101 FAVORITE PLAY THERAPY TECHNIQUES

Volume III

Child Therapy Series
A Series of Books Edited by **Charles Schaefer**

Cognitive-Behavioral Play Therapy
Susan M. Knell

Play Therapy in Action:
A Casebook for Practitioners
Terry Kottman and Charles Schaefer, Eds.

Family Play Therapy
Charles Schaefer and Lois Carey, Eds.

The Quotable Play Therapist
Charles Schaefer and
Heidi Gerard Kaduson, Eds.

Childhood Encopresis and Enuresis
Charles Schaefer

The Therapeutic Powers of Play
Charles Schaefer, Ed.

Play Therapy Techniques, Second Edition
Donna Cangelosi and Charles Schaefer, Eds.

Children in Residential Care:
Critical Issues in Treatment
Charles Schaefer and Arthur Swanson, Eds.

The Therapeutic Use of Child's Play
Charles Schaefer, Ed.

Refusal to Speak:
Treatment of Selective Mutism in Children
Sheila Spasaro and Charles Schaefer, Eds.

Sandplay:
Therapy with Children and Families
Lois Carey

Helping Parents Solve Their Children's Behavior Problems
Charles Schaefer and Andrew R. Eisen, Eds.

Clinical Handbook of Sleep Disorders in Children
Charles Schaefer, Ed.

Clinical Handbook of Anxiety Disorders in Children and Adolescents
Andrew R. Eisen, Christopher A. Kearney,
and Charles Schaefer, Eds.

Practitioner's Guide to Treating Fear and Anxiety and Children and Adolescents:
A Cognitive-Behavioral Approach
Andrew R. Eisen and Christopher A. Kearney

Words of Wisdom for Parents:
Time-Tested Thoughts on How to Raise Kids
Charles Schaefer, Eds

The Playing Cure:
Individualized Play Therapy for Specific Childhood Problems
Heidi Gerard Kaduson,
Donna Cangelosi,
and Charles Schaefer, Eds.

101 Favorite Play Therapy Techniques
Heidi Gerard Kaduson and
Charles Schaefer, Eds.

Saying Goodbye in Child Psychotherapy:
Planned, Unplanned, and Premature Endings
Donna Cangelosi

Short-Term Psychotherapy Groups for Children:
Adapting Group Processes for Specific Problems
Charles Schaefer, Ed.

101 More Favorite Play Therapy Techniques
Heidi Gerard Kaduson and
Charles Schaefer, Eds.

101 Favorite Play Therapy Techniques

Volume III

Edited by

Heidi Gerard Kaduson
and
Charles E. Schaefer

JASON ARONSON
Lanham • Boulder • New York • Toronto • Plymouth, UK

Published by Jason Aronson
An imprint of Rowman & Littlefield Publishers, Inc.
A wholly owned subsidiary of The Rowman & Littlefield Publishing Group, Inc.
4501 Forbes Boulevard, Suite 200, Lanham, Maryland 20706
http://www.rowmanlittlefield.com

Estover Road, Plymouth PL6 7PY, United Kingdom

First Paperback edition 2010

British Library Cataloguing in Publication Information Available

Library of Congress Cataloging-in-Publication Data

101 favorite play therapy techniques / edited by Heidi Kaduson, Charles E. Schaefer.
p. cm.
Includes bibliographical references and index.
1. Play therapy. I. Title: One hundred and one favorite play therapy techniques. II. Title: One hundred and one favorite play therapy techniques. III. Kaduson, Heidi. IV. Schaefer, Charles E.

ISBN 0-7657-0368-8 (cloth : alk. paper)
ISBN 978-0-7657-0799-4 (pbk. : alk. paper)

RJ505.P6
618.92'891653—dc21 2002023647

Printed in the United States of America

To all the children of the world
We thank you

CONTENTS

PREFACE

An amazing resource for play therapy techniques is the children with whom we work. Many of the techniques illustrated in this book were created with a specific child in mind. We have the pleasure of helping children with psychological difficulties, and that also enhances the creativity of many of the therapists who contributed to this book. The contributors of this book of techniques come from a diverse group. There are therapists from child-centered play therapy, cognitive-behavioral play therapy, gestalt play therapy, Jungian play therapy, psychodynamic play therapy, and prescriptive play therapy.

The most important aspect of our treatment with children is the rapport that we establish with each child. Any technique is as good as the therapist using it. Modification of a technique to suit the therapist/child relationship is actually the most appropriate use of this book. We hope to give therapists different techniques to review and use to help in their work with children.

The criteria for selecting techniques for this book is the same as we have had before. We asked that the techniques be specific, practical, relatively inexpensive, and original, or that they involve an original modification to an already existing technique. Therapists from all over the world have contributed their knowledge and expertise to that end.

We have grouped together the techniques into seven sections: expressive arts techniques, puppet play techniques, storytelling techniques, group play techniques, play toys and objects techniques, game play techniques, and other techniques. Each contributor has included an introduction to the technique, a rationale for using it, as well as a detailed description and application to illustrate how the technique is performed with children.

The expressive arts techniques include various media used in expression through art, such as paint, sculpture, clay, markers, drawing, and so on. These media have successfully aided children in expressing traumatic circumstances and other psychological issues where communication was difficult. The group play techniques illustrate different methods of play to use in a group format for children's social skills, anger management, and other support groups. Game play techniques use games bought at stores or self-created games to help children express psychological issues. In game play techniques, the child feels safe to express his or her own thoughts and feelings as if involved in a real issue. This distancing allows for many ages to be helped through play therapy. With the play toys and objects techniques, the therapist is using a specific toy or object to facilitate expression in therapeutic play. Storytelling techniques illustrate the use of stories in helping children to express issues of grief, anger, abandonment, and attachment issues through the metaphor of the story. Puppet play techniques are also used in play therapy to help children express conflict and role play issues regarding family and friends in a safe environment. Lastly, the other techniques section illustrates the use of miscellaneous techniques to be used in play therapy on various topics.

This book will be of interest to anyone who is interested in treating children across a number of disciplines. It allows individuals to see how techniques are used in facilitating expression of psychological issues and working through the same in a fun and nonthreatening manner. We hope that this will help further the therapist's individual creativity and expand the use of play to help children all over the world.

Heidi Gerard Kaduson
Charles E. Schaefer

CONTRIBUTORS

Adeyinka M.A. Akinsulure-Smith, Ph.D., RPT-S, 275 West 96th Street, Apt. 8D, New York, New York 10025-6270

Jean Stirling Albaum, Ph.D., 1408 1/2 Valley View Road, Glendale, California 91202

Virginia B. Allen, Ed.D., Idaho State University, Department of Counseling, Campus Box 8120, Pocatello, Idaho 83209-8120

Judith Anastasia, Reg. Psych., RPT-S, Family Therapy Centre Ltd., 1628 West 1st Avenue, Suite 212, Vancouver, British Columbia V6J1G1

Deborah Armstrong Hickey, Ph.D., MFT, RPT-S, 230 Arabella Way, Oceanside, California 92057

Jeffrey S. Ashby, Ph.D., Georgia State University, 3248 Majestic Circle, Avondale Estates, Georgia 30002

Jennifer Baggerly, Ph.D., LMHC, University of South Florida, 4202 East Fowler Avenue, EDU 162, Tampa, Florida 33620-7750

Betty Bedard-Bidwell, Art and Play Therapist, Betamarsh, Inc., 60 Lighthouse Street, Goderich, Ontario N7A 2J4

Judith D. Bertoia, Ph.D., RPT-S, 6573 Kempson Crescent, Delta, British Columbia, Canada V4E 1R7

Brenda L. Bierdeman, Psy.D., 27 South Platt Street, Albion, New York 14411

Shane Blasco, M.S., College of Education, Georgia State University, Atlanta, Georgia 30303

Maryanne Bongiovani, Ph.D., 950 Chevrolet Drive, Elliott City, Maryland 21042

Nancy Riedel Bowers, MSW, Ph.D., Wilfrid Laurier University, Faculty of Social Work, University Avenue, Waterloo, Ontario, Canada N2L 3C5

Linda Pak Bruner, M.S., 103 Terrace Drive, Atlanta, Georgia 30305

Melissa V. Bush, Ph.D., Richland Family Counseling, 914 Richland Street, Suite B-202, Columbia, South Carolina 29201

Chari Campbell, Ph.D., 126 Lighthouse Drive, Jupiter, Florida 33469

Kyla Chambers, MMFT, 10230 Maeburn Terrace, St. Louis, Missouri 63127

Saralea E. Chazan, Ph.D., Theraplay Institute, 5 East 76th Street, New York, New York 10011

Teresa M. Christensen, Ph.D., LPC-S, RPT-S, University of New Orleans, Education Building 348, New Orleans, Louisiana 70148-2515

Nancy F. Cincotta, CSW, Mount Sinai, Box 1252, One Gustave L-Levy Place, New York, New York 10029-6574

Mary Determan, MSW, CICSW, RPT-S, Encompass, Inc., 2421 North Mayfair Road, Wauwatosa, Wisconsin 53226

Judith A. Detrude, Ph.D., LPC, LMFT, Sam Houston State University, P.O. Box 2119, Huntsville, Texas 77341-2119

Denise K. Filley, MA, RPT, Kansas City Play Therapy Training Institute, 7850 Haskell Drive, Kansas City, Kansas 66109

Dora C. Finamore, Ed.D., RPT, Florida Association for Play Therapy, 4605 Community Drive, West Palm Beach, Florida 33417

Sylvia Fisher, MA, 3490 Buskirk Avenue, Suite A, Pleasant Hill, California 94523

Mary T. Foret, Ph.D., Psychotherapeutic Arts Institute, Inc., 4201 Willow Park Drive, Orlando, Florida 32835

Jennifer Fortier, LICSW, RPT, Sexual Assault and Trauma, 300 Richmand Street, Suite 205, Providence, Rhode Island 02902-4222

Robert W. Freeman, Ph.D., 3511 Raymond Street, Chevy Chase, Maryland 20815

Sandra B. Frick-Helms, Ph.D., RN, RPT-S, 501 Keswick Road, Columbia, South Carolina 29210

Vivian Gentz, LCSW, RPT-S, 5509 South Lewis Avenue, Tulsa, Oklahoma 74105

Suzanne Getz Gregg, Ph.D., LPC, 1309 West Little Neck Road, Virginia Beach, Virginia 23452

Teresa A. Glatthorn, Ph.D., RPT-S, The Art of Communicating, 211 East Mill Road, Hatboro, Pennsylvania 19040

Dennis C. Gold, Ph.D., Susquehanna Counseling Group, 676 Wyoming Avenue, Kingston, Pennsylvania 18704

Paris Goodyear-Brown, LCSW, RPT, 121 McCall Street, Nashville, Tennessee 37211

Corinne H. Greenberg, Ed.D., LMHC, NCC, 8107 Southwest 43rd Place, Gainesville, Florida 32608

Joop Hellendoorn, Ph.D., University of Leiden, the Netherlands, P.O. Box 9555, 2300 RB Leiden, The Netherlands

Linda Herschenfeld, LCSW, RPT-S, Farrington Elementary School, 249 Eastern Avenue, Augusta, Maine 04330

Michelle Hodsdon, MS, 39355 California Street, Suite 209, Fremont, California 94538

David Hudak, LCSW-C, 15 Eastern Circle, Middletown, Maryland 21769

Karen L. Hutchison, MA, RPT, 2050 Encino Vista, San Antonio, Texas 78529

Shelley A. Jackson, Ph.D., LPC, RPT-S, Texas A & M University, Ocean Drive, Corpus Christi, Texas 78412

Susan H. James, Ed.D., Western Kentucky University, College of Education, Department of Educational Leadership, Tate Page Hall 409, 1 Big Red Way, Bowling Green, Kentucky 42101-3576

Jacqueline Johnson, Psy.D., Third Reformed Church, 18 Ten Eyck Avenue, Albany, New York 12209

Janice Jung, M.Ed., RPT-S, 1210 10th Street, Suite 203, Bellingham, Washington 98225

Heidi G. Kaduson, Ph.D., RPT-S, 983 Route 33, Monroe Township, New Jersey 08831

Melissa F. Kalodner, Psy.D., RPT, JFSA, 3909 South Maryland Parkway, Suite 205, Las Vegas, Nevada 89119-7520

H. Mike Kanitz, Ph.D., LPC, NCC, CAC, Central Michigan University, Rowe Hall 208, Mt. Pleasant, Michigan 48804-0038

Sueann Kenny-Noziska, LCSW, RPT, Children's Interagency Program, 23119 Cottonwood Avenue, Building A, Suite 110, Moreno Valley, California 92553

Terry Kottman, Ph.D., RPT-S, NCC, The Encouragement Zone, P.O. Box 1045, Cedar Falls, Iowa 50613

Nancy Kuntz, RN, MN, CPNP, 21391 Visa Estate Drive, Lake Forest, California 92630

Brenda Lawrence, CSW, Box 71, High Falls, New York 12440

Norma Y. Leben, ACSW, LMSW-ACP, RPT-S, CPT-P, Morning Glory Treatment Center for Children, 1205 Pigeon Forge Road, Pflugerville, Texas 78660

Tracy C. Leinbaugh, Ph.D., Ohio University, McCracken Hall 201, Athens, Ohio 45701-2979

Sanda L. Lindaman, MSW, The Theraplay Institute, 1137 Central Avenue, Wilmette, Illinois 60091

Celia Linden, CSW, RPT-S, 11 Webster Avenue, Suite 1, Goshen, New York 10924

Diana Malca, LCSW, RPT-S, CPT-S, 16300 NE 19th Avenue, Suite 208, North Miami Beach, Florida 33162

Jim Martin, MS, 2815 Lake Court, Cumming, Georgia 30041

Claire Milgrom, MSW, RSW, Box 47038 RPO Marion, Winnipeg, Manitoba R2H3G9

Bob H. Milich, Ph.D., 126 Grand Street, Croton-on-Hudson, New York 10520

Wendy M. Miller, Psy.D., RPT-S, 2732 NE Broadway, Portland, Oregon 97232

Neresa B. Minatrea, Ph.D., Western Kentucky University, College of Education, Department of Educational Leadership, Tate Page Hall 409, 1 Big Red Way, Bowling Green, Kentucky 42101-3576

Jo Anne Mitchell, M.Ed., LPC, RPT-S, NCC, 202 Waldburg Street, Savannah, Georgia 31401

Bertha Mook, Ph.D., Universite d'Ottawa, 145 Jean-Jacques Lassier Street, Ottawa, Ontario, K1N 6N5

Peter Mortola, Ph.D., Lewis and Clark College, Campus Box 86, Portland, Oregon 97219-7899

Jodi Ann Mullen, State University of New York at Oswego Counseling and Psychological Services, Oswego, New York 13126

Evangeline Munns, Ph.D., RPT-S, Blue Hills Child and Family Services, 402 Bloomington Road West, Aurora, Ontario L4G 3G8

Ruth Ouzts Cash, M.Ed., NCC, LPC, Desoto Family Counseling Center, 957 Swinnea Ridge, Suite 4, Southaven, Mississippi 38671

Dale-Elizabeth Pehrsson, RPT-S, Oregon State University, School of Education, Education Hall, Corvallis, Oregon 97331-3502

Sharon Picard, Ph.D., 3217 Calle Rosales, Santa Barbara, California 93105

Alvin Ramsey, Ph.D., RPT-S, Center for Humanistic Studies Graduate School, 40 East Ferry Avenue, Detroit, Michigan 48202-3802

Carla J. Reyes, Ph.D., University of Utah, 1705 East Campus Center Drive, Room 327, Salt Lake City, Utah 84112-7148

Cynthia Reynolds, Ph.D., University of Akron, Carroll Hall 127, Akron, Ohio 44325-5007

Margery Lewy Rieff, Ph.D., 108 Third Street, Wilmette, Illinois 60091

Lawrence C. Rubin, Ph.D., RPT, 941 NE 19th Avenue, Suite 204, Fort Lauderdale, Florida 33304

Inés Schroeder, Psy.D., Voices, 1010 Wethersfield Avenue, Suite 302, Hartford, Connecticut 06114

Karen M. Scribney, B.Sc., M.Ed., Eckert, Scribney & Associates, Suite 3, 1300 8th Street SW, Calgary, Alberta T2R1B2

Jerri Simms Shepard, Ed.D., Gonzaga University, School of Education, Spokane, Washington 99258-0025

Mary Lou Sherry, LPC, CSW, 2386 Mt. Hood Lane, Toms River, New Jersey 08753

Cindy A. Stear, Psy.D., Common Boundary Wellness Center, 220 East State Street, Suite 300, Rockford, Illinois 61104-1011

Susan M. Swearer, Ph.D., School of Psychology Program, Department of Educational Psychology, The University of Nebraska-Lincoln, 130B Bancroft Hall, Lincoln, Nebraska 68588-0345

Daniel S. Sweeney, Ph.D., George Fox University, 12753 SW 68th Avenue, Portland, Oregon 97223

Erika L. Surkin, M.Ed., RPT, 363 Valleybrook Road, Chester Heights, Pennsylvania 19017

Kathleen Truax, M.S., M.F.T., 711 D Street, Suite 203, San Rafael, California 94901

Perry Woehrlen, ACSW, RPT-S, 1333 South Cranbrook Road, Birmingham, Michigan 48009

Section One

Expressive Arts

1

The Family Collage

Jerri Simms Shepard

INTRODUCTION

Therapists working in diverse and multicultural settings are often challenged to find ways to help clients express their feelings and tell the stories of their lives. This can be particularly difficult when working with individuals from dysfunctional or troubled homes, but it provides ways for them to talk about family dynamics. Jung (1965) reflected that expressive arts represented an essential connection to the inner world of feelings and images.

I was first introduced to this technique in the late 1980s at a conference on counseling children and adolescents who had been sexually abused. In a workshop forum, participants were given case descriptions, including family information, and asked to reflect on what it would be like to be *this* child in *this* family. They were then asked to create collages from colored paper depicting the child and her or his family. It became obvious that the experiential collage technique was far more meaningful and engaging for participants and observers than simply reading and discussing the case scenarios.

In my work as a school psychologist and marriage, family, child counselor, I began to have my clients describe their families using this collage technique and was amazed at the information provided. I also found that clients created different collages during the course of counseling, representing changed perceptions of their families, as they began to individuate and disengage from the dysfunction of their families.

RATIONALE

The concept of multiple intelligences (Gardner, 1983) explains that individuals have many ways of expressing themselves. Counseling and psychotherapy are usually based on a verbal model, which requires verbal linguistic ability, typical of Caucasian, Western educational practices. Many clients are limited in verbal expression, especially when English is a second language or their cultural backgrounds or orientations are not of the dominant culture. Clients may also be limited in verbal expression when they have been traumatized. In some cases of child abuse, children are threatened with further violence to themselves or their loved ones if they disclose the abuse and identify the perpetrator. In those situations, it is important to find other ways for clients to "tell" what happened. In honoring clients, it is important to provide them with alternative ways for them to tell their stories, and nonverbal techniques, such as art therapies, may prove quite useful. Art can be used as a process of transforming the self through the active formation of an object (family collage). Franklin (1992) reported that for clients to work with art materials is to transform their physical and symbolic potential.

When a client is describing her or his family, it is often helpful to have a framework from which to begin. The collage technique is nonthreatening; clients are not asked to draw or create exacting images. They are asked to tear shapes of colored paper and paste them on paper. The process is simple and quick.

DESCRIPTION

The client is asked to portray her or his family using colored construction paper in a collage form. The family portrayed can be the family of origin or the current family situation. The client is given various colors of construction paper and a glue stick, and is provided a flat surface on which to work. He or she is first told to choose a color to represent the background (climate) of the family. Then he or she is told to tear a shape out of a colored paper to represent each family member, including himself or herself, and place all the torn shapes (often in various colors) on the background sheet. In this way, the client can position family members (as represented by torn colored paper pieces) on the background sheet. When the client is finished, he or she is asked if all the family members are represented. The client is then asked to describe the collage. The therapist uses minimal verbal responses to encourage the client to describe the collage, but does not interpret the client's artwork. I always tell the client that I will record his or her description of the collage and keep it with the collage in the client's file.

The therapist notices the background, the presence or absence of certain family members, how they are represented, and the proximity of members. Clients sometimes purposely leave out certain members or put them on the back of the paper or on a separate paper. The process of constructing the collage is also of great interest; some clients create the collage in minutes, others painstakingly labor over every move or simply cannot finish the project. Careful observation of this process is essential.

APPLICATIONS

This technique is useful with culturally diverse client populations. Collage does not require artistic ability and is nonthreatening to clients compared to some of the art therapy techniques that may inhibit individuals who feel they are not artistic. Even the tearing of the paper is relaxed, rather than having to cut perfect shapes with scissors. Children and adolescents are highly receptive to this technique, which is often seen as more engaging than some of the verbal therapies. Several collages can be created over a period of time, during the course of therapy, to illustrate changes in the client's perceptions of family members. Family collages are extremely engaging for clients and highly informative for therapists.

My psychotherapy practice has included clients who have been abused and/or neglected. I have used the family collage with numerous children, adolescents, and adults at the beginning session as a part of the initial assessment. Children need little encouragement with this technique; however, adults who are self-conscious or skeptical of any art technique may be somewhat resistant. I have countered initial resistance by explaining that visual expression is just another form of language and there is not a wrong way to do the family collage. Most clients enjoy breaking from talking therapy and are curious about their own creations.

In many cases of abuse or neglect, the client does not include himself or herself or a significant family member in the collage. Sometimes a family member is deliberately left out or pasted on the back of the page. I always ask the client if the entire family is represented when the collage has been completed. After the child describes the collage, the therapist follows with nondirective questions. I keep the dated original or a photograph of the original in the client's file.

As an instructor of graduate students in counseling and education, I have my students do many case studies, which always include the family collage as part of the assessment. The graduate students create the collage from the child's perspective with the knowledge he or she has gained as the child's teacher or counselor. I marvel at the insight and emotion my students experience when they create the family collage from the child's perspective. This is a very informative and powerful technique, which crosses all cultures and provides new avenues for understanding clients and their perceptions of their families.

References

Franklin, M. (1992). Art therapy and self-esteem. *Journal of the American Art Therapy Association*, 9(2), 78.

Gardner, H. (1983). *Frames of Mind: The Theory of Multiple Intelligences*. New York: Basic Books.

Jung, C. G. (1965). *Memories, Dreams, Reflections*. New York: Random House.

2

Drawing It Out

Peggy Woehrlen

INTRODUCTION

Children have a difficult time truly understanding their feelings due to the complex and abstract nature of them. A common goal of a child therapist is to assist the child in identifying, labeling, and understanding their feelings. Giving the child a vehicle in which to not only identify their feelings, to draw out those feelings, and to give voice to them, is a powerful way to assist the child in gaining understanding and mastery of their feelings.

RATIONALE

In my work with children and adolescents, I am always looking for ways for my clients to really understand their internal experience. Typically, they may have an intellectual understanding of their emotions, but that's where the understanding stops. Consequently, many children and adolescents will somatize the deeper aspects of an experience just because they don't know what else to do. In working with traumatized children, drawing is an excellent way to enter the process of working through all aspects of their traumatic experience, in particular the "worst moments," because their cognitive skills at those times are shut down due to the overwhelming sense of fear and powerlessness. Applying this concept and technique to a broader range of emotional experiences has been quite successful even with the most resistant child or adolescent. This is due in part to the focus being off the client and on the drawing process.

DESCRIPTION

Sit at a table with the client; supply him or her with white letter-sized paper. The age of the child will determine if you offer crayons, markers, colored pencils, or pastels. A younger child would find crayons most suitable, and adolescents enjoy colored pencils or the artistic potential of pastels.

Therapist: "I would like you to draw a picture of where in your body you experience those feelings." Typically what happens is that the client draws a picture of his or her whole body with only a brief reference to their body experience of the feeling. See figure 2.1.

Figure 2.1

Child: "Um, I don't know. I guess it's like this. I feel my scared and worried feelings in my head." If the child is not comfortable with his/her drawing ability, he/she often rushes through the exercise or comments in a negative way on what his/her drawing looks like.

Therapist: "You know, I really want to understand what it's like for you when you are scared and worried, so draw me a picture over here (pointing to a space adjacent to the first drawing but on the same page) of your head and where in particular those feelings are." I then wait for the child to begin drawing again. See figure 2.2.

Figure 2.2

Usually, the child will pause for a moment to focus on that internal experience and then begin drawing. Sometimes the child will not be able to produce more detail, and so it may be necessary to prompt him or her with a few questions such as: "We have talked about your headaches before, can you draw what those feel like?" "You have mentioned that your thoughts start to race when you are worried; draw what that feels like." The goal at this point is to show interest and support in the client using the drawing process to visually articulate his or her inner experience. If the drawing is still fairly vague, then I will ask the child to put words to the image. I then ask if there is anything about his or her drawing that is new, that he or she didn't realize before and what his or her reaction is to the affect or "feel" of the drawing. Before we move on to the next step, I make certain to ask if there is anything else he or she wants to add to the picture.

Therapist: Next I ask, "Do you experience those feelings elsewhere in your body?" If he or she says no, then the intervention is complete. *Note:* This may be the end of the drawing experience if this is your first time using this technique with the client. I have found with some children that they need to experience this intervention several times before feeling free enough to use it to its fullest extent. If the client says yes, then I proceed.

Figure 2.3

Therapist: I hand the child additional paper and ask him or her, "I'd like you to draw where else in your body you feel those worried and scared feelings" (or whatever feeling is being focused upon). Of course, there is no right or wrong answer to these questions because you want to elicit the child's own internal experience. See figure 2.3. As the client was drawing the feelings in her stomach (butterflies, "growl," jitters, a needle piercing her stomach, "boom," and grouchy critters) I was attentive, interested, and encouraged her to continue until she felt complete in her depiction of her experience.

Child: She sat back in her chair upon completing this intense activity, upon which she had been very focused. "Wow, I had no idea so much happens when I'm scared."

Therapist: "It looks pretty crowded in there. It seems like it would be hard to pay attention to any one thing."

Child: "Yeah. I just think of it as being nasty." And with that comment, the client labeled the picture "Nasty Day." The client again sat back in her chair as if complete with the process. I had the sense I could go further with her in terms of expressing what she had just drawn.

Therapist: "If your stomach could talk (pointing to the drawing she had just done), what would it say?" While I was saying this to her, I gently moved the drawing a bit to the side and put a clean piece of paper in front of her.

Child: She immediately began writing. See figure 2.4. After she completed writing "Stop doing it. I don't like it!" She sat back in her chair as if she felt complete.

Therapist: "I'd like you to read this outloud." The client did so in a very soft, gentle voice. Because the affect of her voice did not match the affect of the writing, I said, "I want you to say this again as if you really mean it."

Child: "Just a minute." The client then wrote over the words more strongly to emphasize the intention, adding the scary drawing and the comment at the bottom of the page. After amending the drawing, she reread the page in an assertive manner, thereby matching her internal experience with her thoughts and her outward expression of them. Again, she sat back in her chair and let out a deep breath.

Therapist: In an effort to consolidate the work just accomplished, I gave her another clean sheet of paper and said to her, "I'd like you to do a drawing of how you are feeling now."

Figure 2.4

Child: Quickly and easily the child completed figure 2.5. As she sat back in her chair this last time, she began to giggle and said, "Boy, I sure like that picture."

Therapist: I had all five drawings laid out in front of her and we quietly looked at them. "You can do this whenever you are feeling upset and don't know another way to let go of your upset feelings."

APPLICATIONS

This is an intervention that can be used with a wide range of ages, from age 5 through adolescence, for a wide range of emotional issues. The quality of the finished artwork is not important. The process of the child

Figure 2.5

drawing out his or her feelings and concretizing them in a visual way is where the clinical value is. I have used this technique with trauma survivors and for bereavement, school adjustment difficulties, anger management, pro social-skill building, and generally assisting children to identify, label, and process their feelings. As long as the therapist recognizes the developmental stage that the child is at and matches the art medium with the age-appropriate language, this technique has significant clinical value. When I performed this intervention with this client, her mother was in the playroom observing the process. With little additional training on my part, the mother now uses this technique at times at home with equal success.

3

Problem-solving Techniques: *Hand-ling* the Decision-making Process

Judith D. Bertoia

INTRODUCTION

In our fast-paced culture, each of us is bombarded with massive amounts of stimulation. Although maintaining a primary focus on circumstances and interactions that require our conscious attention, we must also deal with considerable background activity—the sights, sounds, smells, and so forth of daily living. To maintain our sanity in the midst of this onslaught, we learn to screen from consciousness much of what seems irrelevant. In order to function efficiently within limited time constraints, we manage rapid processing of various possible actions before reaching decisions.

RATIONALE

Children, however, do not have the same level of development in the cerebral cortex as adults do. Because their executive functioning is less mature they often simply react to situations, frequently with behavior that is driven by emotions with little or no thinking involved. Although they may attempt to screen excessive environmental stimuli from consciousness, much of what they filter out becomes stored at an unconscious, visceral level that in fact heigh' ns the child's level of arousal. Thus, their decision-making approach is often based on obtaining immediate emotional and physiological relief. Essentially they react without any cognitive processing. This impulsivity leaves no time to consider the potential consequences of the behavior.

The following decision-making technique is effective for two reasons. First, it interrupts the child's established arousal-escalation patterns and the subsequent urge to respond impulsively to a situation. By following this sequence for *hand-ling* problems, the child disrupts the rapid sequence of thoughts that usually heighten the physiological arousal in difficult situations, the fight or flight response.

Secondly, this technique is based on an image, the child's own hand. The child's first language, the preverbal primary process language, is image-based. By combining the use of an image—especially because this one is based in the body—with the logic of planned decision making, the child always carries a valuable visual aide for problem solving.

This technique can be taught early in the play therapy process if the therapist's style provides for some directed activity. For less directive styles of therapy, the technique can be delayed until an opportune time in play therapy arises. It should be noted that whether the therapist is in a professional role or in character during the play, this is a technique that will require some teaching.

DESCRIPTION

This technique for helping children "get a grip" on the decision-making process involves some simple verbal interactions and tracing their own hand. The activity is easily introduced when a child comes into a session indicating that he or she is facing a difficult choice. For example, a child who must decide between making the regular weekend visit to the noncustodial parent's home or staying in the usual residence in order to attend a birthday party might be told, "This sounds like a good time to learn about *hand-ling* choices."

The child is given a blank sheet of paper with the suggestion, "Because this is *your* situation and you need to *hand-le* the decision making, let's use your hand for our model." The child is asked if he or she would like to trace the left or right hand, and if he or she would like to do the tracing or have the therapist do it. A comment such as "Wow! You've already made two decisions right there" helps the child recognize that he or she does have the capacity for handling problems and in fact does so repeatedly throughout the day. For children who need considerable ego-building and reassurance, it is often useful to comment directly on such small successes.

Once the hand is traced, with fingers spread wide open, the child is asked to describe the problem or situation. The therapist summarizes the issue in one sentence and checks to confirm the accuracy of that statement. Once the child indicates the summary is correct, it is written in the center of the drawn hand by either the child or therapist.

At this point the child and therapist are ready to brainstorm possible options for responding to the situation. The child is reminded that in brainstorming no possibility is too silly or impossible. One choice is written along each finger. For example, the child who must make the decision between going for the usual paternal visit or staying home and attending a friend's birthday party could have brainstormed these choices: "stay home and go to the party," "go to Dad's and miss the party," "go to Dad's if he'll bring me back for the party," "come home from Dad's a day early," and "ask my friend to change the day of the party."

Once five options have been brainstormed, each one is evaluated. This requires imagining and discussing the possible results for each choice. A negative sign is written on one side of the finger and a positive sign on the other. Besides the first finger, which indicates the choice of staying home in order to attend the birthday party, the child might write the positive outcomes as "I get to go to the party" and "My friend will be happy I'm there." On the other side the child may say, "Dad would be really upset if I don't go there." Because of limited space these points are written in abbreviated form and may appear more as "I go to party," "friend = happy," and "Dad = upset." If the child has difficulty imaging outcomes, questions such as "How would your dad feel about that choice?" can be posed.

When all the choices have consequences written beside them, the child and therapist talk about which options are more desirable to the child. Often a choice will have several positive outcomes and only one negative possibility, but the one negative is so frightening to the child that the choice is excluded. If a choice is not helpful, it is also discarded. Helpful choices are chosen and finally narrowed to one selection, which can then be implemented.

At this point the child and therapist may need to discuss how the chosen option will be enacted. This planning stage often involves scripting what might be said and then role-playing the situation. As the activity is concluded, the child is encouraged to think and say, "I can *hand-le* this!"

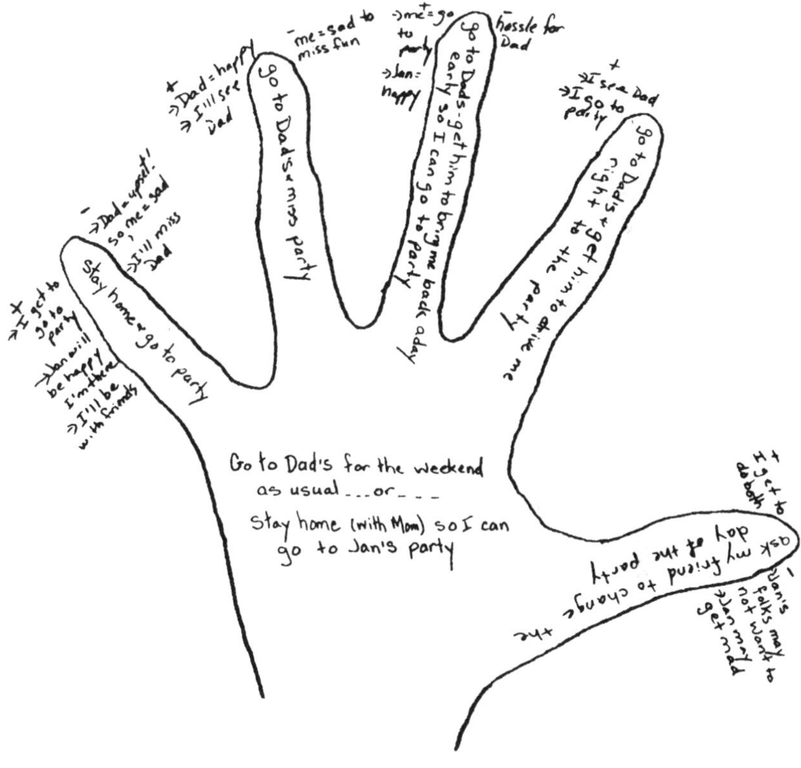

Figure 3.1

The child learns to stop and think before acting, thus interrupting the escalation phase of the arousal cycle. The child also learns a technique for considering several possibilities and for making a decision based on both logical and emotional weighting of options. Finally, the child experiences a sense of empowerment through mastering a new way of *hand-ling* difficult situations.

APPLICATIONS

This technique is a useful life skill for all children. It is suitable for preschool children as well as adolescents and adults. Very young children usually manage this technique better when they are choosing from only two or three options. It is especially useful for impulsive children; however, it will usually take more repetitions for them to master it. With this population it may also be important to help them recognize and monitor the physiological symptoms of their arousal and to teach them other strategies for managing these symptoms such as deep breathing and changing cognitive patterns. For example, the child may have had the physical experience of increased heart rate, flushing or feeling warm, and having sweaty palms. Along with these physical symptoms, the child may have experienced anger, humiliation, rejection, or frustration. When there has been time for any thoughts, they usually fall into patterns of escalation such as "I *never* get anything I want!" or revenge such as "You ruined my plans so I'm going to wreck your day too!"

Once the child recognizes early physiological cues and their rapid escalation as well as the old cognitive patterns that led to purely reactive behavior, however, new calming techniques can be inserted to disrupt the escalation cycle. The child can mentally say, "Stop! Breathe. *Hand-le* the situation." In a crisis the child may have time to think of only two options such as fighting or walking away. However, one consequence of walking away is that the child has time to calm himself or herself and then think of other options for addressing the situation.

Within the context of play therapy, children demonstrate the difficult choices and dilemmas they face on a regular basis as well as their typical patterns of responding to challenging situations. Play therapy therefore becomes an ideal opportunity for teaching an important life skill—the art of decision making—one that even some adults have not mastered.

4

Problem-solving Techniques: The Storyboard

Judith D. Bertoia

INTRODUCTION

Children often find themselves in relationships or circumstances where they wish desperately for an alternative. Usually they are able to articulate the current situation quite clearly and to envision a preferred scenario. Because play is the child's natural language and fantasy is one of the psyche's natural inventive forms of expression, the creative activities of play therapy provide an ideal opportunity for the child to explore the alternative circumstances that he or she seeks to create. C. G. Jung (1971) notes that answers to all problems come from the innovative capacity of the psyche; he indicates that by creating the fantasy from our inner world, we can then move toward concretizing it in the outer world. Unfortunately, many children lack the necessary skills for comparing the two versions of their current and desired reality, analyzing the differences, and then determining the sequence of events necessary to shift from one to the other. Guided by a therapist in play therapy, however, children can master the steps necessary to accomplish this shift.

RATIONALE

The storyboard technique can be used by play therapists to help children begin resolving some of life's problems. By encouraging the child to fantasize possibilities other than the existing circumstances, the therapist fosters the child's creative potential. Once activated, this creative potential stimulates the child's capacity to envision more alternatives, nurtures a sense of empowerment, and guides the process of converting possibilities into concrete form. Through a playful approach to the activity, the therapist can bring a lightness to the heavy emotional tone being carried by the child, not by invalidating the child's experience or sense of distress, but rather by restoring hope that alternatives do exist.

Part of the storyboard's playfulness comes from the cartoonlike format of this technique. The cartoon format is familiar to children in our culture because most of them have seen the "funnies" in newspapers or comic books. This problem-solving activity copies the cartoon form in which several cells visually portray a sequence of events. Most children also have favorite television programs. They are often quite intrigued to know that in the planning stage of many programs a cartoonlike storyboard format is used to guide the action. However, those storyboards are very large multicelled creations.

The same principle of a cartoon sequence is used in the storyboard problem-solving technique with children. By explaining to the child that the storyboard for a television program guides the characters' words and actions toward the desired ending of a program and that it looks much like a cartoon series, the therapist helps the child understand the value of planning his or her action in this similar form.

Actually seeing the drawn sequence in an external, concrete form also increases the child's ability to carry out the actions necessary to achieve his or her goal. Many children, especially younger ones, have difficulty breaking a broad concept into smaller, more manageable steps. For them, remembering the individual components and their sequence is easier when they have an image attached through visual memory. The mental rehearsal process of creating and then repeatedly imagining oneself following the steps of the actual experience is an effective strategy for performance enhancement.

DESCRIPTION

This technique can be introduced in one of two ways: by asking the child if he or she has a favorite television program or comic in the newspaper or by bringing in an example of a cartoon series such as *Calvin and Hobbs, For Better or Worse,* or *Garfield.* The therapist then introduces the child to the concept of a storyboard, that is, to a sequence of events with a beginning, two or more steps in between, and a conclusion. As described previously, many television programs use the storyboard format to outline the scenes needed to help the plot unfold, although the viewers see only the finished product performed by actors. Similarly, comic series use the same concept to tell their stories, and readers do see the final result in cartoon form. In this activity, the child will create his or her personal storyboard in order to facilitate attaining the desired result for the problem under discussion.

The therapist folds a single sheet of $8\frac{1}{2}$ by 11 paper into quarters, sixths, or eighths, pressing firmly on the creases and creating either four, six, or eight cells once the paper is unfolded again. The number of cells depends on the complexity of the situation and the age of the child. If the situation is relatively simple, the child may need fewer drawn steps to envision what must be done to achieve the goal. If the child is fairly mature and able to imagine the subtle shifts among the drawn stages, then again fewer cells are needed. For young children or those who are very concrete and need greater step-by-step guidance, the eight-cell version is usually most helpful.

Once the paper is unfolded, the child is asked to make two simple line drawings. In the first cell, the child creates a representation of the current situation. In the final cell, the child draws the desired, alternate version. Either the child or therapist can print the words or thoughts in dialogue balloons for the child's character. Some dialogue for other characters can be useful, but too much information can crowd the visual effect and confuse the child. Therefore the decision to include extra content should be determined as the storyboard progresses.

The therapist guides the sequence of drawings through posing questions. For example, if the first drawing shows the child fighting with a sibling over who has access to the family computer, and the final cell's drawing shows only the child on a computer, then the therapist could begin by asking where the sibling has gone in the final picture. If the child replies by indicating that the sibling is at a scheduled activity such as soccer practice, then the next-to-last cell can be drawn with the sibling heading out the door to practice. It is often easier to anticipate the next-to-last step than the first step required for changing the existing situation. There is no specific order for filling in the cells and working backward from the goal to the current situation is often simpler for the child. In creating the storyboard, filling in the cells in any order that achieves a completed series is appropriate. The sequence is often determined by the therapist's questions. These questions flow out of the discussion and images, and continue until all the cells contain some activity.

Each child will create unique touches during the storyboard process. In figure 4.1 Margherita added lines to clearly differentiate each step in the process and included numbers to reinforce the sequence of events. As a resourceful child, she was able to articulate a problem and a process for resolving it very quickly. Even in the first cell she anticipated what was needed to achieve her goal—buying the bear she loved—and how to solve the problem of insufficient funds for reaching that goal. As she said, "I know—I'll save up for it."

Although this example is not a serious problem compared to most of those encountered in therapy, it does demonstrate the importance of relationships with other people as a component of children's problem solving. This example helped the child visualize the key elements of her problem-solving strategies. This included sharing the situation with her parents, enlisting the help of others, generating ideas herself, and achieving her goals.

In figure 4.2 Jay demonstrates common themes in children's lives—perceived unfairness and being disappointed by friends. Although Jay's friend Alex had nearly completed his part of their joint project, he was now injured, in the hospital, and unable to contribute more. Jay enlists his mom to help with the final details that were originally Alex's responsibility. When the teacher returns the completed project in the final cell, graded with an "A," she appears pleased for Jay that he was still able to meet the requirements for a long-planned trip. Jay's reactive anger shifts to relief as the storyboard progresses.

Sometimes children will collapse dialogue, thought, time, and events into fewer cells, moving rapidly from problem definition to resolution. They omit details of dialogue, thought processes, and transitional images among events. For very action-oriented children, it is often helpful to have them expand their storyboard to six or eight cells so that the therapist can help them consider their emotional responses to the many different elements of the situation.

It can also be helpful to pose "what if" questions that suggest unanticipated responses by the other people included in their storyboards. For example, knowing how angry Jay was at his teacher's initial "unfair" failing grade and wondering how he might respond to a negative response from his mom, the therapist could ask, "What if your mom is too busy to help? What else could you do?" By anticipating the possibility that other people may not respond according to their story-

1)
THRIFT STORE
2)
MOM, DAD! I have to make $6.00! Fast! I'll call my friend Amy to help me!
3)
Hi Amy! It's Terri, I need you to come over! OK, bye!
4)
What should we do?
Lets have a car wash!
5)
Wow, we raised $8.00!
6)
Done by: Margherita

Figure 4.1

I Said You & Alex had to hand it in together! So You Fail!
What? thats not fair I did my Part!
Where were you we failed our Project.
Sorry, Jay didn't you get my message I was in the hospital. I am nearly done I will it to You tomorrow
Hospital
I'll get mum to help
I know your busy but I need this A. can you help me with this
well, its nearly done and Alex cant do more So I'll help with the Finishing touches
Here, you go miss Alex was in the hospital but we Finished
well done with this A you can go on your the now
STORY By JAY

Figure 4.2

board, children can be prepared for the emotional reactions to the plan not unfolding as predicted and can develop a repertoire of preplanned alternative courses of action.

Once the series is complete, the child and therapist may want to enact and refine the storyboard. It is often useful to have the child repeat the plan verbally. It is also valuable to have the therapist provide a guided imagery activity for the child using the storyboard for directions. This mental preparation provides the child with a model for independent practice and rehearsal.

APPLICATION

This activity is applicable for a wide age range, from young children to teens. It works well with realistic, achievable situations such as having a "grounding" punishment removed, attending a peer's function, or negotiating a time extension for completing an assignment. Obviously, impossible situations such as restoring a dead pet to life or having divorced parents reunite would not be suitable. Children enjoy creating a cartoon about their own life situations, and they benefit from learning a strategy for solving some of life's problems.

Reference

Jung, C. G. (1971). *Psychological Types*. Bollingen Series XX. Princeton, NJ: Princeton University Press.

5

The Pain Sculpture

Brenda L. Bierdeman

INTRODUCTION

Chronic illnesses and chronic pain can leave children feeling helpless, hopeless, and depressed. Talking about their feelings or even trying to describe how it feels to be sick or in pain often makes the children feel worse, or more discouraged, because it forces them to admit that they have felt this way for a very long time, and may continue feeling this way, or worse, for even longer. The Pain Sculpture is a nonverbal play therapy technique that allows children to put their horrible, overwhelming, and even unspeakable feelings into a concrete, tangible form that can later be transformed as the therapy progresses.

RATIONALE

Nonverbal techniques allow children to bypass the conscious processes of protests, speech difficulties, language barriers, defense mechanisms, and rationalization, and access the subconscious directly. They are projective in nature, allowing the children to project onto the clay the image they have of what the pain is like, what it looks like, what it feels like. Using a nondrying clay allows the material to be formed and changed as many times as desired. If the child wants to make the sculpture permanent, the material can be baked in an ordinary oven and that particular representation can be preserved as is. Otherwise, it can be worked with and changed over and over again as the child's perception of the pain evolves, and hopefully diminishes.

DESCRIPTION

The therapist should have available several colors of colored modeling clay, preferably the kind that will not air dry, but can be hardened in an ordinary household oven. Sculpey, Premo, and FIMO are three popular brands, are nontoxic, have no noxious odor, can be found in most craft stores, and are excellent for the task. Sculpting tools are not necessary but may be made available to the child if the therapist desires.

The therapist should introduce the task to the child by showing him or her the clay and asking if the child would like to make something with it. If the child responds positively, the therapist continues to explain the rest of the instructions. Never force a child to play with the clay. The child may not be emotionally ready to do so or may have sensory integration issues that prevent the child from being able to play comfortably with the clay. If the child says no, just put it away and ask again at another time, preferably on another day.

Once the child has responded positively, tell the child that you would like him or her to think for a moment about the pain that he or she is in. Individualize this to the child and circumstances. Children may be asked to think about the worst pain, a specific time they felt a pain, a pain in a certain part of their body, and so forth, or the instruction may be kept quite general. The therapist may suggest that the child's eyes be closed if it is comfortable and might facilitate the thinking and imagery process, but this is not mandatory. You should then tell the child that you would like him or her to show you what the pain looks like by making a model of it with the clay. Encourage the child to use whatever colors are desired and show the child by working a small piece of your own clay that colors may be left separate or mixed together. Try not to place any restrictions on the size or shape or colors of the sculpture. If the child seems willing to do it, but can't think of what to do, you may suggest something like this: *Some children just make shapes and colors, some make specific shapes that might represent (stand for, look like) something important to you.*

Choose simple language that is developmentally appropriate to the child. If the child still seems confused or asks you to be more specific, go ahead and make some suggestions such as these: *Some kids make round things or flat things. Some make a part of a body or a whole body. Some make animals. But you can make any shape or thing you want. Go ahead and use your imagination.*

When the child indicates that the model has been completed, the therapist should give some approving comment. Allow the child to tell you as much about it as he or she can. If the child does not spontaneously offer any descriptions or further explanations, the therapist may say something like this: *Tell me about what you have made.* Because this is primarily a nonverbal task, the child may not be able to describe anything to you, or explain anything about the shape, the colors used, or the meaning behind it. Don't push for verbal explanations. Even if nothing is said, the next questions should be: *Now, what would make it feel better?*

The child may opt to do something to the model or tell you what would make it feel better. Encourage the child to go ahead and do it—if it is possible given the constraints of time and the environment. For example, if the child responds: "I'd like to throw it through the window," you would tell the child that it is not possible to do that here, but you would make a note of it, and then ask the child to think of something else that might make the model feel better.

If the child is not able to come up with anything, you might suggest some possibilities by asking some questions like these: *Would it feel better if the colors were different? Would it feel better if it were smaller? Would it feel better if it were a different shape? Is there something that you would want me to do with it?* If the child answers positively to any of these questions, encourage the child to make the alterations. If the child wants the therapist to do something, have the child direct you as much as possible. Never touch the child's model unless the child gives permission.

APPLICATIONS

This technique can be used with children age 4 and older. The younger the child is, however, the more nonverbal the process will be. It is helpful for children with chronic problems of any type: physical, emotional, or even social. The initial directive must be changed to fit the nature of the chronic problem, for example, *Show me what your (stress/fear/loss/etc.) looks like.* This technique is particularly helpful with children who have difficulty putting their feelings or thoughts into words.

6

In Memory of or a Torch of Love: A Hand-Processing Technique

Betty Bedard-Bidwell

INTRODUCTION

This is a therapeutic technique that can be used to process grief and loss for an individual, group, or family. The technique allows an individual, group, or family to remember a loved one, by symbolically processing their respect, love, involvement, and role for the individual who died as well as providing the opportunity to be part of a ceremony. Everyone can participate and benefit, despite age or disability.

RATIONALE

Bereavement and the processing of one's grief are often difficult, particularly if there is no way to physically participate or contribute to closure. This technique is a creative approach that is processed both nonverbally and verbally; it allows everyone to feel part of the process and/or group, to feel like they have contributed with an end product that is both beautiful and memorable.

DESCRIPTION

Materials

Cardboard

Scissors

Paint

Colored Construction Paper

Sparkles and glitter

Pencil

Paintbrush

Glue and clear tape

Markers and crayons

Steps

1. Cardboard—cut out a round wreath.
   Set aside the middle to make a stand.

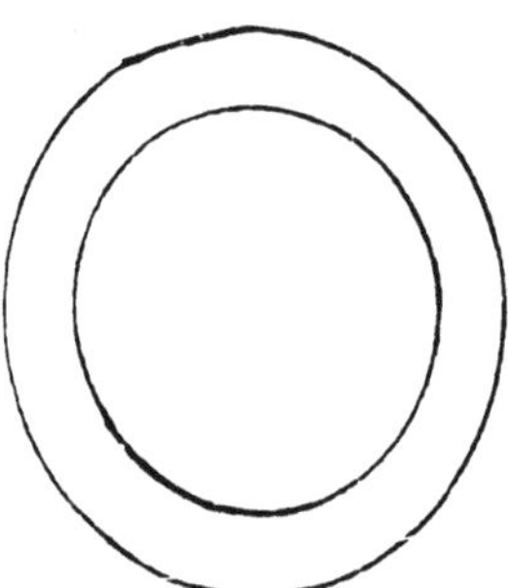

2. Paint circles a bright color following the example provided.

3. Have each child choose a sheet of colored construction paper, then trace and cut out the shapes of his or her hands.

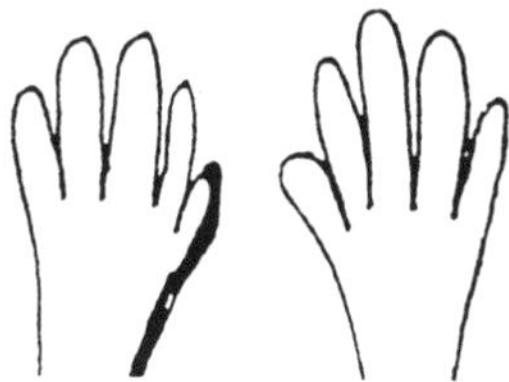

INDIVIDUAL APPROACH "IN MEMORY OF"

a. On the left palm of the hand, write a memory of the person who died.

   On the fingers of the left hand, write five feelings that you have about that memory.

   On the right palm of the hand, write what you learned from the memory you wrote on your left palm.

   On the fingers of the left hand, write how you will be able to make a difference to yourself and others from this memory.

b. Fold the hand over, palm to palm, tape with clear tape, then curl the fingers outward to make a flower. Apply glue on with a brush. Add sparkles.

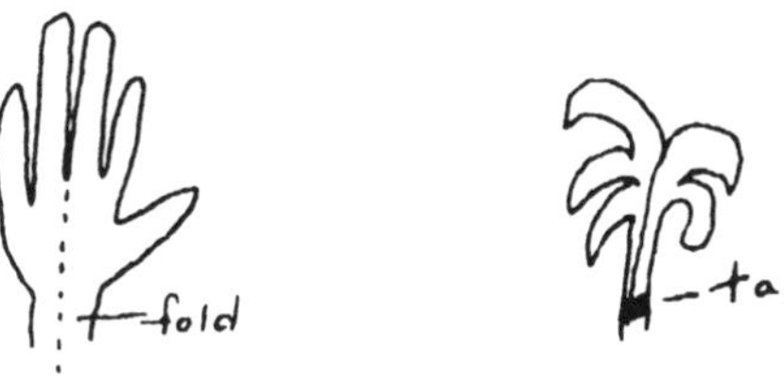

c. Process a set of flowers each week and place them on the wreath until completed or the individual has completed his or her grieving process.

   Flowers are stapled on to the wreath together, palm to palm, fingers pointed outward. Add a photo, a poem, or a picture on the inside circle.

   Staple the inner circle on the back and use as a stand. See the completed wreath in figure 6.1.

Figure 6.1

FAMILY APPROACH "A TORCH OF LOVE"

Same process as for an individual but you would follow a different way of processing. Five ways that the deceased (i.e., Jason) gave to me personally and five ways that Jason gave to our family.

Everyone can participate and process their individual flower, then encourage the family to have their own ritual with the completed wreath.

For a classmate, teammate, friend, teacher, coach, colleague, and so on. Same art process as flower, possibly changing the request to five things they gave to me and five things they gave to the class, the school, or the team.

In a group I would suggest that you process first by having each member give his or her responses so that they can be written on a chalkboard or flip chart. It is easier to process and have a session as a group by beginning in this manner.

I have had great success with this technique. Many of these wreaths were used at the funerals and kept by the family, friends, school, or team.

The Hand-Processing technique was originated by Wanda Sawiki, an art therapist in London, Ontario, who works in a multicultural agency. The Hand to Flower technique has been used by many early childhood educators, day care teachers, and kindergarten teachers in North America. My daughters taught me this technique when they were in kindergarten.

7

The Family Art Project

Judith A. DeTrude

INTRODUCTION

Family therapy is very active, and in order to be inclusive of all members, techniques that can encompass all ages are needed. Encouraging families to take part in activities during sessions is often more effective than "talk" therapy, especially when you are working with various ages and developmental levels within the family. Utilizing play techniques with families is one way to meet diverse needs of all family members.

RATIONALE

The Family Art Project is a technique that is used to introduce "play" to a family as a means of increasing communication and cooperation among family members. It is also an observational tool for the therapist to assess the roles and patterns that are present in the family system. This technique provides each family member with the opportunity to express their dreams at a level that matches their level of development.

DESCRIPTION

A long roll of white paper and markers or crayons are provided for the family. The therapist introduces the activity and then asks the family members to sit on the floor.

Therapist: "We all have dreams about special places where we think we would like to live, but we do not often get the chance to share this dream with others. What I want each of you to do is to find your own spot on the paper (make sure there's enough paper so they can comfortably sit in front of it and not be crowded by other family members). After you have your own special area, I want you to draw or color what your special place looks like. This place can be a house or another building, a lake, a mountain, anything you want it to be. The only rule for this activity is not to talk to anyone else in your family until everyone is finished."

With younger children you might often get the response, "I am not sure how to draw. I need help with this." It is important for the therapist to respond in an encouraging manner and let all the participants know that their idea of this special place can be drawn or colored in any way. However they want to express themselves or use the crayons or markers is all right for this activity.

It is important for the therapist to monitor any talking during this activity and remind everyone of the need for silence. If members are allowed to talk during this activity, it is possible that the more dominant members of the family may direct the artwork of the less assertive members.

When the family is finished with this activity, the therapist helps each member describe his or her own work. Several guidelines are important at this time: One is the need for the member presenting his or her artwork to have the focused attention of all the other members. The therapist will need to make sure this is understood by all the members.

Some leading questions to each person may include: "Tell us about your special place." "What do you think you would be doing there if you could go there right now?" "If you close your eyes, what are the sounds you hear at this special place?" "If you close your eyes, what do you smell at this special place?"

Each person is given the opportunity to respond to these questions while the other members listen. After each person completes the responses to these questions, each family member is asked to give at least one positive comment to the person who has just disclosed. This might take some prompting by the therapist, but it is to be made clear that all responses are to be favorable. When everyone has had the opportunity to complete this activity and receive feedback from the family, the therapist then asks each member to describe what he or she learned about each other through this exercise.

APPLICATIONS

Although this activity is basic, it is a powerful form of play for family members. It gives all members the opportunity to express themselves not only through their artwork but also through the telling of their story. It provides each member with positive feedback from his or her family and structures the relationships so that everyone knows they have been heard and understood. This type of activity would then be encouraged as homework for the family, so that they might continue to practice the communication strategies learned during the session.

This particular activity has been effective in families when there are members (usually children) who tend to be somewhat emotionally isolated or discounted due to their nonassertive nature. It is also effective for the child at the other end of the continuum who acts out constantly. Engaging in the art project provides these children with the opportunity to be heard by the family unit and also receive positive feedback from each member. For the nonassertive child, this is a time when the family can empower this child and provide equal status in the family unit. For the "acting out" child, participating in this activity can help to create a new communication style in which the child realizes the value of listening to others and then is rewarded for the positive interactions versus relying on the old behaviors that resulted in negative consequences for both the child and the family.

This technique was successfully used with a family of four, which consisted of the parents and two adopted girls. The children had been victims of substantial abuse prior to the adoption, which included abandonment without care or food for days at a time. They had recently been in residential treatment prior to starting therapy. Each parent was aligned with one child, the father with the older daughter and the mother with the younger daughter. The parents were critical of the behaviors of the nonaligned child, especially the mother with the oldest daughter.

During the processing of the family artwork, the family practiced giving positive feedback to all members, and this was especially effective between each nonaligned parent and child. Once the foundation of this new communication pattern was worked on in the therapy session, the family was able to practice with similar activities in the home. Each child was able to feel validated by both parents.

8

Sand Painting

Denise K. Filley

INTRODUCTION

In working with groups of children, especially in managed care or limited session settings, I felt the challenge to provide play techniques that allow for addressing multitasks or accomplishing multigoals. One of my major goals with children is that they leave play therapy with a sense that they have some skill, mastery, or accomplishment to boost their hope and sense of believing in themselves. Another goal that comes with facilitating groups is to help the children bond together with others. This technique provides means toward both goals.

RATIONALE

It seems today that most children lack a sense of hope for themselves. I have found that much of this comes from a lack of belief that they have skills, abilities, or mastery of anything in their lives. I attempt to provide them with opportunities to gain a sense of mastery, and thus, a glimmer of hope, for themselves. In a group context, this is often more challenging due to natural tendencies to compare and compete among children. Sand painting offers an opportunity not only for children to express themselves through art; it also is noncompetitive and does not allow for comparison as far as art ability is concerned. There are no "ugly" sand paintings, and it is not possible for any one child to be "better" or more "talented" at sand painting than another, thus putting everyone on an even level and allowing for natural bonding and acceptance to build group cohesion.

Because I also believe strongly in providing sensory experiences for children to keep them in touch with their emotions, sand painting provides a sensory experience that is only limited by the children themselves. The therapist can enhance the experience by providing options in media used for the technique.

DESCRIPTION

Materials

Colored sand in three or four colors (available in craft sections at stores such as Hobby Lobby or Michael's)

Spice shaker plastic containers (the kind with holes in the top to shake the sand through—often available at recycling centers)

Elmer's glue

Plastic mat (clear or white) or trash bag to put under mat and catch loose sand to prevent it from getting into carpet

Matboard or heavy posterboard/cardboard in neutral colors (white, tan, etc.)

Vacuum cleaner (it might be handy afterward)

The size of the matboard should be determined by the number of people in the group who will do the sand painting together. For a group of three to four people, I provide a canvas space of 36–40 inches by 36–40 inches (square). For two people, a canvas space of 15 to 20 inches square is appropriate. The plastic mat or trash bag should be larger than the matboard/canvas space.

I lay the plastic mats/trashbags around in various places (stations) on the floor around the room. I also have one small shaker bottle of each color of sand sitting at each of these stations. I usually limit this to three to four sand color choices. I also place the glue bottle(s) at the stations. I keep the matboards near me and hand them out after I give the instructions. Each person in the group sits on a side of the canvas. I let them decide this naturally as they set down their canvas and take their places around it. (This technique is usually done sitting on the floor).

The instructions to the groups are to create a picture/painting together using the glue and the sand. Each group works through how they will do this (develops social skills). Usually the groups paint their picture with the glue first, then shake the sand onto the glue to color it. When each group is finished with their painting, they make a decision about keeping the sand colors separate as they have them painted or running the sand colors together. This decision determines how the extra sand will be shaken off the matboard. If they want to keep the sand colors separate, they must take hold of two sides and quickly flip it over to shake off the excess sand. (One warning, sand often flies through the air with this method.) If they want their sand colors to mix or run together, they simply lift up one side, tilting the board at an angle and the excess sand runs down the board and onto the plastic mat. The sand colors run together and stick as they hit the glue on the way down.

After all groups have finished their painting, we discuss the process they used to decide their method, whether everyone felt included, and the group process. I share the observations I made of the group interactions among members (leaders, those who stayed laid back, those who infringed on others boundaries, etc.). When the glue has dried, we cut the picture up and each person takes a portion of it home with them to keep the connection to the group. This also reminds them of their mastery of the technique and the beautiful art they created. I truly have never seen an unattractive sand painting.

APPLICATIONS

The therapist can guide some of the direction of the group process. You can decide when setting up the stations if you want to place only one bottle of glue for the entire group to share or if you will place one bottle per person. This creates interesting group process dynamics and problem-solving opportunities for the group. When one bottle is provided for the entire group, you can observe how sharing is worked out, if they take turns, does one dominate, does one sit back? It is also important to observe how the members share the space on the canvas. Does each person keep "his or her own space" or do they share space and each person feels free to paint all over the mat/canvas? I also observe group communications—do they discuss what they will paint, is it a planned picture, or does someone just start rather abstractly and others add on? It is important to also observe how the individuals and groups interact with the sensory aspect of the activity. Some will have adverse reactions to using the glue or sand. Others will want to touch it, maybe even smear the glue around to create interesting designs. All of these observations should be part of the processing with the groups to help them learn and connect their sensory input, behaviors, and emotions.

The following are some variations to create more sensory experiences: Instead of using sand, use media that can create other sensory experiences such as smelling or tasting. You can use colored chalk, potpourri, sugar, or the candy from Pixie sticks to paint with. You could also use glitter, confetti, or any number of other media. Be creative and don't limit yourself. Instead of glue, you could also use pudding for the wet compound to sprinkle the painting media onto; however, the pudding does not dry, so these pictures end up being thrown away and not taken home. The process, though, is the powerful part of it. I encourage the participants to experience the sensory levels of the media, such as tasting if it is food, before painting with it.

I use this technique with almost all my groups, no matter the goal or purpose of the group. Most any age level or developmental level, except the very young, can do this. Adults, too, enjoy this and are often in awe that they created a piece of art for the first time in their life that they think is beautiful. Family problem solving, interactions, communication, and so on can be observed by using this simple assessment technique for family therapy. It can also be used as a variation on the many scribble techniques used to build rapport between the therapist and the child or between parents and children. The limitation for this technique's uses is only in what the client and therapist set.

9

Sensory/Kinetic Hand Family Drawing

Denise K. Filley

INTRODUCTION

A common challenge working with children today, especially children who have suffered loss of attachment, abuse, or neglect is their lack of connection. The Sensory/Kinetic Hand Drawing provides both a sensory and visual way for children to regain connection and change the directions of relationships and emotions in their life. This technique provides an easy option out of drawing people figures such as those used in the Kinetic Family Drawings (Burns and Kaufman, 1970). This opt-out is important as most people have anxiety about their figure/people drawing abilities.

RATIONALE

The loss of connection for children exists on many levels. They have lost connection with people, relationships, social systems, and, especially, they have lost the connection between their sensory intake and emotional content. They may experience sensory events and take in information through touching, hearing, tasting, smelling, movement, and feeling. Their past life experiences, however, have caused them to shut down the connection from this sensory input to their emotions in order to protect themselves. I wanted to provide a positive technique that would remove the fear of sensory input, be fun for the child, and create a new connection on multiple levels. Hands, including the blood that flows through them, are a symbol for our relationships and connections in life. As I considered that probably 95 percent of connecting is done through our hands (shaking hands, touching someone's hair, waving, and so on) and that four out of the six sensory modalities require touch, usually with our hands, I developed the use of the Sensory/Kinetic Hand Drawing. This technique allows children sensory input from touching and the visual picture of connection. With some variations, it can also allow physical, safe connection with people in the child's life as well. Another value of this technique is that it is simple and children of almost any developmental level can participate in it.

DESCRIPTION

Material needed include white paper and markers, crayons, or other writing media. To add a more sensory experience, this could also be done with other media such as paint, pudding, or clay, but I prefer to keep it focused on the content and keep the sensory level simple so as not to overwhelm the child. (If the child is a tactile learner, however, I would opt for one of the more tactile media.) Here, I will discuss this technique done in the context of a family session. In an individual session, the child could trace his or her own hand or the therapist could do this.

Each child has a parent or adult caregiver trace his or her hand on the paper, just like we did in grade school to make those Thanksgiving turkey pictures. The child can then trace the adult's hand on a separate piece of paper. On each finger of his or her hand tracing, the child will identify one family member. He or she does this by either writing his or her name or, my preference, drawing a picture of that person or a symbol for that person. At the wrist he or she can, depending on the therapist's goal for the exercise, write or draw other important people in the child's life or something that connects the family together (sports, music, yelling, alcohol, whatever it might be to them). In the palm or "heart" of the hand he or she will put either: a positive symbol to represent his or her family, or something his or her family does together, or be creative and create what you think would be best for him or her to express there. As the child is completing the drawing, the adult also completes his or her drawing. As the drawing process occurs, discussions are ensued about connections in our lives with people, experiences, and how they affect us, and our interactions as well as our emotions. Each person is then allowed to share his or her drawing and discuss, led by the therapist, his or her perspectives and connections. It is important to talk about the sensory aspect of the exercise such as how it felt to have someone touch your hand while tracing, how hard it was to keep your hand still while tracing, did it tickle to have the crayon or marker trace your hand, and so on. For the child, explore the sensory and control issues of him or her holding down the adult's hand and tracing it. Explore the same venues of sensory experience from this different perspective.

APPLICATIONS

This technique can be done in individual sessions, family or group sessions, and so on. It is especially effective in working with children who have attachment issues such as children who have experienced foster care or adoptive placements. In using this with foster or adoptive placements, it assists children in pulling together as a whole all the pieces that make them up, including their biological connection. They can assimilate all the people who have invested in them without feeling as if they have to deny or betray any of those relationships or experiences. As well, it assists children with abuse issues who tend to shut down their sensory input connections from their emotions, which further impairs their ability to connect with others and themselves.

Another aspect of this technique is that it is advantageous for use with children who have different primary learning modalities: tactile, visual, auditory. This technique addresses all three levels of learning. Because the therapist can guide where the technique goes and how long is spent on any one level of learning (tactile, auditory, or visual), this technique can be tweaked and tailored to each individual client and his or her learning style. If a child is more tactile, more time can be spent on the sensory-making aspect of the hand or by using more sensory media to create the hand picture and less time on the auditory discussion. (Tactile learners take in more through the experiences without discussion.) These specifications to how the technique is structured can be done for each learning style.

I have primarily used this technique with abused children or children who needed to form attachments. I used this with a 4-year-old boy who lived with both parents, but his connection with his father had just not meshed. The father had a difficult time connecting with his son at a child's level and expected the son to interact at a level more as an adult. The boy had begun to demonstrate his anger and frustration with this relationship. His behavior at preschool escalated to throwing chairs at a teacher. Affectively, he looked pretty apathetic to things around him. By using this technique we were able to identify that the son felt no positive connection with his father and that he was craving some child-level interaction with Dad. We were able to help the father value his son for his playfulness as a child and get them to have at least one or two activities a week together that they could both enjoy. Another example comes from a colleague.

A therapist friend, after I taught her this technique, shared the most beautiful example of using this technique with two sisters, aged 7 and 9, who had been through four foster placements (in four years) and were currently in an adoptive (almost final) placement. The session was done with the girls and their adoptive parents. Each parent paired up with a child. They took turns tracing their hands. The therapist described that much giggling and touching occurred. In each finger, the girls wrote the names of the foster placements and at the wrist they wrote the birth mother and father's names as they discussed life and blood connections. (The adoptive parents did the same exercise with their family.) The therapist reported that watching the interaction was very moving to observe—the anger and sadness at birth parents' names, memories of each of the past placements, hopes and dreams shared about their future. Both girls added hearts to the paper they were tracing on. At the end, the older girl commented that the hands should be connected so she drew a line so all four did connect (they did all four hands on one large page). During the session the bond for this family was emotionally deepened. This technique took the entire session. At the end, they rolled up the picture, tied it with a bow, and sent it home with the family.

This technique has many applications and can be adapted by the therapist to meet the goals, sensory needs, and learning styles of each client.

Reference

Burns, R. C. and Kaufman, S. H. (1970). *Kinetic Family Drawings (KFD)*. New York: Brunner/Mazel.

10

All Tangled Up

Paris Goodyear-Brown

INTRODUCTION

This technique was the result of one session's collaboration between this therapist and a 4-year-old girl. It is true that our clients are our best teachers. This 4-year-old client had many worries, but when I asked her to list them for me, she turned to me in frustration and said "They're all tangled up!" It became necessary for us to find a concrete tool to help us not only number the worries, but judge them in terms of their intensity. The client provided the metaphor, and I provided the yarn.

RATIONALE

Preschool-age children are just beginning to put words to their feelings and their feelings vocabulary normally doesn't extend past happy, mad, and sad. However, some of our preschool clients have worries that plague them and are expressed behaviorally because they do not have the vocabulary to express them verbally. Children with many worries (the kind of children who will probably come to the attention of a therapist) spend the majority of their energy simply feeling overwhelmed. They are not yet able to tease out one worry from another and compartmentalize it. These children need help untangling their worries. Play therapists can help these children to separate their worries into manageable pieces. This helps the child feel more in control of his or her emotions. Moreover, these children do not have the skills for quantifying the intensity of their worries, at least not verbally. They can identify big and small, but they are not particularly good at expressing degrees of emotion. With an adult client, you might ask, "Which of these worries do you want to work on first, second, and so forth." A preschool-age child might be able to tell you about his "biggest" worry, but his powers of articulation fail at further illumination. The worries must be expressed concretely and then they can be manipulated jointly by the preschooler and the therapist until they are resolved.

DESCRIPTION

The therapist begins by taking a ball of yarn, preferably one that is "all tangled up" and showing it to the child. Introduce the exercise by saying, "Everyone has worries, but sometimes they get all tangled up and then it's hard to fight them one at a time. This ball of yarn is tangled up just like your worries. Let's start untangling them." Then the therapist should use an example of her own to model the activity for the child. "Sometimes I worry about people leaving me." (Try to make your example related to an issue in the client's life.) Then the therapist pulls out a length of yarn from the tangled ball. Say, "I worry about that this much" and cut a piece of yarn to a length that mirrors the intensity of the concern (that is, longer for a "big" worry and shorter for a "little" worry). Children will be able to show you varying degrees of anxiety in this way.

Ask the child, "What's one of the things you worry about?" The child names a worry, perhaps "I worry that my parents will get divorced." The therapist encourages the child to cut a length of yarn that reflects how much or how often the client worries about this particular concern. Once the child has named five or more worries and cut various lengths of yarn, the therapist then says, "Let's stretch these worries out so we can see them." The therapist then ties one end of one piece of yarn around something in the room (for example, the leg of the chair). The child is given the other end and asked to tie it off somewhere else in the room. The therapist helps the client do this with each piece of yarn until what looks like a three-dimensional spider web has taken over the office. The therapist then helps the child take a step back and look at the big web of worries. The rest of the session is spent dealing with each thread of the web. Once a strategy for dealing with a particular worry (thread) has been decided upon, the child gets to cut that thread down . . . progressively making the spider web less complicated, until it disappears completely.

When I did this technique with my 4-year-old female client, she loved it. She had great fun tying the pieces of yarn to various pieces of furniture in the office. This client had been adopted, and her largest worry was that her adoptive parents would abandon her as her birth parents had done. The intensity of this worry was made poignantly clear to me as she unwound length after length of yarn. The one strand was so long that it had to be tied off in several places and criss-cross the room several times in order to be pulled taut as part of the web. I asked the client if she believed that her parents knew how much she worried about things. When she said she wasn't sure, I asked if it would be all right to bring her parents into the room so that they could see the web of worries. We brought her parents in (although this proved difficult because part of the web was tied off on the doorknob) and their understanding of their daughter's pain was deepened by experiencing the three-dimensional web.

APPLICATIONS

This technique can be modified to deal with any number of subjects. Clients could untangle feelings, sort out cognitive distortions, analyze negative self-talk statements, or generate a web of new, self-esteem-building statements. This technique can also be modified for a group setting. In that case, I would use a spider puppet as the focal point of the exercise and let the children take turns stringing up their "worry yarn" with the spider puppet while verbalizing the worry to the group. Strategies for dealing with each worry could then be generated by the whole group.

11

Scavenger Hunt of Relaxation Tools (SHORT)

Teresa A. Glatthorn

INTRODUCTION

Anxiety issues in children are sometimes difficult to treat and often require a multifaceted approach. What works to reduce anxiety in adults may or may not work with children. Furthermore, what works to help a given child who is anxious about one situation may not reduce another child's, or even the same child's, anxiety in another situation. In addition, chronically anxious children often feel helpless and disempowered. Paradoxically, many of the anxious clients I have worked with become *more* anxious when asked to simply relax and learn to "let go" in relaxation training. These children need to *do* something when they are anxious in order to feel in control of their anxiety and relaxation. This scavenger hunt empowers anxious children (as well as adolescents and adults) through the assemblage of a set of individualized tools for reducing their own anxiety.

RATIONALE

Many anxiety-reduction techniques are based on the belief that the state of anxiety is not compatible with relaxation, pleasure, humor, feeling strong and capable, or experiencing other strong positive emotions (Wolpe, 1973). Because each individual responds to his or her own variety of anxiety reduction cues, and because anxiety often precludes the ability to remember anxiety reducers, I often use the Scavenger Hunt of Relaxation Tools (SHORT) as an activity in an early session with very anxious clients of all ages to "make SHORT of anxiety." It empowers clients by having them begin to gather for themselves the anxiety-reducing tools that work for them and keep them in one place so that they are available when needed. Some traditional relaxation tools, such as progressive relaxation, may be part of it (Hawton, et al, 1998; and Wolpe, 1973), as well as effective distractors, sensory awareness tools, symbols, playful items, and other tools for relaxation and empowerment. SHORT is a powerful, playful activity in which people of all ages feel comfortable participating and from which they feel they derive great benefit.

DESCRIPTION

The activity starts with the decoration of a box. (A large shoebox or a box of similar size works well.) The box is decorated as simply or elaborately as the therapist and client desire, from covering it with construction paper or wrapping paper to a detailed collage of pictures and words. Relaxation and empowerment should be reflected both in the completed product and in the assembling process. In other words, all activities used to create it should be fun and relaxing, not anxiety producing (i.e. no art if there is performance anxiety about art and *no perfectionism or "failure"*!)

While decorating the box, a conversation naturally evolves about what makes the person feel relaxed, confident, competent, happy, and so on. This prepares the client for the scavenger hunt, which actually occurs between sessions. The therapist invites the client to gather at least one relaxation tool for each of the five senses, including as many objects as possible without overwhelming him- or herself. All content should represent relaxation, fun, pleasure, humor, strength, pride, confidence, and empowerment. Clients should be empowered to use their own materials and ideas to decorate the box as well as to fill it.

Some favorites include pictures, comics, sayings, soaps, candles, tea, candy, stones, stuffed animals, Play-doh, music, prayers, Kooshes, bubbles, and markers.

Words or pictures can be put on 3 by 5-inch cards to represent things that cannot be put in the box. For example, a picture of a piano might represent making music, while a nature scene or an acorn might symbolize walking or exercising in nature, and a bath bead could help recall the relaxation of a warm bath.

Each time the client learns a new skill, activity, or phrase that helps him or her, some representation of it is added to the box. Between sessions, whenever the client feels anxious or stressed, he or she is encouraged to look through his or her box and use an idea or combination of ideas that could help him or her feel better.

The greater the variety of positive feelings evoked (relaxation, empowerment, pride, and so on) the more effective this tool is. For young children and children with limited ideas, the scavenger hunt can be "assigned" as a parent-and-child project and ideas generated during box decoration can be written down as a reminder. Parents and therapist alike need to respect the client's choices of items to include. For example, although an ice pack may soothe the parent, a warm ("hot") pack may be more soothing to the child.

APPLICATIONS

A 7-year-old girl was fearful in her own house (a 150-year-old farmhouse) and refused to travel independently between the first and second floors. Cognitive approaches failed to comfort her or enable her to increase her independence. The first week after completing her SHORT box, this little girl could run quick errands up- and downstairs alone if she carried a favorite cuddle toy and sang (quite loudly!) a silly song she learned in school—a combination she invented after perusing the materials in her SHORT box.

A perfectionistic 12-year-old girl, who had recently survived an impulsive suicide attempt, found creating the box to be a great way to reduce anxiety in her early sessions. It kept her hands occupied and focused the conversation productively, but away from the suicide attempt itself, until enough rapport was developed to address the latter more directly.

In the process, this client was tempted to repeat her usual perfectionism. With encouragement, however, she was able to use the phrase "It's good enough" to cope with tiny details that did not come together perfectly. "It's good enough" became an important tool to include in her SHORT box.

She revealed little of herself at first. Her fascination with frogs, which were populated all over her box, however, led to our researching frogs.

This gave rise to an even more empowering tool, when we found that the brightly colored frogs (her favorites) carry poison in their skin. Left alone, the frogs were harmless, cute, and sweet; however, any creature that bit the frog died very quickly from its potent poison. The client, afraid to stand up for herself to peers when being teased, did not want to be the cause of anyone else's pain. The frog metaphor helped her see that if she merely spoke up in response to their attack, any repercussions the taunters experienced were their *own* fault, not hers.

The preparation of the SHORT box was a safe opportunity to begin to practice letting go of the anxiety related to perfectionism and led to a metaphor that empowered her to be strong in scary circumstances. She also used many of her other SHORT tools for empowerment and relaxation in other circumstances.

References

Hawton, K., Salkovskis, P. N., Kirk, J. and Clark, D. M. (Eds.). (1998). *Cognitive Behavior Therapy for Psychiatric Problems*. New York: Oxford University Press.

Wolpe, J. (1973). *The Practice of Behavior Therapy*. New York: Pergamon Press.

12

Invisible Feelings

Sueann Kenney-Noziska

INTRODUCTION

A common area of clinical attention when working with children is assisting children in identifying and expressing their emotions. Although this seems like a simple concept, it can often be a challenge to reach a guarded child or assist a child in acknowledging certain emotions. This technique creates a way for the therapist to lower the child's defenses while facilitating recognition, identification, and expression of various feelings.

RATIONALE

Most children entering treatment can benefit from developing an understanding of their emotions. For a depressed or anxious child, emotional issues are typically a focal point of treatment. For other children, like the child with attention deficits or learning disabilities, processing emotions surrounding issues such as rejection or isolation can be an important secondary treatment focus. Unfortunately, by the time children are referred for treatment, they are typically guarded and reluctant to discuss emotions that are difficult, embarrassing, or uncomfortable. It is often the task of the therapist to devise a creative way to reduce the child's defenses and create a safe environment for the child to process his or her emotions. This technique not only creates an opportunity for children to identify their feelings, but also provides an opportunity for children to process situations that trigger emotions as well as explore coping skills.

DESCRIPTION

Materials needed for this activity include an 8½ by 11-inch sheet of white paper (placed horizontally) and Color Changeable Markers™ by Crayola. The package of Color Changeable Markers™ includes a clear marker and several colored markers. The clear marker writes "invisibly" on the paper and does not appear until the area that was written on is colored with one of the changeable colored markers. Prior to the session, the therapist uses a black marker to divide the paper into three columns of equal size. A heading is created for each column by drawing a line across the paper approximately 1 to 1½ inches from the top of the paper. After the paper is divided, the therapist uses the "invisible" clear marker to write an emotion in the heading section of each column. The therapist should include emotions that may be difficult for the child to express. For example, if a child struggles with depression, the therapist will want to label one column "sad." The other columns can be labeled with different emotions such as "happy," "mad," or "scared." Because each feeling is written with the "invisible" marker, the paper will not appear to have any writing.

When the child enters the session, the therapist asks the child to read what is written on the paper. Because the words are "invisible," the child will likely make a statement reflecting the fact that nothing is written on the paper. The therapist's challenge will be to playfully build the intensity of the intervention by engaging the child and eliciting the child's assistance in finding the "missing" words. The therapist can accomplish this by looking puzzled and making statements such as "Hmm, I know something was written on this paper. I wonder what happened to the words?" Obtaining the child's assistance in searching the room to find the "missing" words can also be done.

After the child is engaged in searching for the "missing" words, the therapist provides the child with the changeable markers. The child uses the markers to color the heading of each column and reveal the "invisible" feelings. The child is then invited to list situations or events that elicit each emotion in the respective column. If the child chooses, the therapist can assume the role of "secretary" and the child can "dictate" what the therapist writes.

Processing this activity creates many clinical opportunities. First and foremost, the intervention provides an opportunity for the therapist to normalize and validate the child's emotions. The therapist may also join with the child as emotions are shared and processed. In addition, the intervention can be expanded by introducing and exploring coping skills to address the emotions processed during the session.

APPLICATIONS

This technique is primarily utilized in individual therapy but may be modified for group or family work. The therapist should tailor the emotions utilized in the technique to meet the child's individual treatment needs. Instead of listing different emotions for each column, the therapist can modify the technique to include different environments in which a specific emotion is triggered. For example, if a child struggles with anger management, the therapist can label the columns to encourage the child to identify triggers to anger at home, at school, and while playing with peers.

The playful nature of this intervention creates a nonthreatening environment for the child to express emotions and is useful for a variety of clinical issues. In particular, the technique appears to work well for children who are struggling with mood instability commonly seen in depression and anxiety. Aggressive children may also benefit from the use of this technique, particularly if coping and problem-solving skills are explored in conjunction with the intervention.

The use of the Color Changeable Markers™ creates a playful and intriguing therapeutic medium that lowers defenses while captivating the child's interest. Highly guarded children often become engaged and are able to identify and process their emotions as a result of the playful nature of this intervention.

13

The Use of Metaphor for Careful Preparation in the Play Therapy Process: Unloading a Garbage Bin of Feelings

Nancy Riedel Bowers

INTRODUCTION

Many children and their family members enter the play therapy process with uncertainty and, at times, resistance to the relationship that is about to commence. As is indicated by Risë VanFleet (2000), "Parental resistance to play and filial therapies is perhaps most likely to occur at the outset" (p. 37), resulting in false impressions about what play therapy is about and what it can accomplish. This can be overcome by a careful preparation process, assisting the child and family in their understanding of how the expression of feelings, a major goal of play therapy, can enhance self-growth.

RATIONALE

Play therapists can prepare the child and family for the relationship that develops in the therapeutic process. It is a mutually shaping therapeutic process, "fragile in nature . . . a process that moves in harmony" (Riedel Bowers, 2001, p. 221). It is likened to a "delicate balance" with the therapist gradually becoming attuned to the child's wish to overcome the pain from his or her world. Gradually, the child (and family) develop a sense of trust in the therapy situation.

The child, in the early relationship development process of play therapy, uses the medium of play to express feelings and memories. Play is a link between the imagined and real worlds of the child and, through play, the child develops "a voice" or a way in which to communicate and express him or herself within the outside world (Bowlby, 1953; Gross, 1901; Landreth, Baggerly & Tyndall-Lind, 1999). With this voice, the child develops a sense of security and safety within the early process of play therapy, gradually being prepared for the sharing of painful feelings.

It is the use of play as the metaphor through which the child develops a sense of comfort and clarity in the early play therapy process that is the focus for this description of the therapeutic technique, "unloading a garbage bin of feelings." This activity facilitates an early understanding of what the play therapy process has in store for the child. The importance of metaphorical beginnings is stressed in this presentation, similar to the use of play as metaphor in play therapy terminations (Gil, 1991; Glatthorn in Kaduson and Schaefer, 1997).

DESCRIPTION

Play as Metaphor

Play acts as a form of metaphor for the child's expression of emotions, wishes, and fears. Meares (1993) suggests that "One requires a language that will somehow describe his inner life . . . emotions are always expressed in terms of metaphor . . . they may be a means of helping to enlarge and make real something of the inner zone" (p. 159). Play has an "'as if' or non-literal quality" (Schaefer, 1993, p. 1), thereby allowing the child to intuitively act out aspects of his or her life.

The natural medium of expression that play provides (Axline, 1947) facilitates the use of symbolic interpretation within the play therapy process. Through this symbolic activity, using the metaphor of play, the child is able to grasp the meaning of the play therapy process and is able to develop an investment in the early relationship with the play therapist. The building of the emotional communication between child and therapist in the early attachment process of psychotherapy provides a cathartic experience for the child and family (Bowlby, 1988; Schaefer, 1993). It also encourages a belief in the play therapy process, which ultimately enhances its effectiveness.

Emptying the Garbage Bin

One such intervention effectively used to develop an early attachment between children, families, and therapists in the play therapy journey is the activity of filling one's own "garbage bin" full of feelings and gradually unloading some of these emotional states and perceptions. This activity provides clarification about the early therapy process and, consequently, early resistance in the play therapy process can be prevented.

More specifically, the therapist in the early relationship development process asks the child (and family members) to choose a number of "feeling faces" to be selected from a grouping of cut-up squares that clearly illustrates dozens of feelings, positive and negative in nature, with accompanying word descriptions. For instance, the feeling for "happy" would depict a face with a smile and underneath the round face would be the word, *happy*. These faces can be made by the therapist ahead of time or can be designed, drawn, and cut out by the child during the early relationship development process.

The child is encouraged to fill a small toy garbage bin that has a lid with as many feelings as he or she has indicated are part of his or her life. The therapist might join in the activity by filling the bin with crumpled up newspaper or other representations of "garbage" to metaphorically illustrate the "filling of one's life garbage bin." The lid can be placed on the bin and can be superficially forced (by the play therapist) to pop off indicating how full one can be of memories, fears, and feelings. The child can be encouraged to add more feelings to visibly illustrate the process of the garbage bin becoming "too full" and needing to be "unloaded."

In order to further clarify one of the goals for play therapy, should that be a desired intention of the play therapist, the child may be encouraged to choose one or more unpleasant emotions and may set them as a goal for "unloading" or therapeutic change.

At the conclusion of this process, which may be brief for those who are unable to address their affect due to the depth of traumatic life events, the therapist may summarize the activity and verbally connect the metaphor of "emptying your garbage bin" to the goal of play therapy. This takes the "as if" quality of the play metaphor and applies it to the real world.

APPLICATIONS

This technique is helpful with children involved in many play therapy techniques as well as with adolescents and adults usually involved in a more talk-oriented therapeutic context. It allows the child to literally see the process of choosing his or her feelings, loading them up until "the bin" is full, and then unloading them in an empowering way. It is a mirroring process, providing an opportunity to look from the outside in.

Supporting the need for a mutual engaging and clarifying experience in play therapy, Nemiroff and Annunziata (1990) suggest:

> When kids play, the therapist can understand their feelings and their worries. That's because children play their feelings better than they talk about them. Child therapists help them understand their feelings while they play. Children's problems seem to get better when they understand their feelings. That's because kids sometimes have feelings they don't know they have.

The metaphor of the garbage bin, the filling of it, and the unloading process facilitate some clarity about what play therapy is, what it can facilitate, and how it can prevent suspicion and resistance for all involved.

References

Axline, V. (1947). *Play Therapy*. New York: Ballantine Books, Inc.

Bowlby, J. (1953). *Child Care and The Growth of Love*. Middlesex, England: Penguin Books.

Bowlby, J. (1988). *A Secure Base: Clinical Applications of Attachment Theory*. London: Routledge.

Gil, E. (1991). *The Healing Power of Play*. New York: The Guilford Press.

Gross, K. (1901). *The Play of Man*. New York: Arno Press.

Kaduson, H., and Schaefer, C. E. (Eds.). (1997). *101 Favorite Play Therapy Techniques*. Northvale, NJ: Jason Aronson.

Landreth, G., Baggerly, J., and Tyndall-Lind, A. (1999). Beyond adapting adult counselling skills for use with children. *The Journal of Individual Psychology* Vol. 55 (3).

Meares, R. (1993). *The Metaphor of Play*. Northvale, NJ: Jason Aronson.

Nemiroff, M. A., and Annunziata, J. (1990). *A Child's First Book About Play Therapy*. Washington, D.C.: American Psychological Association.

Riedel Bowers, N. (2001). *A Journey within a Journey: A Naturalistic Study of the Early Relationship Development Process in Non-Directive Play Therapy*. Unpublished Doctoral Dissertation: Wilfrid Laurier University, Waterloo, Ontario.

Schaefer, C. (1993). *The Therapeutic Powers of Play*. Northvale, NJ: Jason Aronson.

VanFleet, R. (2000). Understanding and Overcoming Parent Resistance to Play Therapy. *International Journal of Play Therapy* Vol. 9(1).

14

The Cargo Train

Jacqueline Johnson

INTRODUCTION

Symbolism is a powerful tool in psychotherapeutic work with children because symbols communicate experiential patterns or themes that are difficult for children to articulate with words. Play therapists purposefully apply symbolism to assess and assist children with deep expression of meaningful but elusive psychological constructs. Therapists also can easily instruct or convey relevant therapeutic ideas through concrete and representational objects.

RATIONALE

The use of concrete objects to represent complex concepts or internal processes encourages reflective exploration of therapeutic themes through multiple sensory channels. The Cargo Train is a therapeutic tool that translates abstract ideas into tangible items. It is richly symbolic and can serve as a didactic and therapeutic instrument throughout phases of psychotherapy with children. This tool is especially useful when there is a step-wise progression in skills, as in self-esteem enhancement and social skill development, or when self- or group monitoring is paramount to therapeutic gains. It also assists with depicting the simultaneous existence of opposing or complementary actions, emotions, or thoughts. the therapist may use the tool as a way for children to review progress, rehearse skills, or revisit specific themes. The therapist may think of the train as representing the child, and his or her navigation of ecological contexts such as school, home, and community settings, including the necessary physical, emotional, and perceptual shifts that occur across these settings. The train also represents the development and maintenance of the child's therapeutic gains. The train's cargo is the substance (for example, feelings, skills, abilities, talents, and so on) that the child possesses (contains), carries, and demonstrates (retrieves or unloads) through his or her navigation across contexts. The machinery of the train, much like the human body, needs fuel to run efficiently. The therapist and child may name food, sleep, and other sources of physical, social, and emotional nourishment within this analogy. The Cargo Train's richness as a didactic and exploratory tool becomes evident through a child's response to it.

DESCRIPTION

The therapist and the client can co-construct the train and its cars through a number of expressive methods and art media. Use the following illustration of the engine and cargo car to guide construction. Materials such as quart- and pint-sized milk, cream, or juice cartons, miniature cereal boxes, egg cartons, toilet paper tubes, or tea tins can be used to form the basic train body, train cars, and additional features. Train cars serve as containers of the cargo that will be added during therapy sessions. Small thread spools (glued to each car), pipe cleaners, garbage bag ties, plastic straws, or coffee stirrers can be used to attach train cars together through perforating and twisting, taping, or gluing. Bottle caps, buttons, milk caps, or foil-covered or painted cardboard circles can become wheels. Cardboard wheels fastened to a milk carton by thumbtacks or fasteners work particularly well because they allow the wheels to turn. Painted cutouts in felt, construction paper, or cardboard can be glued to cover the engine car. The child's name or other identifying information can adorn the finished engine car. Film canisters make excellent cargo that can be placed in train cars. The outside of the canisters can be labeled appropriately (for example, categories of feelings, skills, competencies). The inside of the canister is ideal for magazine cutouts, written or picture labels, or other symbolic references to the cargo. The therapist can supply a variety of materials, introduce the activity of making a cargo train, and describe appropriate parallels while guiding the child's construction. Once construction is complete, the train's cargo becomes the central feature in play therapy.

APPLICATIONS

The cargo train's play therapy application is multifaceted and restricted only by limits of individual imagination. The cargo is symbolic of a school-aged child's accessible and nascent repertoire of social and emotional behaviors. As such, the train can depict the child's observable and reported emotional and behavioral regulation, and it can make a visible record of a child's therapeutic progress within and outside of play therapy sessions. For the purposes of restorative work with the child client, the therapist can help the child identify, develop, rehearse, or review ("load") adaptive responses that are represented by and added to the cargo. Thus the train is a tool to utilize throughout the phases of assessment, intervention, and generalization. Example applications of cargo include:

1. Representation of the acquisition of systematic steps in social skill training (e.g., the canister labeled Making Friends includes "introduce self" on a strip of paper or contains a symbolic picture of a greeting).
2. Depiction of step-wise progression of desensitization to fearful objects through unloading appropriately labeled canisters at each junction of progress.
3. Representation of various talents, skills, and abilities that become identified over time as part of self-esteem enhancement. Canisters contain the competencies either in categories or "locations" where they are demonstrated.
4. Representation of group cohesion, direction, and dynamics involved in group therapy (e.g., a canister labeled Taking Turns includes the names of all group members). The construction of the cargo train assists with the development of cohesion and reveals dynamics very quickly. Group members can identify

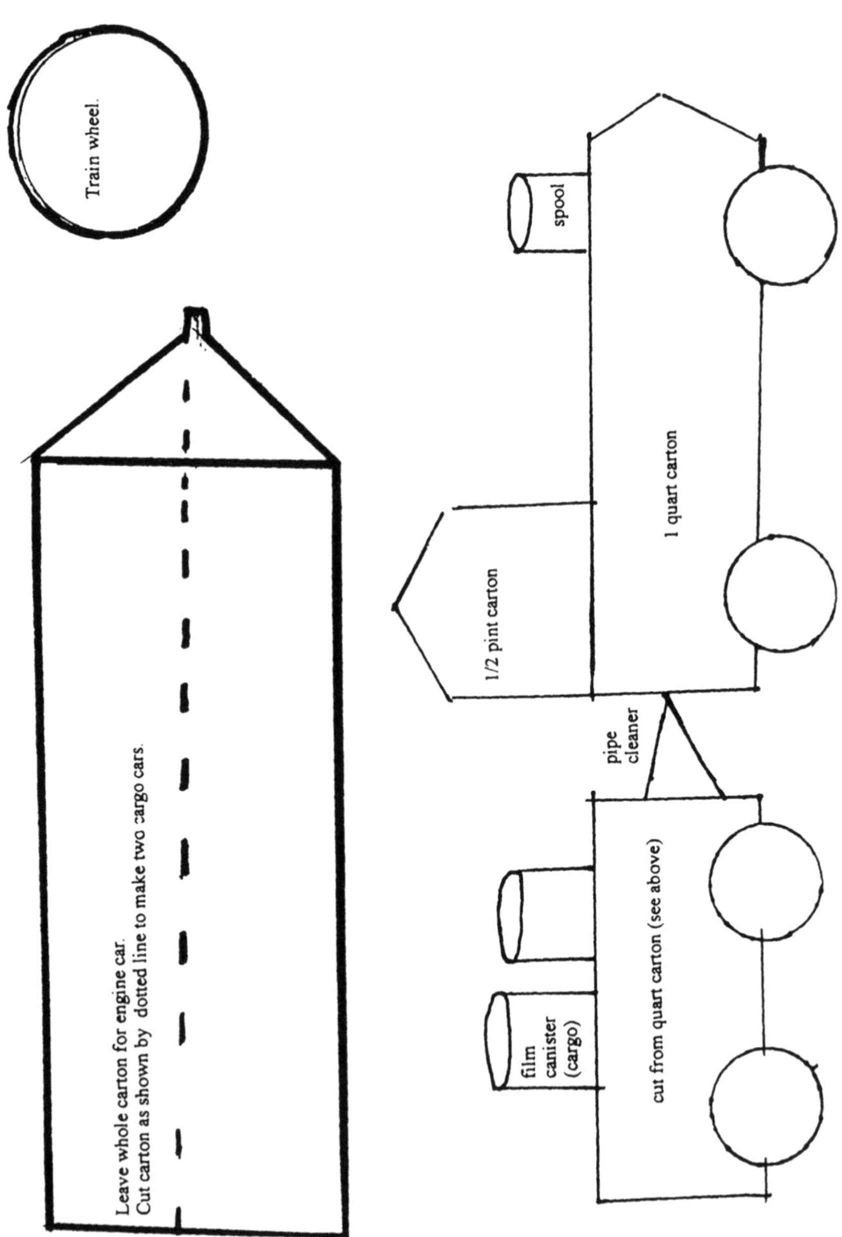
Train wheel.
Leave whole carton for engine car.
Cut carton as shown by dotted line to make two cargo cars.
spool
1 quart carton
1/2 pint carton
pipe cleaner
film canister (cargo)
cut from quart carton (see above)

Figure 14.1

what they each believe are important aspects of group functioning and label canisters accordingly.

5. Depiction of self-monitoring skills, new or complex skills with component parts for children who are impulsive, inattentive, or learning disabled.

15

Water and Oil—Do They Mix?

Diana Malca

INTRODUCTION

Play therapy is a method of helping children help themselves. According to Axline (1947), "Play therapy is based upon the fact that play is the child's natural medium of self-expression" (p. 9).

In play therapy the child has the opportunity to play out his or her feelings, thereby feeling accepted, respected, and most importantly, heard. Unlike indirect play therapy, throughout directive play therapy the therapist assumes the responsibility for guidance and interpretation. The following technique is directive, because the presenting problem, at times, requires an immediate alleviation and understanding.

RATIONALE

Divorce is devastating for children and their parents as well. It entails a process of loss and mourning. Children suffer from it, but mostly from the process and its outcome. There is a vast amount of literature for both children and parents about divorce, and there are divorce groups, workbooks, and board games. However, divorce is a complex concept that entails complicated and painful facets, and it is an abstract concept difficult to grasp.

The following technique is a visual experiment that symbolizes the reality of what the child is going through. This technique will help the child understand that the divorce is not his or her fault, as well as comprehend the reasons for the divorce, without having to discuss the adult reasons.

The goals of the following technique are:

- Understanding the trials that have been made by the parents to work things out.
- Taking away the blame from the child.
- Facilitating communication regarding the divorce.

DESCRIPTION

Materials

- Water
- Oil
- Sugar
- Watercolors, food coloring
- Transparent cup
- Spoon

This technique works well for all family members involved. It may be done with the child alone or with siblings and one or both parents.

The therapist tells the children that an experiment is going to be done. The child is asked to pour water into the cup and then add oil. The therapist may describe what is seen or question the child as to what he or she sees. The oil is floating, the water is below, and they are not mixing. The child is asked to stir and then comment on what happens. If siblings are in the session, they may take turns in stirring the water and oil. Again it is described as the stirring continues that the oil and water may look as if they are blended, but they always separate when the stirring stops.

A question is then asked. "Whose fault is it—the water's or the oil's?"

Many reactions arise at this point. Some children blame the water, some the oil, and some the lack of enough stirring. All of the above challenges are confronted softly, by adding more oil, if the child blames the oil; more water is added if the blame is on the water; finally, letting the child stir as much as he or she may wish.

When the child realizes that it is not anyone's fault, and any trial is in vain, then a connection is made to his parents' divorce. It is no one's fault. The constant stirring was the constant trial the parents made to make the marriage work.

In order to provide the child with a solution to the enigma, the child is then introduced to substances that mix and actually combine. Trial may be done with water and watercolors, water and sugar, oil and color, and so on. It is important to teach that there are substances as well as people who do mix, blend, and are able to stir and remain that way. And there's nothing better than ending the session with a sip of water and sugar!

APPLICATIONS

This technique may be applied with children of divorce. It may be applied when the parents are about to get divorced or if they have been for many years. The technique may also be applied with sibling rivalry; as the siblings may understand that they are different, thereby loved differently by their parents.

Reference

Axline, V. (1947). *Play Therapy*. New York: Ballantine Books.

16

Group Drawing

Jean Stirling Albaum

INTRODUCTION

When children first enter a play therapy group they feel shy, intimidated, and unsure of what will occur. It is important to introduce a sense of trust, safety, and fun during the first session. A group drawing is a novel, motivating, and nonthreatening activity to use when building rapport and introducing group members to each other for the first time; it utilizes drawing, a familiar activity to most children, and crayons, a comfortable and well-liked material. It is a technique that is appropriate for use during the introductory session of play therapy groups that have been formed to address either general or specific life situations or problems.

RATIONALE

Children cannot begin to express and explore their experiences, thoughts, and feelings in a group setting until they feel a sense of trust, safety, and rapport with both the leader and the other children in the group. It is important to introduce and create a climate of safety and trust during the first session. Once this climate has been established, communication and expression of thoughts and feelings can follow.

DESCRIPTION

The therapist and the children sit at a table that is a comfortable height and allows enough room for each child to draw without getting into any other child's space. After the initial introductions have occurred, a single large sheet of drawing paper and one box of crayons are placed on the table. The following rules for the activity are then explained: (1) The paper will be passed around the table with each group member, including the therapist, allowed two minutes to draw; (2) The whole group will create a single picture. Each person will either add to what has already been drawn or add something that goes with it; (3) There will be no "put-downs" of what any other group member contributes to the picture; (4) No one may draw anything that either threatens to destroy what has been made by another group member (such as an airplane bombing the house made by another child) or ruin what is already on the paper (such as scribbling over what has been drawn by someone else); (5) Because we want each person's part of the picture to be completely his or her own, there will be no talking while anyone is drawing; (6) After each group member has had a turn and the picture is finished, we talk about it.

(Note: If the therapist can arrange to be the last to draw, he or she will be able to add any necessary sky, ground, clouds, or similar background to pull the picture together into a coherent whole.)

When the drawing is complete, the therapist asks each child to talk about the picture. Questions similar to the following can be asked: What kind of picture is this? What kind of place does it show? Is it a happy place? Is it a sad place? Is it a scary place? Are there other feelings that the picture suggests? If you could be anywhere in the picture, where would you like to be? If you could become anything in the picture, what, or who, would you want to be? Why? How would it feel to be that person, animal, or thing? Is there anything else that anyone would like to say about the picture?

APPLICATIONS

This activity is appropriate for children of all ages who have been referred for a wide variety of presenting problems. Although it has been designed for use with play therapy groups, it can be adapted as a rapport building exercise between a therapist and a child in a one-to-one setting. This technique allows children to become acquainted with the therapist and with other children in a group in a nonthreatening manner. It is useful in most therapeutic settings and utilizes readily available materials.

17

The Solution Drawing

David Hudak

INTRODUCTION

Solution-focused and narrative therapies are becoming increasingly popular in our culture not only because they are brief therapies satisfying managed care, but because they focus on building clients' strengths and competencies rather than being overly focused on pathology. When there is more "solution talk" than "problem talk" occurring in therapy, clients tend to feel hope and a sense of control over problems that previously felt overwhelming (Ahola and Furman, 1992). Solution-focused therapy zeroes in on assumed skills that clients already possess and gets clients to imagine what the future would look like using these skills toward a solution to their problems. Narrative therapy is aimed at using language to restory problems that may be entrenched or "scripted" in a negative way, to allow clients a more positive outlook and hope for change. Combining both of these therapies with play can be empowering to child clients. The Solution Drawing technique is one example of this endeavor.

RATIONALE

Most children are willing to draw, and drawing can be a useful projective tool to get children to express how they think and feel (Oaklander,

1988). Drawing a solution illuminates and crystallizes an experience of positive change a client achieves. When this type of drawing is created in therapy, I find that children feel a sense of accomplishment. They have now produced a concrete strategy to solve a problem. A drawing also provides an accessible record for clients to take home as well as a tool to utilize in later stages of therapy. Clients can readily use the solution to practice at home or where and when there is a need.

DESCRIPTION

The solution drawing can be used at any time during therapy. It is particularly useful when a child client and therapist are discussing a problem. Their parents often apprise children as to why they are being brought to therapy. They will give explanations such as "because I fight with my sister, or because Dad doesn't visit and that makes me sad." After the therapist "maps" how the problem is influencing the child's life, he or she can ask about unique outcomes and examples of when the child coped well with the problem (Epston and White, 1990). Solution-focused therapists would ask, "Are there times when you aren't arguing with your sister, and if so, what are you doing differently?" (Pellar and Walter, 1992). These questions guide the therapy conversation to focus on alternative stories that script the child in a more positive light or help children realize that there are behavioral solutions to their problems that they may already be using. More often than not, children can come up with examples of being able to ward off problems. When the child client is able to identify times when he or she has coped better, the therapist asks with enthusiasm and interest, "How did you do that? How did you get yourself to not argue with your sister?" Asked in this manner the child feels esteem, competency, and hope to solve his or her problem. The child will then tell the therapist a potential solution to how he or she prevented arguing with the sister. For example, if the child says, "I just minded my own business and played by myself," the therapist asks the child to draw a picture of this. When the drawing is complete, the therapist writes down, either on the drawing or on a separate piece of paper, the child's account of his or her solution. This affirms a sense of competency and shows belief in the child's ability to solve his or her own problems. During the writing phase, the therapist assists the child to flesh-out and restory the problem in a context of managing to deal with the problem effectively. I like to begin using sentence completions:

Therapist: This is a picture of . . .

Child: Me minding my own business playing with the Legos.

Therapist: This helps me not argue with my sister because . . .

Child: I'm ignoring her making faces at me.

There are other questions borrowing from narrative and solution-focused therapies that can be useful after the basic solution drawing and story are created, such as the narrative technique of externalizing the problem. This technique addresses problems as acting on a child externally rather than internally. For example, when a child says, "I'm really mad!" the child almost becomes the feeling and discord is almost inevitable. Instead of asking about "being mad," the therapist can pose the following question:

Therapist: Do you think if you mind your own business and ignore your sister you will keep anger from bossing you around (Epston and White, 1990)?

Child: Yeah, maybe, because then I would be the boss of the anger.

Therapist: Exactly!

Or, a solution-focused technique that is future-oriented involves the following type of question:

Therapist: As you leave here today and take your drawing to practice minding your own business and ignoring your sister, how will your parents be feeling about you (Pellar and Walter, 1992)?

Child: Good. They like when I control my anger.

As described, once the solution drawing is created it can be used as a springboard for exploring more positive scripts and outcomes for child clients.

The following case example involves an 8-year-old, third-grader, Sam, who is very bright, though not athletic. He is teased by certain classmates and has a handicapped older sister who is very outgoing. The chief complaints are that he seems depressed, is very easily upset, has anger "meltdowns," and makes threats that he wants to die. The solution drawing he created and storied with the therapist's help is clear, articulate, and focused:

"I get mad sometimes, and have different ways of dealing with it. One way is counting backward. This works because it gives me time to think

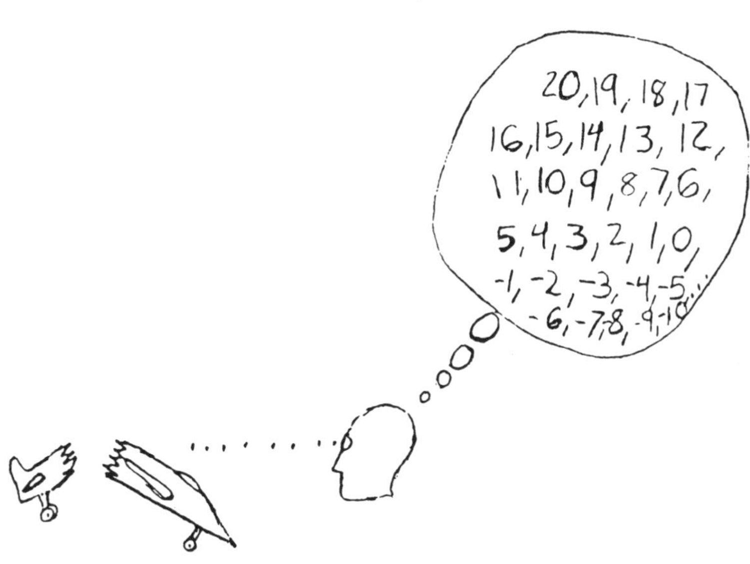

Figure 17.1 Sam's Solution Drawing

about the problem. Then I can think that maybe it's not so important and maybe my life doesn't depend on it. Also, if you're occupied with doing something, like counting, you forget what you were mad about."

Although Sam is just beginning therapy, he has made a good start getting in touch with skills he already possesses to solve a problem with anger. Because Sam was reluctant to come to therapy, I did not want to overwhelm him with too many questions to consider. I did use language to externalize the problem, such as "Do you think that if you use your solution of counting backward, it will keep anger from bossing you around?" I also gave him a future-oriented task, "During the next week I'd like you to notice all the times when you are able to keep anger from bossing you around, and let me know what you discover when you come back." This task assumes and focuses on building competencies. Children often return the next week with positive stories about how they used their skills and solutions to "keep problems from getting the best of them."

APPLICATIONS

The Solution Drawing technique can be used with children with a broad range of problems. I've even had success using it with traumatized children once trust and safety have been established. It is particularly productive with children with artistic skill who like to draw; however, I'm amazed at the willingness and effort that "nondrawers" will make. Drawing is a fun way to unleash the expressive side of children. The solution-focused and narrative techniques described here can also be used with other forms of play, such as puppet play, sculpting, and ball play (Hudak, 2000).

References

Ahola, T., and Furman, B. (1992). *Solution Talk*. New York: Norton.

Epston, D., and White, M. (1990). *Narrative Means to Therapeutic Ends*. New York: Norton.

Hudak, D. (2000). Therapeutic use of ball play in psychotherapy with children. *International Journal of Play Therapy* 9(1), 1–10.

Oaklander, V. (1998). *Windows to Our Children*. New York: Center for Gestalt Development.

Pellar, J., and Walter, J. (1992). *Becoming Solution-Focused in Brief Therapy*. New York: Brunner/Mazel.

18

Saying Good-bye: Breaking the Links in a Chain

Brenda Lawrence

INTRODUCTION

Endings for children are difficult and painful. Feelings of anger, abandonment, and unfairness with not having control or choice in the termination of therapy are common. Having the child be an active participant in the end of treatment can help this necessary and inevitable situation become an empowering event. This technique was shared with me several years ago by my creative and knowledgeable supervisor at the time. I have used it with success ever since. Construction paper, scissors, and a stapler are all one needs to build a visual prop to assist the child and therapist with saying good-bye in a healthful and playful way.

RATIONALE

Most children enjoy the use and manipulation of art materials; they often find it relaxing and just plain fun. The act of making, creating with one's hands is certainly less threatening than just talking about an upsetting experience and loss such as termination of therapy embodies. Children more quickly adapt to changes when they are given ample time and warning of what is coming. Abstract concepts, such as time, can mean little to youngsters whose thinking is still very in the moment. They can gain a sense of mastery and control when adequately prepared for the termination of therapy.

DESCRIPTION

Several weeks before a young child's last session, the therapist begins preparing him or her for the inevitable good-bye, talking about why and when therapy will end. Three or four weeks before that last date of therapy, construct together a simple chain out of colored paper. On each link is written a date. On the first link is the present date, with the following date on the next link, and on and on until the last link has the date of the final session. These links are stapled together to make a chain. Each time the child comes in for a session, he or she breaks away that link for that session. On the final day of therapy, the child will break away the remaining link. Using this technique, the ending for the child is not a surprise.

APPLICATIONS

This technique can be used with all young children (ages 4 to 8); however, children with separation issues will especially benefit from the gradual, more self-paced ending that this play technique affords. Very young children have little understanding of the concept of time. The visual, tactile, hands-on creation of the chain as well as the breaking away of the links adds an element of concreteness to the otherwise abstract quality of time and its passage. In addition, the child's active participation in the ending of therapy enables the child to more fully integrate the feelings that naturally arise at this time at a pace that is comfortable and safe. It engenders a sense of control and choice.

Five-year-old Sarah, a selective mute child in kindergarten, was referred to me for treatment. Our work together was time-limited (six months) due to the nature of the school-based program. Treatment ended at the end of the school year. Sessions were twice weekly for the first three months and weekly for the following three months. Sarah's family was actively involved in the therapy. Sarah was able to overcome her select mute symptoms in this treatment period. Sandplay therapy, drawing, and bioenergetic techniques were the primary modalities employed. Endings and losses were difficult for Sarah. Her grandfather had died and her father had been separated from the family for a period of time due to a work situation. Sarah did not want therapy to end. The Breaking the Links in a Chain technique was a useful device for this child. She assiduously created the chain and wrote all the dates herself. We found just the right spot to store the chain safely between sessions, high on top of a cabinet. Saying good-bye was not easy, but the chain was instrumental in making the break a healthier, more empowered process.

19

My Storybook

Inés Schroeder

INTRODUCTION

Children often have been given ample opportunities to interact with books. When children are young, adults read to them at home or at school. As they grow older, reading becomes a part of the children's lives. Providing the opportunity for children to create their own books gives the children a chance to use their creativity while addressing the issue for which they are brought for treatment.

RATIONALE

Children learn many things from the books that are read to them as well as those that they read on their own. Children tend to accept the stories within the books and enjoy the fantasies that are created. Books are a nonthreatening way to approach a child regarding issues in treatment. Often, therapists use books to highlight issues the child may be facing in his or her own life. This provides the therapist with the opportunity to help children understand that others face similar problems and normalize the children's issues that are to be addressed in treatment. The following activity takes the use of books one step further by having the child create a book.

DESCRIPTION

This technique is best used once rapport is established and the child has had time to process the issue that initiated his or her treatment. The therapist can use some bibliotherapy within sessions prior to introducing this project, but it is not necessary.

The therapist explains to the child that they will create a book together that discusses the important things the child knows about the issue of focus in treatment. The child is given instructions that he or she is the expert in this issue and can explain to others the important things children face when confronted with the problem. Although the therapist will not share the book with others, the child will have a finished project to take and then share with those he or she wishes.

Allow the child to decide how the story will approach the issue, from reality to fantasy styles. As the child writes or dictates the story, the therapist can aid in guiding the storyline to include a focus on information, feelings, and strategies to overcome the problem. The child should be praised for capturing important elements and explaining the feelings that occur. Each page of the story can have one to two sentences written on it. When the storyline is complete, the child can then add art to follow the words. The art can be in the form of colored drawings, illustrations showing examples of what the words on the page mean, pictures of people's expressions feeling the feelings indicated in the story, or collage work from old magazines or cards that exemplify a pertinent point. The final product can be bound at a local printer for a nominal fee or rings, string, yarn, ribbons, or brats can be purchased to connect the pages together.

This project can be completed with the use of a computer or written by hand. The computer can be utilized with children who can spell on their own because it provides an added air of professionalism. At times, the therapist can pose as the client's "secretary," documenting his or her words as he or she speaks. Each of these techniques helps to highlight to the child that his or her words are important and what he or she says is valid.

An example of the use of this project was with an 11-year-old African-American female who had recently witnessed the sudden death of a younger sibling due to an illness. She was having difficulty processing the loss as well as fears regarding her own health. The creation of the book she titled *I Lost My Brother* assisted her in focusing on the various elements that happened during the event and shortly after it. We wrote the story on the computer, and then placed one sentence at the top of each page. When we printed out the story, it was 17 pages long. She was really excited about the length!

During the following sessions, she chose which topic or topics to focus on in therapy by picking one to three pages to illustrate. She had flexibility to pick whichever pages she felt ready to discuss regardless of their order in the book. One example of what she wrote on one page commented that she had wanted to tell him some things before he died. Below, she drew a box and began to compose a letter to him ("Dear ________,") sharing those thoughts she wished she could have said. A different page stated that people have many feelings about death. Below this sentence, she cut pictures of different expressions on people's faces from old magazines to illustrate the variety of feelings. On another page, she was able to voice the fear that she too would go to the hospital one day unexpectedly and die. On this page, she drew a very sad picture of herself.

This project allowed her the opportunity to discuss the events as well as the feelings about the loss and the fears about her mortality. We were able to proceed at a pace she felt comfortable with as well as touch on each of the issues she experienced through the loss. Some issues were difficult for her to share at home. This technique allowed her the place to process while helping her to understand that others need help to process these issues too. She felt good about being able to share with "other children" who would learn from her experience. Once the project is complete, the therapist can take the book to be bound at a local printer with the client's permission. The look on her face when she saw her professional book was priceless. She invited her mother to come to a session and read the book together and process the emotions that she had experienced. She then had a book to take home with her to share with whomever she wished.

APPLICATIONS

This technique is useful for children at a variety of age levels with various problem issues. Children who cannot write can dictate the story.

The length of the story varies from child to child, as does the style of the story. Some children discuss the issue using animal characters in a fictional setting. Some use fictional settings and times. The wonderful thing about the activity is that it brings structure and manageability to the problem issue that may have at one time felt overwhelming to the child.

20

The Feelings Chart

Maryanne Bongiovani

INTRODUCTION

This activity is based on the Color Your Life technique developed by Kevin O'Connor (1983). It is a technique that allows children to be more aware of their feelings and to think and talk about the feelings they are currently experiencing in their lives.

RATIONALE

Children enjoy playing games. Playing a game about feelings would be less threatening to most children than having a direct conversation about feelings. Using this game at the beginning of therapy allows the therapist to obtain valuable information and allows the child to feel comfortable with the therapist and the therapy process.

DESCRIPTION

The therapist takes an 8½ by 11-inch sheet of paper and lays it lengthwise on a table. The paper is then divided vertically into eight even sections by drawing lines from the bottom of the paper to the top of the paper. At the bottom of each section is written the name of a feeling. The feelings happy, sad, angry, scared, proud, and stressed are usually included. The other two feelings could be ones that the child wants to include or the therapist could add two additional feelings that would fit the child's particular situation. For example, if a child is having difficulty with sibling rivalry, the feeling jealousy might be added to the chart. If a child is anxious about going to school or moving to a new location, the word *nervous* or *anxious* might be added to the chart.

The child is given a box of colored crayons or markers. The child is asked to pick a color that he or she wants to represent each feeling. First the child chooses a color to represent happy. A mark with that color is made under the word *happy* on the chart. Next the child chooses a color to represent sad and a mark with that color is made under the word *sad* on the chart. This is continued until the child has selected a different color for each of the feelings listed.

The child is then told to look at each column and decide how much of each feeling he or she is currently experiencing in his or her life. A lot of a feeling means that a lot of the column will be colored. If a particular feeling is not currently being felt very often, the color in that column may not go up very high. For example, if the child says he or she is feeling very happy, he or she may color in the whole column with whatever color he or she chose to represent happy. The child might say that he or she does not feel much anger or sadness and in that case, the child may draw only a thin line at the bottom of the columns labeled with the words *sad* and *angry*.

After the child has colored each of the columns, the therapist and child can discuss what the child thinks is causing the feelings that he or she is having. For example, the child can talk about what is causing so much or so little happiness and sadness. If the child is unable to express why he or she is having certain feelings, the therapist can help the child with this and postulate what might be causing the feelings that the child is having. The chart can also lead to discussions about how to deal with some of these feelings. By looking at the intensity of feelings on the chart, the therapist can also discuss with the child better ways to cope with various feelings and perhaps discuss ways to make some of the feelings either more or less prominent in the child's life.

APPLICATIONS

This technique is a good introduction to therapy and a good assessment tool. At the beginning of therapy, it is important to talk about feelings because many children either have not done this very often or are not comfortable with this type of discussion. With many children it is difficult for them to talk about their own feelings. It is easier for them to talk about the feelings other people have, and this can be a good starting point. First make sure the child can identify various feelings and give examples of what type of situations might cause different feelings in other people. Once children can do this, and they are fairly comfortable talking about feelings in others, it is important that children are able to transfer this knowledge to themselves. The therapist should then make sure that the child can properly identify his or her own feelings. The feelings chart is a good introductory technique to see how well the child can talk about his or her own feelings.

The chart also helps the therapist understand what feelings the child is having and how intense the feelings are. It is a technique that can be used throughout the therapy to measure improvement or to evaluate the impact of new problems should they arise.

This technique has been used with children as young as 4. At this age, the child still chooses the colors he or she associates with the various feelings, but sometimes the young child prefers the therapist to do the coloring. Older children sometimes like to construct the entire chart themselves and to print the feelings at the bottom of the chart as well as color in the chart.

This technique has also been used successfully with adolescents. It is a good introduction to the work of therapy and a good way to get sometimes reluctant teenagers to start talking about their feelings. Some adolescents are self-conscious talking about their feelings and this activity is a good ice-breaker. The adolescent can be coloring in the chart as he or she talks about his or her feelings. This means the adolescent is looking at the chart and is not having direct eye contact with the therapist. This sometimes helps an adolescent feel less self-conscious. Once the adolescent has talked about his or her feelings in a nonthreatening way a few times, it becomes easier, and often the self-conscious teenager will be able to talk about feelings face to face with the therapist in just a few sessions.

The feelings that a child or adolescent talks about when doing the chart can be helpful in setting treatment goals and in measuring the outcome of these goals. As the therapist talks to the child about his or her feelings and the possible reason for the feelings, it can give the therapist an indication of what is uppermost in the child's mind at that particular time and it can help the therapist understand the reason for some of the symptoms the child may be having. The chart indicates some of the emotions and feelings that the child is struggling with, and as therapy progresses, the charts can be repeated and compared to see how successful therapy has been in reducing feelings such as sadness, anger, and stress and in increasing feelings such as proud and happy. As the therapist sees the various intensities of the feelings change, treatment goals can be adjusted to focus on whatever is most important at any point in time.

Reference

O'Connor, K. J. (1983). The Color-Your-Life Technique. *Handbook of Play Therapy* (Eds.). C. E. Schaefer and K. J. O'Connor, pp. 251–258. New York: Wiley.

21

Teddy Bear Feelings

Mary Determan

INTRODUCTION

A common issue for me in my work with children and adolescents is their inability to verbalize their feelings. When I am questioning children directly about their feelings, I find that children have a difficult time answering. At times they seem to be guarded against or unable to connect with feelings. Children also seem to find it very difficult to talk about feelings that are threatening to them. In trying different interventions in my practice, I have found that this Teddy Bear Feelings technique has been a fun and productive way to help children become more in tune with their feelings. The concept of teddy bear feelings was developed to help children match feeling with color, which then helps them to identify and express their feelings. It gives children and adolescents a playful way to talk about and share their feelings. This technique can also be used to help children talk about those feelings that they are having difficulty communicating. It helps them identify and verbalize situations they are having problems with and helps them learn options and skills for approaching similar situations in the future.

RATIONALE

I was looking for an activity that gave children and adolescents an opportunity to have fun and be creative in sharing and expressing feelings. Beanie Babies were a very popular toy at this time, so I decided to make felt teddy bears, about the same size as Beanie Babies, and pick colors that could vary in shades, like dark blue, medium blue, and light blue, to reflect feeling words. I have found the therapeutic value of this activity is that it gives the child the ability to choose and describe the color that best matches his or her feeling.

DESCRIPTION

The pattern I chose to best make the teddy bears I imagined was the McCall's Crafts pattern #897. See figure 21.1. The reason why this pattern seemed so suitable to me was because it lends itself to a child's creativity. To try to have these teddy bears appeal to children like the Beanie Babies have, I downsized the pattern on a Xerox machine, so the finished teddy bear measures from ear to toe seven to eight inches. The bear has five small doll joints, two eyes, and a sewn-on black nose. The head, arms, and legs are all jointed and moveable. I arbitrarily decided to make 12 teddy bears, chose bright colored felt as my material, and gave each a matching color ribbon. All 12 teddy bears lay in a basket on the floor in the play therapy room where they are easily noticed. Children seem to be very attracted to these teddy bears and will often spontaneously involve themselves with the teddy bears in different types of play. This allows for the therapy approach to begin. Because of the various colors of teddy bears and the opportunity for the children to be creative moving the joints to position the bears in their play, their defenses are reduced and they are more likely to talk about their feelings. As the child interacts with the bears, the child spontaneously acts out thoughts and feelings, some of which he or she was aware of but couldn't put into words and some feelings unknown to him or her that become unlocked.

This technique may be used as a directed activity by the therapist or a nondirected activity in response to the child's play. Along with the bears I use feeling stickers that have 12 feeling faces per sheet. In a directed activity I would ask that the child match the feeling stickers to the colors of the bears. When using this technique I find that the children are often very careful and take time to match the feeling sticker with a color. This

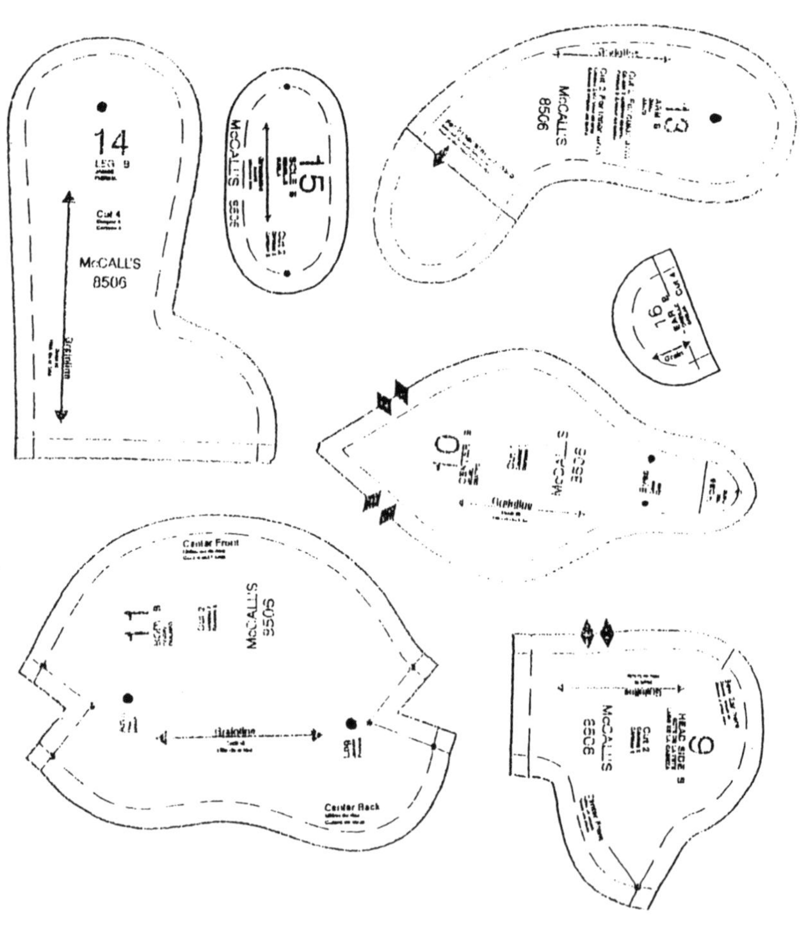

Figure 21.1
McCall's Crafts #897

initiates much thought into the meaning behind their feelings. We then begin to talk about and explore these feelings. I would ask questions such as, "Can you tell me more about why you picked the color red for angry? Can you tell me a time that you felt angry or red? Does angry ever have a different color?"

This gives the child the okay to identify and verbalize these feelings. At times when a child is having more difficulty talking about these feelings, this allows him or her to explore the meaning behind the color and feeling that the child has combined. The nondirected activity happens naturally. Sometimes the teddy bears are already wearing feeling stickers, and the child may choose to leave the stickers as they were. This allows for questions and interactions regarding the purpose and choice. Many times children change the feeling stickers to better match the colors they feel are more appropriate. Often the child will spontaneously discuss why he or she is changing the stickers and will begin to use them in play relating the feeling he or she chooses. Children will use this opportunity to express their feelings, fears, and concerns. I find that this activity can help me teach children how to cope with stress, how to relax, and how to focus thinking. This intervention can teach children how to solve problems, be assertive, and think and behave in an optimistic and positive manner. This exercise promotes open communication and allows for cooperative efforts toward problem resolution. A catharsis of negative and other overwhelming feelings may result from this intervention and can promote better understanding of self and others.

APPLICATIONS

This technique was designed for the play therapy office and is used with children and adolescents struggling with issues of depression, hyperactivity, anxiety, aggression, and peer conflict. This technique can be used in individual, group, or family therapy. It has been very beneficial when used as a directed activity as well as nondirected activity. Children have responded very positively to this activity resulting in increased communication, increased self-esteem, and improved avenues in relationship building. In my office the bears have also been used as people acting out different issues and have been included in family drama, playground drama, and doctor/patient drama. In my practice I have seen children divide the bears into positive and negative feelings. In one session a young adolescent female was discussing family discord at home with the "whatever" attitude. I asked her to use the stickers and teddy bears in a way that would represent her current emotional state. She matched the stickers to the colored bears and divided them into what became known as positive and negative feelings. She chose to place all the light colored bears on the right side of her and all of the dark colored bears on the left side. We discussed this process and her choices for a while and decided that the goal was to begin to mix all the colors in the middle. This young lady began to relax and started to share feelings, discussing ways to meet her goal.

I have found this technique to be successful in allowing both the child and the adolescent to be very creative in their expression of play and feelings. This technique can be used in the therapy office, at home, or at school to help children dramatize satisfying and constructive means of handling feelings and the accompanying stressors.

References

Hills, Maureen. (1996). McCall's Crafts #897. New York: Little City Bears & Co.

Stickers Available in English, French, German, Spanish, and Hebrew. 120 per pack. Faces include confident, suprised, confused, ecstatic, hopeful, happy, angry, frustrated, disgusted, lonely, sad, and hysterical. $3.00 each. You can order them from Creative Therapy Associates, Inc. Fax (513) 521-5592, phone (800) 448-9145.

Mary Determan, M.S.W., C.I.C.S.W., R.P.T.-S., Encompass, Inc., 2421 North Mayfair Road, Wauwatosa, Wisconsin 53226, (414) 453-8380

22

Make a Family "Drawing"

Heidi Gerard Kaduson

INTRODUCTION

Many therapists are confronted with the problem of using drawings as an assessment tool when the child they are treating has moderate to severe fine motor problems. Children might draw for the therapist, but they might be worried about whether the drawing is "good" or "right." If they cannot hold a marker, crayon, or pencil with ease, they might produce a very quick rendition of the request to draw their family. This could be only stick figures or heads. In cases such as these, therapists might be inclined not to use this valuable tool because the child is resistant or incapable. In order to gather the information given by a drawing, and especially a family drawing, the Family Collage technique was created.

RATIONALE

Drawing has always been a valuable tool for making a child feel at ease in the first session of play therapy. When a child has fine motor difficulties, is perfectionistic, or feels like he is not a good artist, however, the child may be reluctant to attempt the drawing or do it so quickly and without detail that it does not allow for analysis and interpretation. In cases such as these, it is most helpful to assist the child by providing cut-out magazine pictures and letting the child paste the faces, bodies, and so forth onto the page to reflect his family.

DESCRIPTION

In advance of any intake with a child who has fine motor difficulties, the therapist would cut out 20 to 25 pictures of each of faces, shirts, pants, skirts, dresses, shoes, sneakers—items that children draw in family drawings (table, chairs, ball, and so on). It is helpful to also use a feeling word chart with line drawings for feelings so that it does not reflect any cultural or ethnic bias. The pictures used should be of a variety of expressions and styles.

The therapist would create boxes for each object, such as, a box for faces, hair, shirts, pants, skirts, dresses, shoes, and "things" that might be drawn by other children when each item is being created. A box the size of a shoebox would be helpful so that most of the pictures can be seen when the child looks in the box. An 11 by 14-inch piece of paper and a glue stick are provided so that the child can easily choose and glue what represents a picture of a person or his family doing something, without feeling the pressure of actually drawing. If the child wants to draw additional information, he is encouraged to use whatever materials he would like. In many cases, the child will go through the boxes and search for a specific look or similarity to his perception of the family. The therapist can assist the child if asked in order to facilitate the production of the family collage. A stack of magazines is also kept nearby so that if the child wants to add something that is not in any of the boxes, he or she can look through the magazine and have the therapist cut it out. Fine motor problems may also restrict the child when cutting.

During the production of this work, many children feel an instant rapport with the therapist, and some children will talk about whom they are making and why that person is looking a certain way. The freedom from fear of performance is gone, and the child is more likely to present some information for the therapist's interpretation.

APPLICATIONS

This technique is especially useful for children who are anxious or perfectionistic, which results in an entire session being taken to do a drawing, or for children who clearly have fine motor problems and do not draw for fun or otherwise. This can also be used successfully with preschool children with a little assistance from the therapist for gluing the pictures down.

Joey, age 8, was referred for behavioral problems associated with Attention-deficit Hyperactivity Disorder. He had been evaluated by an occupational therapist, and his fine motor skills were delayed. His parents had also informed the therapist that he does not like to color or draw, and they have fights with him regarding this homework. On the day of his intake, he was agitated in the waiting room. He had been to other therapists before, and he anticipated the drawing part of the session. When he entered the playroom, he sat at the table and asked what the boxes were used for. The therapist opened them up to show him the faces, hair, clothes, and items boxes. He immediately started to look through them as the therapist asked him to make a picture of a person. He willingly put together the person with glue, illustrating a sad-faced boy holding a book. He commented during this production that he hated reading and wished that the teachers would stop telling him to read things. He only liked Pokemon™ things to read (which meant he looked at the pictures). The therapist then asked him to create a picture of his family doing something. He put together his mother, father, and sister playing a board game, while he put himself on the bottom of the page playing with the cat. Since the therapist did not anticipate the addition of animals, Joey asked the therapist to draw a cat. When he finished his production of the pictures, the therapist was able to gather much more information by asking about the people in the picture, what they were doing, how they usually played together, and the boy's feeling of being left out while playing with the cat.

By using the Family Collage technique, rapport is immediately established and the fear of "drawing" is removed. This playful technique lends itself to groups and individuals so long as enough items are cut out.

23

My Brain

Jennifer Fortier

INTRODUCTION

The challenges of psychotherapy with children are twofold. There is the challenge of finding out what problems exist in the child's life, plus the additional challenge of getting a young person with partially developed communication skills to express him- or herself in a way you can understand and respond to. Standardized screening tools completed by an adult in the child's life, such as the Child Behavior Checklist, or by the child herself, such as Beck's Child Depression Index, do help. But the child's true feelings can be difficult to ascertain because the child may not be able to respond to written questionnaires or direct verbal questioning. The My Brain technique is an activity that can be used with both young children and adolescents to identify and communicate their thoughts, hopes, fears, and dreams.

RATIONALE

It is as important to help a child express his or her feelings as it is to help him or her identify them. Expressing feelings is difficult for children who are unfamiliar with doing so, confused, or guarded. "My Brain" deals with problems of expression by doing the following:

- Incorporating both the positive and negative aspects of the child's life
- Focusing on the child as the "expert" in therapy
- Encouraging the child's fascination with his or her brain and how it works
- Helping the therapist develop a treatment focus with the child
- Reducing the child's defenses by focusing first on thoughts in her head versus feelings about her life
- Serving as a pre- and post-test that the therapist and child can review together.

(Note: Requesting that the child elaborate on some of his responses during this technique is suggested in this chapter, but is optional, depending on the child's situation and the therapist's preference.)

DESCRIPTION

The therapist sits on the floor or at a table with the child. The therapist needs a piece of paper and an assortment of markers. The therapist draws the profile of a child's head covering the left three-quarters of the paper with a black marker at the beginning of the session with the child. This outline of the head should be very large and therefore does not need to be to scale. If anything, this is often a source of humor between the child and therapist to break the ice, and it humanizes the therapist for the child, showing the child the therapist is not perfect. The therapist writes across the top of the page: My Brain Thinks About . . . ?

Therapist: I made this drawing of your brain for what we are going to do today. I made it really big to show how incredibly smart you are. (Or, if child is fairly new to the therapist: because I can tell you are pretty smart.) Your brain holds a lot of different thoughts inside it all day long and even at night, too, when you have dreams. Some of these thoughts may be about people, places, or things. Some are about things that have happened to you, good or bad; things that are impor-

Exhibit A.

Figure 23.1

tant to you in your life every day now; and things you may look forward to in the future.

Your brain is always thinking about things, even though you may never talk about any of these things at all. So, only you know what those things are, and they're different for everyone. Let's see if you can come up with some things your brain thinks about, and we'll write them down here (along the side of the paper) as you think of them.

Child: I think about playing outside after school.

Therapist: That's great. Lots of kids think about that. Let's write that down. (Write or have the child write the items as a list in the order that they're mentioned.)

Child: I think about my dad.

Therapist: Okay, what do you think about when you think of your dad?

Child: I don't know. I guess if he might come get me to live with him.

Therapist: That's an important one to list. (If the child cannot elaborate or is reluctant, the therapist states: okay, we'll just write down "dad," and you'll know what that means.)

The therapist continues to write or have the child write what he or she thinks about. Younger children should have shorter lists because it will be harder for them to follow the concept later on with too many items to focus upon. Children's responses have included: family members they cherish, miss, or worry about; people and pets who have died; school grades and problems; making friends and social difficulties, including being teased or bullied; an illness they have; whether they are loved; things they have nightmares about; things they wish for; food; "being good" or getting into trouble; getting hit or hurt; finding a family; problems of incontinence; a personal trait they dislike; an offender who abused them, and people finding out about the abuse.

Teenagers often expand topics to those corresponding to their stage of life including: dating and sex, being popular or accepted, getting out of the house, living on their own, and other future plans.

If the therapist is aware that the child has not mentioned but is struggling with particular problems and is here for help on those issues, it is important for the therapist to encourage that the child consider them.

Therapist: I noticed you haven't mentioned the abuse yet, but I know that's a pretty big thing that's happened to you lately. Even though kids don't want to think about it much, a lot of times it still comes into their minds. Is that something that should go on your list too? (Generally kids acknowledge this and will add it if they hadn't already.) The therapist can bring up these issues that were not volunteered, and then suggest a couple of other unmentioned, benign issues for the child, such as going to a place the child likes or eating a favorite food.

When the child is satisfied that his or her list is complete, the therapist asks the child to pick a different color marker for each item on the list, marking each item with that color. This may involve a check, dot, star, or any shape of the child's choice. (Children often carefully choose colors that symbolize something about that thought.)

Therapist: Now that each thought has a color, you're going to be able to color your brain, and we can see how much you think about the different things on your list. Using the color for each thought, color inside this drawing of your brain how much your brain thinks about it. For instance, if your brain hardly ever thinks about fighting with your sister, that means only a tiny bit, and you would just color a tiny amount in your brain. If you think about it some of the time, you'll color a spot for it that's not really small or big, and if your brain spends a lot of time thinking about that, you'll color a whole bunch of that color in your brain.

Child: How should I color it? (Many kids start immediately before the directions are finished, but some want more guidance.)

Therapist: Your brain is your space to use however you want. You can scribble in the colors, or color blocks, blobs, sections, or shapes. If you decide you need more of one color because you realized your brain thinks of it even more than you showed at first, you can add more of it in another spot. When you are all done, your whole brain should be full, and it will look kind of like a puzzle.

The therapist sits silently with the child while he or she finishes filling in the brain, just listening and reflecting comments the child may make during this time. Once they are absorbed in the process, plenty of children have decided they needed more room to indicate the magnitude that certain issues consume their thoughts and may ask for permission to color into the entire profile, outside the head, and even over on the back of the paper. These options should be supported by the therapist.

Therapist: It looks like you've finished. Let's look at your brain now. What do you think?

Child: I think about a lot of things. It looks cool.

Therapist: Your brain is amazing! Let's see if we can figure out what's in it. Can you tell me about it?

The therapist lets the child lead the discussion of what each of the blobs of color represents if possible. Otherwise, the therapist can remark on various parts of the design in an effort to encourage some elaboration.

Therapist: I see there is a big spot of red over here, and it looks like red is the color for "Mom and Dad fighting." (This is continued until all of the parts are addressed.)

Therapist: Now that we know all the things your brain is spending time thinking about, which things are really important to you right now and which need less attention, we can figure out together how to help you with them. If it's something you don't want to spend as much time thinking about, we'll work on making that smaller, and if there are things you'd rather have room for or want to spend more time thinking about, we'll work on adding those or making those bigger. I'll ask you to color your brain again much later on so we can see if anything has changed.

APPLICATIONS

This intervention can be used in sessions with the child to address his or her struggle of spending so much brain power on negative events, especially those that cannot be changed by the child, and to help him or her begin work on how to make room for other more positive, satisfying things. It helps children to become more self-aware and identify issues that may be difficult for them to verbally express. The exercise initially allows the child to express those thoughts and emotions with some separation (through "the brain") and explore the idea of being able to control what his or her brain focuses upon and how to use the brain as a positive force. It helps the child form a basis for imagining hope for the future, visualize how that improvement would look symbolically in advance, and then, later, observe evidence of their success.

24

Tune It In, Tune It Out

Celia Linden

INTRODUCTION

One of the challenges the play therapist faces is finding activities that can be adapted to a variety of symptoms that are simple enough to use without elaborate setup. Techniques that can reinforce important therapeutic notions are extremely valuable to have readily available in session. These types of techniques can assist the therapist in creating meaningful metaphors for the child to participate in and generalize well outside of the playroom. Due to their simplicity, they allow for spontaneity within the confines of the playroom and provide opportunities for engaging in the therapeutic process without complex setup or complicated planning.

RATIONALE

Cognitive behavioral techniques are extremely useful in treating children with various disorders but the challenge to the therapist remains making these ideas fun, playful, and meaningful. The more engaging and enticing the activity, the more likely the child will benefit from participating. In this particular technique the element of dramatic play combined with artistic self-expression offers the child opportunities to participate on many different levels depending on his or her comfort while maintaining the overall value of the exercise. Cognitive behavioral elements utilized in this activity are aimed at making the material concrete, goal-oriented, and useable both within and outside the confines of the playroom.

DESCRIPTION

To use this technique you will need the following things:

Markers or crayons

8.5 by 11-inch paper (or larger)

Tape recorder or videotape

To introduce the framework that underlies this activity, the therapist will begin by explaining how radiowaves are broadcast. The idea that these waves are sent from towers as signals that are received by the individual radio that is tuning them in can be illustrated with a real radio if necessary. The therapist will help the child understand that these signals are heard clearly if the dial of the radio is set to a particular frequency and not heard at all if not tuned in. For instance, if you choose to hear a certain type of music, you tune to a station that broadcasts that style. If you want to hear the news, you tune into a news station by changing the frequency on the radio dial. This metaphor can be simplified for the younger child or expanded upon for the older patient. In order to proceed with the next part of the activity, the client needs to understand the basic manner through which signals are broadcast and the notion that the person can choose which "message" or style of music he or she wishes to hear by actively tuning in or out any particular frequency.

The therapist will then ask the child to identify two opposing cognitions he or she is struggling with. For children with obsessive compulsive disorder, these can be the logical and illogical thoughts. For children with depression, these can be their positive and negative cognitions. For oppositional children, these can be their arguing and nonarguing thoughts. This piece of the activity needs to be specifically tailored to the individual child's struggle to maximize the benefit and can be adapted to encompass a wide variety of symptoms. Two radio towers are drawn at this point to illustrate the idea that these two different types of messages come from different places in the brain or "frequencies" on the dial. Drawing a radio dial is also an effective way to demonstrate the stations and label their "frequencies."

The next part of the activity involves the child creating two radio stations with call letters to identify each opposing message he or she hears. For example a 10-year-old patient who had obsessive compulsive disorder named one station WALAD because it broadcast All Logic All Day. She named her other station WCTAN because her symptoms, which she identified as "Crooked" Thoughts, came out At Night. Once the stations have been identified and their formats discussed, the child and therapist can create commercials enticing the listener to tune in. In this part of the activity, the child is able to identify the reasons these messages or "stations" are meaningful to him or her. Here the therapist illustrates the benefit of "tuning in" the station with the positive message, the logical thoughts, or whatever the therapist is working on and "tuning out" the other one. The most persuasive commercials should be for the stations that broadcast the messages that are being emphasized in treatment. This section is especially important for diagnostic reasons as well and will give the clinician information if the child is not able to make a persuasive enough argument for the desired station. If the child is having difficulty "tuning in" the appropriate station, the therapist can explain how an antenna is used to help pick up desired frequencies. A satellite, antenna, or "extra" power cables can be added to the radio tower to boost the station's ability to broadcast or to assist the radio's ability to receive the appropriate signal.

Once the stations have been labeled, commercials have been designed, and the messages clearly received, the child and therapist can make up specific radio programs to reinforce the goals of treatment. One such example would be an "ask the expert" segment where calls are taken from the "listening audience" and callers seek the counsel of the patient "expert" when struggling with similar issues. If the child is unable to play the role of the expert, the therapist, a peer, or parent can step in and help out. An "ask the audience" program could be utilized if the child is having difficulty with a particular issue, and the therapist, peer, or parent can role play the extra people as needed. Musical segments can be incorporated as well to reinforce messages the child can use outside of the therapy session. Songs can be original or words of familiar tunes can be rewritten to address specific issues. The child may also choose to add a theme song or jingle for one or both stations. One young patient who struggled with obsessive thoughts that any change in her life would make bad things happen used a song from a popular rock group that stated "we could all use a little change" as part of her theme song for her logical thoughts radio station. It was popular at the time of her treatment and served as a reminder of her goals to her and her family outside of the therapy room.

Theatrical presentations including puppet shows, readings from relevant bibliotherapy, game shows, such as the *$25,000 Pyramid*, or any other type of program could be added to the format of the radio station to reinforce information that is relevant. Programs can be recorded or videotaped to share with family members or for future reference. The activity can be expanded or simplified as needed depending on the goals of treatment and the needs of the child.

APPLICATIONS

This activity is particularly useful for children who struggle with obsessive compulsive disorder but can be tailored to any pathology where two opposing cognitions are operating simultaneously. This activity is also appropriate for group work and can be used for social skills training, divorce, or bereavement groups.

25

Working with Play Images of Fearful Children

Bertha Mook

INTRODUCTION

Play therapists of various theoretical orientations are familiar with play images created by children in therapy. The author follows a phenomenological approach to play therapy which fosters the creation of play images and therapeutic communication through imagery (Mook, 1999). This chapter will provide a brief rationale for the use of play images with anxious and fearful children in the context of a supportive therapeutic relationship. The actual working with play images of fearful children in play therapy will be described. This will be followed by a section on application that includes a clinical case illustration.

RATIONALE

Communication through imagery lies at the core of a phenomenological approach to play therapy. Images are seen as primary representations of the child's emotions and lived experiences. Through images, the child expresses personal meanings of his experiential life-world in comparison to words that express socially shared meanings. Play is seen as the child's most natural language and his preferred form of self-expression. In the to-and-fro movement between the child and his play objects, the child does not only play with *them* but they also play with *him*. The child is easily lured into a playworld by the appeal of his toys, and out of their mutual interrelatedness play images are evoked and imaginative play unfolds (Mook, 1999).

Anxious and fearful children are often afraid to express themselves freely in play. Such children are guarded and defend themselves against threatening feelings and experiences by denying them or pushing them out of awareness. They need a safe and empathic therapeutic relationship and a therapist who invites and encourages them to play. This context enables fearful children to reveal threatening feelings in play through the play images created in their playworld. For example, a fearful child may project his fears in the play image of a ghost that causes a little boy to have nightmares, or in a frightening gorilla that terrorizes innocent farm animals. Play images have a projective character to the extent that they serve as vehicles for a child's denied feelings and experiences. As such they shield him from himself and from the significant others in his real world for he knows that he is "only playing." The therapist needs to preserve the anonymous character of the playworld for only then does the child feel free to reveal himself through it. Therapeutic communication should take place within the playworld and through the created play images until the child has fully projected and expressed his fears and is ready to talk directly about them.

One way of helping a fearful child in play therapy to work through his projected feelings in play images is to lead him to concretize a selected play image into an actual image by asking him to make a drawing, a painting, or a clay model of it. Concretizing a play image turns a fleeting image into a concrete and enduring substance. By shaping or modeling it himself the child draws on his own embodied perceptions, feelings, and actions and comes face to face with his projected fear. This process deepens his experiential involvement and increases his sense of mastery and control. The concretized play image can be reintegrated into the child's playworld and further explored by the child and the therapist. The therapist's goal is to bring the fearful child to an identification with his or her denied self as projected in one or more central play images.

DESCRIPTION

In order to evoke and work fruitfully with play images of fearful children, the playroom needs to be well equipped with materials that lend themselves to projection and creative expression. This includes a sandbox, running water, drawing materials, paints, modeling clay, a vast array of miniature toys, and a puppet theater with puppets.

Within a supportive therapeutic relationship, the play therapist invites the child to play and encourages him or her to use imagination. The therapist facilitates the emergence of an imaginative playworld by becoming an active participant in the child's play. She provides suitable play materials, shows a keen interest, and selectively verbalizes the child's play actions. At the child's request, the therapist may join the child directly in the playworld by enacting roles of the play figures providing that the child creates the play images and the play story. As the play images and the imaginative play unfold, the therapist communicates with the child through the actions, thoughts, and feelings of the play figures and takes care to respect the anonymous character of the playworld (Hellendoorn, 1987; Mook, 1999).

The fearful child tends to project his or her fears in one or more play images in imaginative play. For example, the heaped-up sand in the sandbox becomes an active volcano ready to erupt at any time, or the pool becomes a dangerous place for the family of dolls to swim in because of a lurking crocodile in the water, or the villagers are warned that there are monsters in the forest that pose a threat. The therapist listens carefully to the play story as a whole and looks for a play image that shows a high level of emotional involvement and self-identification. Such an image is usually strong, vivid, and original and means a great deal to the playing child. The therapist selects a play image that reflects these characteristics and seems to represent the child's denied experiences in a relevant and satisfactory way. She must be careful not to select a play image that is too frightening or emotionally overwhelming to the child. For example, the play image of a suddenly erupting volcano that kills the sleeping villagers in its wake is very intense and utterly destructive. In this case, the child will need the therapist's support and protection in dealing with the fall-out of the play image.

Once a suitable play image has been identified, the therapist asks the child to draw, paint, or make a clay model of it in order to concretize it into a substantial image. She may suggest a specific medium depending on the nature of the image and its role in the play. Alternatively, the child may choose a medium depending on the appeal of the art materials. The therapist facilitates the process of the concretization of play images by providing the art materials, communicating her interest, and providing technical assistance when called for. Children often need the therapist's active participation in giving shape to an emotionally loaded play image.

The therapist and the child may then shape the play image together, which is supportive to the child and draws them both into a deeper experiential involvement (Lubbers, 1988). Once the play image is concretized, it is reintroduced into the child's playworld. Clay models can easily be integrated in an ongoing imaginative play and tend to play a central role in it. Painted play images can be elaborated upon through storytelling or direct questioning. In both cases, the therapist helps the child to work indirectly through his or her projected fears.

APPLICATIONS

The technique of concretizing play images in the context of play therapy may be helpful with all types of emotionally disturbed children. It is especially indicated for anxious and fearful children and for those who have suffered traumatic or crisis experiences leading to partial denial or other defensive behaviors. The following brief case description provides an illustration.

Mark was an 8-year-old boy who suffered from overwhelming fears. He was afraid to be alone, afraid of the dark, and above all, afraid of monsters who threatened him day and night. These fears emerged after a traumatizing experience wherein he witnessed a violent attack on his later divorced parents by outside intruders. Mark was a soft and affectionate child who forcefully denied these painful experiences.

In play therapy, he revealed his longing for peace and friendship but created at the same time a playworld in which the human and animal figures of his village were either all good or all bad. Set apart from the others was a monster family consisting of a father, a mother, and two babies. Mark conveyed that they were the powerful rulers of the village but insisted that they were good creatures and unaware of their monster status. He was thus able to create the play image of monsters but only if they were masked and believed to be benevolent. Mark was very drawn to these complex monsters. As this play image was clearly of a projective nature and seemed central to his own problems, the therapist led the child toward a concretization of it. She suggested that they make a monster family out of clay to make them look "more real." The child was eager to do this, and with the help of his therapist he became deeply involved in the process of molding and shaping the figures of a monster family. They were immediately introduced in his play and became key figures in a series of subsequent play stories. At a later stage, Mark decided to make another figure out of raw materials and called him Mr. Unique. This figure was given the important mission to unmask the monster family and to reveal their true identity to themselves and to the rest of the villagers. Once this was accomplished in the play, Mark no longer needed the monster family, and his own fears of monsters dissipated. Soon afterward, Mark started to talk directly to his therapist about his frightening experiences and his anger and was able to solve his problems in more realistic ways.

References

Hellendoorn, J. (1988). Imaginative play techniques in psychotherapy with children. C. E. Schaefer (Ed.). *Innovative Interventions in Child and Adolescent Therapy*. New York: Wiley.

Lubbers, R. (1988). *Psychotherapie Door Beeld en Begripsvorming*. Nijmegen: Dekker & Van de Vegt.

Mook, B. (1999). Phenomenology, analytical psychology, and play therapy. Brooke, R. (Ed.). *Pathways into the Jungian World*. London: Routledge.

26

Stories in the Sand

Erika L. Surkin

INTRODUCTION

Stories in the Sand combines sandtray techniques and digital technology. The client and play therapist create a "book," which allows them to capture and build upon the emotional experience from one session to the next.

After the sandtray scene is created, the therapist elicits any verbal comments the client may wish to offer. These comments are captured with the use of a tape recorder. The therapist then uses a digital camera to photograph the tray. Later, the photographs are loaded into a computer. The tape-recorded comments are transcribed and combined with the photos to illustrate details of the scene, then printed out in advance of the next session. The next session begins with the therapist reviewing the book with the client. The words and pictures are the client's own, recapturing the therapeutic work and enabling continued exploration of the metaphor. It is vital for the therapist to avoid interfering with the client's sandtray experience. Those clients who are reluctant to be recorded should be offered a written record of their verbalization; others may prefer to write, rather than dictate, their descriptive responses.

RATIONALE

Sandtray techniques are widely used by play therapists to promote expression of emotional and social issues from the client's perspective. Metaphors used by children and adults have personal meaning, which the therapist interprets through clinical expertise and experience with the medium. Frequently, clients revisit their metaphors to work through troubling aspects of their lives. This work may span several sessions as difficult emotional issues and unconscious conflicts are resolved. There may be a loss of continuity from one session to the next, which makes the therapist's task more difficult. Drawing or photographing the scene at the end of a session may help, but it may not re-create the emotional experience for the client. Stories in the Sand is particularly helpful in doing just that: It recaptures the moment when the last therapy session ended and facilitates continued exploration of the sandtray experience.

DESCRIPTION

The clinician should have a filled sandtray with appropriate miniatures or toys. (Many children place a variety of toys in and around the box; some place dollhouses and castles into the sand to communicate their themes.) A tape recorder with a lapel microphone is required. A digital camera with some capability for fine detail, a flash, and a zoom are preferable. The ability to take close-up shots of sandtray details is particularly helpful. Obviously, a personal computer is necessary, loaded with photo loading and photo management software. Binding of the book may be as simple as a report cover with a sliding spine or a loose leaf notebook.

Stories in the Sand works most effectively after the client has created several trays and become comfortable with some type of verbal comment on the scene. Before using this technique, the client should have several introductory sessions with the sandtray experience, as outlined by other authors (Bradway and McCoard, 1997). Once the client is familiar with the sandtray and is comfortable with the medium, the therapist may ask for a verbal reaction or description of the scene depicted. Some clients may offer an extended description of their work, while less verbal clients provide a simple description of important parts of the scenario. These descriptions provide important clues for the clinician in interpreting the tray.

The therapist should give the client an introductory explanation. Prior to creation of the tray, the therapist offers the client the opportunity to create a book of the sandtray work with continuing chapters to explore the themes. A sample book helps to capture the excitement and imagination of the client. This introduction should *not* involve study of someone else's work, but a quick look at the sample to understand the finished product. (The goal is understanding the process, not imposing a topic upon the client.) The therapist should create a sample book with an everyday scene, such as a family waking up and going through the usual process of washing, dressing, and leaving the house.

At this point, the client should be invited to create a scene in the sand. Once the client has completed the tray, the microphone is attached and comments are recorded. (Reassurance that the tape recording will be used only for transcription purposes is important to preserve confidentiality.) Once the client has described the tray, the therapist should ask what would happen next. The client should then move the toys to illustrate the story progression. Because the tape recorder is running the clinician is free to snap pictures. Some clients may enjoy directing the photographer while others prefer uninterrupted time to play out the scene. Each week, the client is invited to enlarge the book, adding chapters to the story.

The therapist's work in transferring the client's words and pictures to the computer begins with a word processing program. A colorful and whimsical font may be used to emphasize the imaginary nature of the work. Children particularly enjoy colorful print; their participation in this part of the process may include use of a favorite color. After the photos are downloaded from the camera, a cut-and-paste process is used to create the book. Use of a photo management program, such as Microsoft Picture It! (Microsoft, 1997–2000) helps with touch-up and sizing of the photos. Some clients enjoy editing their book; others merely enjoy reading through the finished product.

APPLICATIONS

The book is useful for many purposes. For the therapist, it is a convenient and clear record of the client's progress and clinical issues. For the client, it is a personal and powerful creation. Many children lack self-confidence in their ability to make up a story or use their imaginations. The book may become a source of pride and a record of accomplishment. Some enjoy taking a copy to read at home, which promotes further therapeutic work beyond the therapy session.

Parents of young clients are always curious about the work done in sessions. The books provide them with a window into the therapy sessions and the inner world of the child. Many parents recognize the meaning behind their children's metaphors, providing the clinician with valuable insight to aid diagnosis and treatment.

Directive play therapists may help the child find new coping mechanisms or story resolutions by asking the client to make up an alternative ending for the story. Another intervention suggestion is to have the client rewrite the book from the perspective of a particular character. The client may also create a title, a book jacket summary, a description of the author, and a cover with a photo of a preferred sandtray picture.

References

Bradway, K. and McCoard, B. (1997). *Sandplay—Silent Workshop of the Psyche.* London and New York: Routledge.

Microsoft Corp. (1997–2000). *Microsoft Picture It!* Publishing 2001 [Computer Software]. Redmond, WA: Microsoft Corp.

27

High-Tech Therapeutic Storybook

Erika L. Surkin

INTRODUCTION

This technique combines several ideas in an effective way to help clients understand an impending medical procedure, reduce fear, and improve postoperative progress. Prior to therapy, the clinician ascertains details of the client's medical treatment. Use of appropriate and realistic toys is important in the initial sessions, during which review of each medical procedure takes place. As therapy progresses, the child is encouraged to play a variety of roles, from doctor to parent to patient. Eventually, the client and therapist create a book using digital photographs of their play to depict the medical experience. The child takes the book home to be read each day prior to the event. This technique combines therapist, parent, and child as a team to approach this difficult experience in a positive and informed manner.

RATIONALE

Creation of therapeutic stories has proven to be an effective technique to reduce anxiety (Kelly, 2001). Children may participate in creation of the story through drawings and words. Therapists reduce children's fears through detailed review of the impending event, creating a book to help children through a difficult experience. Similarly, play therapy enhances abreaction through appropriate play materials provided to simulate and work through emotions experienced during a child's journey through medical treatment.

As children play through such an experience, they gain mastery over their fears, are educated about the steps of the procedure, and experience some sense of control over a difficult event. Play therapy is particularly effective in facilitating the child's expression of deep-seeded feelings and fears, over and above the verbal discussion. Once these factors have been revealed, the book can address this source of anxiety in a direct manner.

DESCRIPTION

After a thorough diagnostic interview with parents or caregivers, the therapist should contact medical personnel to gain detailed information about the child's medical procedure. Such information should include prehospitalization requirements, including presurgical tests, restriction of food and drink prior to admission, each step of the admission process, as well as details of anesthesia and methods of administration. The child should be clear about hospital rules regarding presence of the parent, particularly if there will be an overnight stay. Postoperative pain, injections, IV treatment, location of bandages, and subsequent scarring are important to the child. It is imperative that children be honestly prepared for the level of pain to be experienced, particularly because imagination tends to inflate such an aversive experience in the absence of such preparation.

After this information is gathered, the therapist should gather play materials that represent the medical equipment in as realistic a manner as possible. The therapist might use Playmobil™ toys or large dolls with real medical equipment to take the child through the medical procedure. Over many sessions, the child and therapist play out the entire medical experience. As the sessions progress, repetition is important to desensitize fears and ensure thorough understanding of the event. The client should be encouraged to direct the play, assuming a variety of roles. The ensuing play from the child's point of view may reveal unexpressed fears. Once therapy goals of anxiety reduction, education, and a sense of control for the child have been accomplished, the storybook can be created. The child can be encouraged to play out the "story" independently, while the therapist records the child's words using pencil and paper or tape recorder. The therapist may take the role of a doctor's assistant to remind the child of any missing details and to include those aspects of the procedure that are particularly anxiety-provoking for the child. A digital camera should be used to record the play. The clinician then produces the book through word processing and desktop publishing. The child is given a copy to be read by parents at home each day prior to the medical procedure.

This technique was used successfully with an 8-year-old boy facing major surgery to remove a benign growth in his inner ear. Although hospital staff provided education about the surgery, the child was anxious and resistant to the operation. Five sessions were necessary to educate the child and to achieve anxiety reduction. Through repeated sessions, he expressed his anxiety about injections and postoperative pain. His greatest fears, failure to "wake up" after surgery or awakening during the operation, were expressed after four sessions. Once the latter fears were shared and addressed in therapy, his mother reported dramatic lessening of anxiety and resistance.

The final session consisted of the child's independent creation of the story, while the therapist recorded his play with tape recorder and camera. The book, with a title cover consisting of the child's name and photo, was given to the family. Each night prior to the procedure, the parent and child read the book together. The boy was subsequently able to manage the operation successfully with a rapid recovery.

APPLICATIONS

Although this technique was effective when used with a child facing surgery, other medical procedures may also be traumatic for children, including injections, dental visits, bracing, and casting. Preparation for upcoming life changes, such as relocation, a new sibling, separation from parents, divorce, and illness and death of a loved one may also be addressed in this manner.

Reference

Kelly, M. M. (2001). *Take-Home Stories from the Playroom*. H. G. Kaduson and C. E. Schaefer (Eds.). *101 More Play Therapy Techniques* (pp. 22–24). New Jersey and London: Jason Aronson Inc.

28

Anger Wall

Karen M. Sribney

INTRODUCTION

A common identifying issue in the referral of children into therapy is anger. Often these children are identified as having inappropriate responses when they feel angry or display their anger in a way that feels much "too big" for others to support them with. As it is often difficult for young children to discuss many of their feelings verbally, this activity allows them to utilize their drawing skills and some very basic verbalizations to enable all involved to better understand a child's feelings of anger. This technique was taught to me by my supervisor, Diane McGregor, C. Psych., as I completed my internship; it has always been a useful step in enabling children and adolescents to better understand their anger.

RATIONALE

Often, when children come into therapy to "work on their anger," it is revealed that they have spent a lot of time focusing on this issue either through anger management groups or one-on-one support with an adult. The focus of these previous interventions often appears to be what the child should do once he or she is feeling angry to cope with that feeling more appropriately. The intent of the Anger Wall technique, instead, is to support the child in identifying the kinds of situations that bring on one's anger at different levels. The hope, then, is that once the child is aware of what makes him or her angry, he or she will be better able to put into place the coping strategies that he or she has been taught in the past. Also, if the child is able to identify situations where the anger is "small," these coping strategies will help to thwart his or her anger from building to a level that feels unmanageable.

DESCRIPTION

Using a large roll of paper, lift the loose end of the paper leaving the roll on the floor and begin rolling the paper vertically up the wall asking the child to tell you "when the paper is as big as your anger." When the child tells you to "Stop," cut off the paper and tape the ends to the wall. then take a dark felt pen and draw two lines horizontally across the paper at about one-third the way up and two-thirds the way up so that the paper is divided into approximately three equal parts (see figure 28.1).

Finally, ask the child to draw pictures or symbols that represent three different stages of being angry, at least one on each of the three parts of the paper. The first stage representing mild anger (at the bottom) should be a symbol of what it is like for the child when he or she feels "ticked off." Second, a symbol of what it is like for the child to feel moderate or "medium mad" or "angry" and third, what it is like when he or she feels "enraged."

Have smaller pieces of paper or recipe cards ready and ask the child to tell you ten things that make him or her angry. After you have written these situations on the cards, place a piece of tape on the back and ask the child to stick them to the Anger Wall at the level of anger that the child feels (i.e., a child might identify that his or her mother nags the child in the morning to hurry up all the time and this makes him or her feel angry). Once the child has placed all of the situations on the Anger Wall, it provides a visual representation of where most of his or her anger is felt and a brief discussion of that visual representation can occur.

Discuss with the child what he or she notices while looking at the Anger Wall, where the majority of anger situations are, what kinds of situations most commonly make him or her angry, and so on. One can then explore where a child feels each level of anger in his or her body, and using your own pen, write these on the Anger Wall at each level. Further,

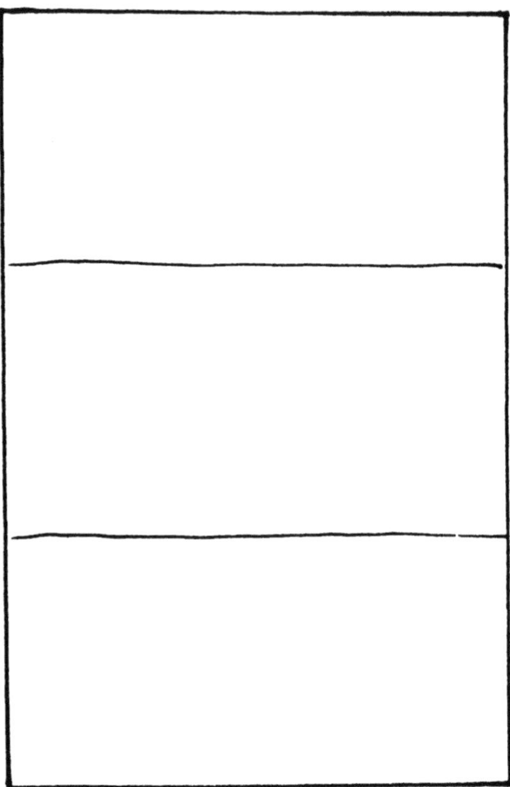

Figure 28.1

help the child explore deeper what kinds of coping strategies he or she has found most successful for each level of anger. Finally, the child can be asked if he or she would mind showing the Anger Wall to the parents or guardians and explain what was learned.

For a more cathartic experience, some children have found it beneficial to throw wet sponges at their Anger Wall to have a specific and safe place to direct anger while being supported by the therapist. To complete this part of the Anger Wall, fill a bucket with warm soapy water and toss in five of six sponges (sponges should be about the size of a large softball). Suggest to the child that he or she throw the sponges at the wall, aiming at specific anger statements. Help the child verbalize angry feelings through this process, (such as "I feel soooo angry when . . ."). Help to validate and expand these feelings by throwing sponges yourself and making statements with your throw (such as "Yeah! Sally feels soooo angry when . . .").

The room will begin to get very messy during this process, so this part of the Anger Wall is not for those therapists who prefer very orderly playrooms. Children will often turn this into a "target game" and "aim" for specific problems. This part of the Anger Wall encourages physical movement, which increases self-expression. Additionally, the activity is *fun* adding to further release of feelings. As children "get into it," they will often laugh uproariously. With water running down the Anger Wall, the child's drawings and self-statements begin to wash off. This becomes a great metaphor for "washing away" anger.

29

The Jungle (or City) Adventure

Lawrence C. Rubin

INTRODUCTION

In the course of supervising play therapists working with children and teens in foster care, a common theme has emerged. These clients, who have numerous behavioral and emotional symptoms, particularly anger, anxiety, and interpersonal difficulties, have lived in various state, county, and private foster facilities. They have witnessed a parade of parents, therapists, lawyers, and caseworkers involved in their lives, and as a result suffer deep confusion, insecurity, and abandonment fear. There is little predictability or certainty in their lives, and their fears are acted out in ways that serve only to undermine their current placements and relationships.

Their therapists, often overwhelmed by children's complex histories, often feel at a loss to connect with and offer security to these clients, and fumble with generic play therapeutic techniques that are more symptom-related. The Jungle (or City) Adventure technique is a mutual drawing/construction technique that derives (loosely) from the typical shopping mall map, which provides directions to the various stores by use of a little "You Are Here" marker and a pathway. Therapist and client work together on a large sheet of news print to construct (with crayon, popsicle sticks, figures, animals, and clay) a map of the client's life, including the various facilities and people connected to him or her. The client fashions a figure of him- or herself and has it travel the road connecting the various facilities, describing and talking with the characters involved. The journey may be through a jungle for young children or a city for older children and teens. The technique is designed to provide the client (from age 5 through adolescence) some understanding and control over the events in his or her life since leaving home.

RATIONALE

This technique is therapeutic for several reasons. First, it is a relationship builder, because the client and therapist work together to depict and animate the various living arrangements he or she has had. Second, it is an ongoing technique, requiring considerable development in order to capture the depth and complexity of the client's history. Third, it incorporates role playing (between the client and various actors in his or her life) and thus removes the burden of tedious question and answer. Fourth, it is portable. Fifth, it allows for a backdrop against which all other symptom-focused techniques can be employed. Finally, it aims to provide a foundation in understanding for a client who has had little security and predictability since being removed from the birth home.

DESCRIPTION

The technique is introduced to the client as a journey they will take together through a jungle or city, with the client as the tour guide and the therapist as the student. The client and therapist use a large piece of news print, and in the upper left-hand corner draw the client's birth home as a treehouse or regular home (complete with parents, siblings, and extended family). Younger children may use popsicle sticks (colored with marker) or puppets to depict family members, case workers, and therapists, while older children may use human figures or drawings to represent these characters. For the younger client, animals of varying temperaments may be used to depict people with similar real or perceived personalities, such as a lion for a scary houseparent, a playful monkey for a friendly foster-sibling, or a wise owl for a helpful judge. Older children may use animals or human figures in a similar way. Additionally, the client is encouraged to create one figure who has been a constant or a helper, so that figure can accompany client and therapist on their journey, answering difficult questions along the way. The goal of the technique is not to find a way out of the jungle or city, but to reconstruct the journey of the client's life, allowing for conversations and the expression of feelings and questions along the way. Each house (or jungle tree house) is connected by a road, drawn in a color that is special to the client, depicting his or her life. The client is encouraged to create a unique marker out of clay that represents the location on the map that he or she is discussing, the ubiquitous "You Are Here" marker found in shopping mall maps. The therapist is encouraged to bring his or her own creativity to bear in the process of making the three-dimensional map into a living document.

APPLICATIONS

The technique is not designed for use with specific symptoms or behavioral problems, but instead as an ongoing grounding process for clients whose lives have been disrupted by numerous or just a few upheavals. It is introduced as a technique that is always available and can be returned to when current symptoms appear related to abandonment, separation, or impending relocation. Older clients are encouraged to engage more fully in conversations with the characters in their stories, as opposed to young clients who may use the input from the therapist or special figure that they created. This technique has been used by therapists working with children ages 6 to 10, who are currently in foster care and who have had a history of multiple placements, with and without termination of parental rights.

30

Combining Art and Sandtray Therapies with Sexually Abused Children

Carla J. Reyes

INTRODUCTION

Children who have been sexually abused exhibit a variety of social, emotional, sexual, behavioral, and psychological problems. Depending on the therapist and his or her theoretical or philosophical orientation toward treatment of sexually abused children, therapy may focus directly on the traumatic event that brought the child into therapy or can be less directive focusing on current functioning in the family, school, or community. The combination of art and sandtray techniques can be used with a variety of approaches. I was trained in this technique while I was working in a child abuse agency. I believe the model was adapted from a Violet Oaklander training seminar and shared with us.

RATIONALE

Play therapy has provided a way to bridge the gap between the adult therapist and the child. The "playing out" of feelings is child-centered in that it is used to develop an emotional environment, which, along with acceptance and reflection of feelings, allows the child to reorganize experiences, feelings, and attitudes while progressing toward healing

(Corder and Haizlip, 1989). Play therapy offers children a nonthreatening place in which to express themselves and make sense of the world around them. Play is recognized as a primary and inherent part of children's lives, through which they can also learn, communicate, and interact with others naturally (Sweeney and Landreth, 1993; White and Allers, 1994). Through play therapy, the child attempts to understand the rules and regulations of the adult world. A child can transform this adult-world reality into understandable personal terms by developing symbolic representations of that world. Through play, children are able to experience worlds and identities outside their own, possibly providing alternative ways in which to view life events. A child, particularly one affected by sexual abuse, can take an active part in reconstructing previously overwhelming situations. Children can attain mastery over feelings of guilt and shame through re-creating past traumatic events (White and Allers, 1994), using toys as their vocabulary and play as their voice (Harper, 1991). "Playing out" feelings and experiences creates a natural, active, and self-healing process in which children can engage. Play therapy facilitates the growth and development of the child's own efforts to become more adequate, cope with problems, and make choices (Sweeney and Landreth, 1993).

DESCRIPTION

Art and sandtray therapies take place in a semi-structured session; the entire session is needed for this technique. Materials for the intervention should be readily available, with drawing materials within reach for the child. Once the child is comfortable in an area where he or she can begin drawing (e.g., on the floor or at a table), the therapist begins the process by encouraging basic relaxation breathing. Have the child close his or her eyes and breathe deeply, clearing thoughts about the activities of the day and concentrating on breathing. After a few minutes, the therapist helps the child focus on any feelings that emerge. Have the child imagine the feeling and what it looks like while keeping her or his eyes closed and continuing deep breathing. The child is not asked to label this feeling or feelings. The feeling may or may not get labeled concretely later during the exploration process. Once the child has imagined what the feeling looks like, the therapist asks the child to open his or her eyes and begin to draw the feeling on the paper. Plenty of drawing materials—crayons, markers, pencils, chalk, and so forth should be available.

Colored paper is also fine, but white paper more clearly shows the intensity of the drawing.

The child should be encouraged to draw until it appears the drawing is complete. The therapist then begins to process the drawing with the child. The therapist begins by asking the child, "Tell me about your picture." From the response given, more open-ended questions are asked. This is where the child leads and the therapist follows the child's path in this exploration of feeling(s). The therapist may ask the feeling to talk to the child, to give it a voice. The therapist might also ask the child to talk to the feeling; or if there is more than one feeling ask the child to give each one a voice and have them talk to each other. The therapist should be sure to ask about parts of the picture the child doesn't mention, as well as reflecting to the child what the therapist understands so the child experiences the therapist being with him or her, understanding his or her feeling(s) during this process.

Once it seems the child has explained the drawing, the therapist becomes more structured, asking the child then to move to the sandtray objects, letting his or her hand choose some figures. It helps to stress that the child does not have to think about it, just let his or her hand wander over the objects and let the hand choose. The child may take a few sandtray toys, place them into the sandtray, and go back for more. The selection of toys is completely up to the child. Once the child has selected the items, the therapist asks the child to create a scene in the sand. The child may change his or her mind about including a toy previously selected or may switch a toy for one still on the shelf. When the scene is complete, the therapist once again asks the child, "Tell me about your scene." The same types of questions occur as when exploring the drawing. With the therapists' guidance, the child might want to explore giving different characters names, voices, and, depending on the situation, move the characters to see how that might change the child's perspective. The therapist might ask the child, "What would happen if this character did this?" then ask the child to act out the event in the sandtray. The therapist may also want to be more active and take on a role or voice for one of the characters. This may take place in the form of taking a different perspective or responding verbally to one of the characters the child gave a voice to. These questions are not an investigation, but a gentle exploration of the child's work, to gain a better understanding of the child's worldview. If the child is not able or chooses not to be verbal, the therapist may try interacting silently with the figures.

Drawing appears to touch the feelings a child experiences, and the sandtray allows the child to further articulate in play how that feeling may be affecting her or him in everyday life. The scene seems to create a scenario where the child has just experienced that feeling and then is given the opportunity to explore it further and act it out or possibly learn a new perspective. The voices and movement of characters allow the opportunity for a corrective experience during the therapy session. Sandtray therapy can be a powerful intervention, carrying the drawing a step further to a deeper processing level for the child.

APPLICATIONS

This technique can be used with children with a myriad of presenting problems. It is particularly useful with sexually abused children because the flow of the play with a mixture of semi-structured and child-centered focused play allows the child to take charge of the session but also have some structure available. This combination of techniques allows creative outlets of art and the more tactile, action-oriented play with the sandtray, thus tapping different creative elements of the child during one session. It also allows the opportunity for the child to take steps toward creating a corrective experience in a safe, supportive environment, creating both a therapeutic and empowering experience for abuse victims. Combining art and sandtray therapies allows the child to experience a difficult emotional state; label this feeling, which is often hard for children to do; and then cognitively process these emotions again in a safe, nurturing environment.

References

Corder, B. F. and Haizlip, M. D. (1989). The role of mastery experiences in therapeutic interventions for children dealing with acute trauma: some implications for treatment of sexual abuse. *The Psychiatric Forum* 15 (1), 57–63.

Harper, J. (1991). Children's play: The differential effects of intrafamilial physical and sexual abuse. *Child Abuse and Neglect* 15, 89–98.

Sweeney, D. S. and Landreth, G. (1993). Healing a child's spirit through play therapy: A scriptural approach to treating children. *Journal of Psychology and Christianity* 12 (4), 351–356.

White, J. and Allers, C. T. (1994). Play therapy with abused children: A review of the literature. *Journal of Counseling and Development* 72 (4), 390–394.

31

The Feeling Wall Activity

Sharon Picard

INTRODUCTION

Many children who come to psychotherapy have difficulty with verbal affective communication. They do not know how to describe their emotions or their emotional experiences using words. Frequently, they live in homes with adults who do not talk about their feelings. When children are unable to express themselves, they may act out aggressively, tantrum, become anxious, or withdraw. By encouraging affective communication, a therapist can provide a child client with the skills needed to express his or her emotions and needs to adults and peers.

RATIONALE

The Feeling Wall activity helps children begin to associate feelings with their experiences. Children are encouraged to discuss emotional experiences. This activity also has a physical or movement component to it so that children are not just sitting down to talk about their feelings. They are moving actively about the room. The Feeling Wall activity works well at the beginning of a play therapy session to encourage the child to talk about his or her week. It provides the therapist with the opportunity to hear about the child's week through his or her eyes. If the therapist knows of certain emotional events that may have taken place during the week, this activity can be used to inquire about them.

DESCRIPTION

To create the Feeling Wall, the therapist needs white 11 by 14-inch construction paper, a variety of markers, tape, and at least one nerf ball. The therapist sits down with the child and asks him or her to list some feelings that he or she has felt over the past couple of days. After a child names a feeling, the therapist asks the child which color would go well with that feeling. Then the child or therapist writes the name of the feeling on one piece of paper. The child is encouraged to draw a face that reflects that particular feeling. This process continues until between eight and ten feelings have been identified in different colors. Some feelings that usually get picked and work well during the game are happy, sad, mad, scared, excited, confused, worried, and lonely. If the child says a word that is not a descriptive feeling, such as "good," the therapist can suggest "happy" as the feeling behind "good."

Once the feelings are written out, the therapist tells the child that they will be using these papers to talk about some feelings. The therapist and child tape the feelings up on one wall. Then they take turns throwing the ball at the wall. When the ball hits a feeling, the person who threw the ball tells about a time that he or she felt that way during the past week. The therapist may want to go first in order to give a good example. If the thrower misses the paper, he or she can take the turn over. Once a feeling has been hit by the thrower, it cannot be used again. This way the child will not just pick *"happy"* ten times.

The interaction may sound like this:

Therapist: I can't wait to hear about your week. Okay, we are going to take turns throwing the ball at the wall and hitting the feelings. Once you hit a feeling, you can't use it again.

Child: (Throws ball at the wall)

Therapist: All right! Great shot! You hit *"sad."* When did you feel *sad* during this week?

Child: When I had to leave my friend's house to come home.

Therapist: You were having fun there and didn't want to leave?

Child: Uh-huh.

Therapist: What did you do when you were sad?

Child: I told my mom I didn't want to leave.

Sometimes this game can lead to problem solving such as in the following example:

Child: (Throws ball at the wall)

Therapist: You hit "*scared*." When did you feel *scared* during the past week?

Child: When it was dark in my room.

Therapist: Oh, you were scared in the dark in your bedroom.

Child: Yeah.

Therapist: It can be scary in the dark sometimes. What's scary about your room?

Child: I'm scared there's a monster in my closet.

Therapist: Do your parents let you use a night light in your room?

Child: Yeah, but it burned out.

Therapist: Oh, maybe we can talk to them about fixing that. Is it okay for me and you to talk with them about that when we are all done in here?

During his or her turn, the therapist may want to use examples that are relevant to the child's life to encourage the discussion of these events. As therapy progresses, the therapist can use the activity to discuss emotional experiences more in depth. Once children associate a feeling with an experience, the therapist can use this activity to discuss what they do when they are *happy* or *sad* (such as smile or cry).

APPLICATIONS

This technique works with children who are verbal and old enough to begin to associate feelings with experiences. Depending on the client, therapists may not want to ask about feelings that occurred in the past week. They may want to broaden the discussion to the child's whole life or limit it to just the particular day. If a significant event or emotion gets brought up during the game, the therapist can leave the activity to focus more closely on that event or emotion. Once the Feeling Wall is in place, the therapist can go back to it at any time during the remainder of the session to encourage a child to discuss something that he or she is having difficulty talking about. The child will associate the Feeling Wall with discussing feelings and may approach it on his or her own as a way to talk about a difficult emotion.

32

Shapes and Directions

Sharon Picard

INTRODUCTION

With the growing interest in infant-preschool mental health issues, it is likely play therapists will see their client base becoming younger and younger. Many toddler and preschool children who come to psychotherapy have difficulty following directions and taking turns. This is often the cause of conflict with their peers and adults at child care or preschool settings, as well as a source of frustration for their parents. This game is a parent-child, family, or group activity.

RATIONALE

The Shapes and Directions activity helps build a child's ability to follow directions and take turns during a simple game. It encourages playful parent-child interactions, which I believe to be one of the most therapeutic components of therapy with toddlers and preschoolers. This game makes following directions fun. It also provides the therapist with the opportunity to observe parent-child or family dynamics and interactions. Opportunities for limit setting are also likely to occur during this game. The therapist will have the opportunity to model appropriate limit setting for parents of young children.

DESCRIPTION

To create the Shapes and Directions game, the therapist uses colored construction paper and cuts out shapes of familiar objects and animals. On the back of each shape, the therapist writes an instruction. It is helpful to laminate the shapes so that they last longer. Instructions should be written in easy-to-understand language for young children. The following is a list of sample instructions for toddlers:

- Show us your foot.
- Pretend you are a cat.
- Pretend you are a dinosaur.
- Tell us your name.
- Pretend to drink some juice.
- Point to your tummy.

The following is a list of instructions for preschoolers:

- Tell us your favorite food.
- Hop on one foot three times.
- Turn around in a circle three times.
- Sing a familiar song.
- Tell someone a secret.
- Make a sound like your favorite animal.

The therapist may want to use corresponding shapes such as a cat with the instruction, "Pretend you are a cat" or an ice cream cone with the instruction, "Tell us your favorite food."

To begin the game, the therapist has everyone sit in a circle and places the shapes instruction-side down in the middle. Each person takes a turn picking a shape and acting out the instruction. The adults may read the instructions for the children. The therapist should encourage playfulness in the others by overacting out the instructions. If a child is feeling shy, all group members can perform each activity to encourage the child.

When children have difficulty waiting for their turn, they can be redirected to observe the person whose turn it is. One such interaction may sound like this:

Child: (Reaches for a shape during someone else's turn)

Therapist: Whoops, it's not your turn (puts shape back in the middle), but let's see what Mom is going to do (stated enthusiastically)!

APPLICATIONS

This technique works with toddlers and preschool children. It is designed as a parent-child, family, or group activity. The children do not need to be verbal, and activities can be based on things that the therapist knows the child can accomplish independently. This game teaches children to follow directions and take turns. It provides opportunities for limit setting when children break the game's simple rules. The therapist will also get the opportunity to model appropriate limit setting for parents of young children. This technique has been used with a variety of children including clients who presented with Asperger's Syndrome, autism, no language skills, extreme tantrum behavior, and difficulty with peer interactions.

33

Feeling Sculptures

Ruth Ouzts Cash

INTRODUCTION

Children involved in counseling are often resistant to discussing their feelings. Their limited vocabularies prevent them from identifying and expressing their emotions. Structured play activities provide children with a tangible outlet for their frustrations and facilitate self-disclosures. The Feeling Sculptures activity can be used with children of all ages who are experiencing a variety of difficulties. Building feeling sculptures is an empowering way for children to express emotions that they may otherwise conceal.

RATIONALE

Children feel more comfortable when they engage in play. By incorporating play techniques into the counseling process, the therapist is better able to establish rapport. Once trust and rapport have been established, children are more apt to disclose sensitive issues.

Children often have cognitive and verbal limitations that prevent them from communicating their feelings. By initiating a structured play activity, children can exercise their creativity and enhance their decision-making abilities. As a result, they become more empowered and self-aware. Play activities provide children with the safety and freedom they need to express themselves.

DESCRIPTION

The therapist sits at a table or on the floor with the child. The child is given a small styrofoam tray or plate (I prefer using empty meat trays from the butcher shop), a bowl of gumdrops candy (assorted colors), and a box of toothpicks. The therapist begins by asking the child to identify a different feeling for each color of gumdrops (e.g. red = angry, white = sad, and so on). The child is then asked to make a sculpture that represents the feelings he or she has inside. The sculptures are made by inserting toothpicks into the styrofoam, attaching a gumdrop to the tip of the toothpick, and inserting additional toothpicks into those gumdrops. The gumdrops can be connected side by side or on top of one another. (The sculptures can get really tall!) The child is given about 20 minutes to build the sculpture. Once the sculpture is built, the therapist processes the activity by asking about the identified emotions. Specific processing questions include: (1) Tell of a time you felt ________. (2) What do you do when you feel ________? (3) Which of these feelings (represented in the sculpture) is hardest to deal with?

The child is allowed to keep the sculpture and may decide whether he wants to eat it.

APPLICATIONS

This technique may be used with children of all ages, however young children are usually able to list only two or three emotions and may need some assistance identifying feelings. Older children are capable of generating more elaborate feelings. I have used this technique with abused children, children with attachment disorders, children with ADHD, and children with divorcing parents. Children enjoy exercising their creativity and feel empowered by the opportunity to construct their own sculpture. Because children label the represented feelings, they decide which emotions they wish to disclose. The follow-up questions are relatively nonthreatening. Thus, children are likely to disclose sensitive information.

I was counseling a 9-year-old child with an attachment disorder. Her parents separated a year prior to her involvement in counseling but reconciled a few months later. Since the separation, the child was reported to be very depressed, to have difficulty displaying and receiving affection, and to exhibit "tantrum" behaviors. During these episodes, she often threatened suicide. Initially in counseling, the child disclosed suicidal ideation, however these feelings later subsided.

The Feeling Sculptures activity was implemented in our fifth counseling session. The child was asked to identify feelings for each of the gumdrops. She labeled the yellow gumdrops as love, the white ones as peace, the orange ones as hope, and the red ones as "money." She was encouraged to consider feelings associated with money.

Therapist: I wonder if you could tell me some feelings that have to do with money.

Child: Well . . . I get mad when my mom won't give me any money but gives my sister money. She lets her do whatever she wants to, and I can't.

Therapist: So, it really makes you mad when you get treated differently than your sister.

Child: Um-hmm.

Therapist: Are there any other feelings you can think of?

The child was then asked to build a sculpture using the feelings she had identified. She was encouraged to include any other feelings that she thought of while building the sculpture. I provided tracking and reflective statements as she built the sculpture. For instance, I stated, "You're working really hard on that" and "You're trying to decide exactly where you'd like to put each one." The child smiled frequently as she built the sculpture. At one point she responded, "Wow! Look how tall I made it." I then reflected, "You feel really proud."

Upon completion, the child's sculpture contained mostly white and yellow gumdrops (peace and love). There were a few red gumdrops (mad) and a few more orange (hope).

Therapist: Wow. I see lots of white and yellow gumdrops. I believe those were peace and love gumdrops.

Child: Um-hmm (nods yes). My mom took me to school today, and my sister and I didn't fight.

Therapist: So things at home haven't been as upsetting this week as they were last week.

Child: No ma'am.

Therapist: I also notice there are a few red gumdrops and a few orange gumdrops.

Child: Yeah. The red ones are there because I get mad sometimes. Well, I get mad a lot. But I haven't really gotten mad this week. There is this girl at school who always gets in trouble with the teacher, but I didn't sit by her so I didn't get in trouble.

Therapist: Oh, so you decided you would rather not sit by her?

Child: Um-hmm (nods yes, pauses). Oh, yeah. The orange ones are there because of hope. I hope I don't have another bad week like I did last week.

The child became very verbal when asked to describe her sculpture. This led to a discussion of the frustration that she felt at school and at home. She later suggested that she sometimes felt really mad, as if she would "explode." The child and I talked about the rivalry she had with her sister and the frustration and pressure she felt to perform well in school.

34

It's My Party

Jodi Ann Mullen

INTRODUCTION

Given children's communication style, direct questioning in the context of psychotherapy is often met with defensiveness. Children will avoid answering questions. Building rapport with children in psychotherapy is based on breaking down defensiveness. One way to build rapport is to allow children in therapy the opportunity to feel a sense of power and control. The It's My Party game is frequently used with children I treat—children who have been traumatized by abuse and neglect. It allows the therapist to understand the relationships that are important to the child. The It's My Party game gives the child the power to be the author of his or her own story.

RATIONALE

Children communicate their experiences to others through play. When, in the context of therapy, a child is given permission to play, the need to be defensive diminishes. The child is able to communicate feelings, thoughts, and information in a medium that suits the child. The therapist who uses play and games can engage the nondefensive child in therapy.

DESCRIPTION

The therapist meets the child at the child's level physically—either by sitting on the floor or in child-sized chairs. The therapist has the following materials: index cards, markers, balloons, construction paper, and tape. The materials for this game are easily augmented. The therapist sets the premise of the game and then follows the child's lead. The child is introduced to the game:

Therapist: We are going to play a game today called It's My Party. You will be having a pretend party in here. You get to decide all about the party.

Child: Can I invite my mom?

Therapist: You can invite whomever you want. You can also invite as many people as you want for pretend. Should we start putting together a list?

Child: Here's the paper. Write down Mommy, Grandpa, Leah . . .

Therapist: Okay, I got those three. I'm not sure I know who Leah is?

Child: Leah is my best friend.

Therapist: Is there anyone else you want to come to your party?

The therapist continues to collect names of people to invite to the party. The child may invite pets and famous people too. The therapist or the child records the list of invited guests. If the child cannot think of anyone to invite, the therapist can offer suggestions.

When the child is satisfied with the list, the therapist and the child can begin to make invitations and place cards, depending on the child's direction.

Therapist: Okay, you have everyone on the list that you want to invite. We can make invitations and cards that say their names.

The therapist and child work together to create the scene for the celebration. The guest of honor is the child and the child decides what to celebrate. Together they may blow up balloons and make decorations and pretend treats.

Therapist: We finished making place cards for all the important people to celebrate with you.

Child: I wish this were a real party.

Therapist: It would be great if you could have a party like this for real with all the people who are important to you there.

Child: Yeah, it would be fun.

Therapist: It's disappointing that this isn't for real. We can blow up some balloons and make a pretend cake.

Child: Let's make a sign that says "Happy Birthday, Taylor."

The party planning and play can last for part of a session or over several sessions. Remember that the child will be sharing with you information about relationships. The therapist will therefore gain a perspective of the child's phenomenological world. Understanding the child from his or her own perspective will allow the therapist to establish a strong relationship in which the child feels free to share.

APPLICATIONS

This technique is helpful with all children. Children who have little opportunity for celebration are eager to engage in this game. It is also useful for the therapist. The therapist who hopes to get a sense of the child's phenomenological world, but has little information regarding the child's history and family, will begin to understand how the child makes meaning of his or her world without relying on direct questioning.

35

The Lotion Game: A Theraplay Technique

Margery Lewy Rieff

INTRODUCTION

Successful treatment of any child hinges on the therapist's ability to establish a trusting relationship. Often children feel a need to protect themselves from incoming stimulation, which makes it difficult for them to take a risk or to let someone get close. Such a child may feel anxious, fearful, inhibited, shy, and withdrawn or may be oppositional or overactive and aggressive. Using lotion and other messy substances in playful ways can help the child learn to accept different kinds of appropriate touch.

RATIONALE

Sensory defensive children are less willing to trust a new adult. Using lotion provides a nice continuum of tactile stimulation that enables the child to achieve better self-regulation. The technique begins with basic nurturing and ends with a very stimulating activity. Through these activities the child learns to regulate sensory input with the intervention of an attuned caring adult. Such simple materials as lotion and cotton balls can be used in a variety of fun ways. The therapist needs to be able to tolerate messes.

DESCRIPTION

The therapist sits on the floor with the child. The child may be on the therapist's or parent's lap. A Theraplay session often begins with the therapist counting the child's "boo boos" and taking care of the child's hurts by lotioning them. After nurturing the child, the therapist may put lotion on a cotton ball and stick the cotton ball on her nose. She and the child will try to blow the cotton ball off her nose to a signal. The signal may be when the therapist winks her eye. The therapist sticks out her tongue, wiggles her ear, fills up one cheek with air, and then winks her eye. The child and therapist both try to blow the cotton ball off the therapist's nose. Facial signals are used to help the child attend to nonverbal communication and enhance the child's eye contact. After several rounds, the therapist starts to throw sticky, lotion-covered cotton balls at the wall and encourages the child to do the same. In the spirit of fun, a child may wildly dip his hand into the lotion jar, fling lotion onto the wall, and then skate on the lotion in bare feet. Although this behavior could be misconstrued as oppositional, this would be a major step for a sensory defensive child.

APPLICATIONS

Different parts of the Lotion game can be used gently and with adaptations for all children. With some children, just counting the hurts would be appropriate. With others, as they become less defensive, they can tolerate more sensory experiences. By the adult making the lotion games playful, the child becomes more willing to try the messy activities.

36

Drawing in Three Dimensions: Transcending Time

Nancy F. Cincotta

INTRODUCTION

This is an activity that can be helpful in identifying and dealing with issues that may emerge when viewed in the context of time, specifically the past, the present, and the future. Many themes in children's lives are ongoing (e.g., issues about their appearance) and can be captured in this exercise. Children get excited about the idea of the three dimensions and are generally very easily engaged in this activity.

RATIONALE

This exercise gives the clinician a sense of what the child identifies as important, how the child thinks about matters significant to him or her, his or her ability to prioritize and isolate a salient feature of his or her life, his or her ability to project to the future, as well as an understanding of the child's sense of him- or herself in the context of the present (past and future). For example, if a child is depressed it often becomes apparent in his or her inability to project to the drawing of the future.

Depending on the age or the particular emotional profile the child, if the exercise is too "expansive" (in that it is seeking something about any aspect of life), or if in the course of the activity the clinician learns that the child is unable to identify something, the child can be assisted by further limiting the activity. For example, the activity can be framed as identifying something important in the past in school, something important in the present in school, and something that he or she thinks will become important in school in the future. If there was a need to be even more specific, the clinician could limit this exercise further, that is, if a child was having a problem with a particular teacher the child could be asked to draw something about last year's math teacher, this year's math teacher, and what he or she would hope for in next year's math teacher. The activity affords the child a forum in which to tell a story about him- or herself either directly or indirectly. It can be seen as autobiographical when it is completed.

DESCRIPTION

You ask the child to divide a piece of paper into three sections. Then you ask if he or she would draw something important from the past on the first panel, something important from the present on the middle panel, and something he or she thinks will be important in the future on the last panel. This exercise causes the child to identify and isolate one thing. It also prompts thinking about life in relation to time, with an implication that things change. It normalizes the fact that things change over time in everyone's life.

APPLICATIONS

This activity is good to use with children who have experienced a life transition (adoption, divorce, and death) or have an uncomfortable situation (illness, housing, and school). It can also be used as part of an assessment process over time with the same child. Done once a month the clinician can actually create a story for a child of his or her life, writing down the explanation the child gives with each picture. If the child is over the issue, the child can write the information either on the back of the drawing or in a special book. It becomes a type of "life book" chronicling a period in the child's life. When done with a parent and child together, the parent will often include the child in the drawing as "something important to him or her." This has an added benefit for the child who can conceptualize (in a very concrete way) his or her importance in the family.

This technique presents the clinician an opportunity to intervene in the story, or not, depending on the framework of the clinician. It can be used as an activity independently or as a stepping-stone to gain further evaluative information from the child. Upon discussing the information the child brings forth in this activity, the child will often easily segue into other information.

The technique can be used over time, with children of all different ages, in families and in groups. It takes on different meaning depending on the context in which it is used. With a group of school age children, the stories can be hung up around the room. It can be geared to a particular topic to help the group members connect with each other. If you are using this technique in a group and plan to share information among members, it is important to let children know that you will be sharing information as this may alter what they choose to draw. Also, sharing the story behind the drawing is optional; it allows children to feel freer to express themselves.

Some children are very self-conscious about their drawing (this tends to increase with age). All children can be given permission to draw in whatever way they feel comfortable: in real characters, abstraction, designs, or words. This is an exercise about the things that come to mind and not about the quality or the type of drawing. Sometimes children will come up with their own ways to design this activity still keeping with the general idea of transcendence through time. Examples of topics for drawing:

Draw a picture of where you lived before.

Draw a picture of where you live now.

Draw a picture of where you want to live in the future.

Draw a picture of your family when you were little.

Draw a picture of your family now.

Draw a picture of your family as you imagine it in the future.

Draw what used to be your favorite thing to play with.

Draw your favorite thing to play with now.

Draw what you think you would like to play with in the future.

Draw those who were your friends when you were little.

Draw who your friends are now.

Draw who you think will be your friends next year.

Draw what happened when you had a problem when you were little.

Draw what happens when you have a problem now.

Draw what you think will happen when you have a problem in the future.

If, for example, you are running a group for children whose parents are divorced, this allows relatively easy entry into information and can serve as a less threatening way to begin the group process. The topic and the framing of the activity can depend on the particular reason you are working with the child, or it can be limited to the theme of a given session. Sometimes patterns among themes in one's life and even the need or ability to make changes can become more apparent to the child and the clinician when reviewed over time.

37

Family Interaction Diagram

Kathleen Truax

INTRODUCTION

Art and play are the natural languages of children, and much of what is therapeutic in psychotherapy takes place within the metaphors of art and play. It is also helpful to children to talk about their situations and feelings, but it is sometimes difficult to move from metaphor to conversation.

RATIONALE

Nondirective art and play can lead to talk about difficult situations and a child's feelings about them, but sometimes an art exercise or game can promote a conversation more quickly. It can also be helpful to suggest art or games to children who may not spontaneously engage in elaborative play or drawing. Inhibition can spring from a variety of sources. A child may come from an emotionally impoverished environment, not feel secure enough to freely explore and express himself, or be so well defended against self-revelation that even spontaneous art and play are threatening. Other children have emotional, cognitive, or temperamental styles that result in the nondirective process being slow and laborious or repetitive and "stuck." Children aged 6 to 12 tend to like diagrams and "keys," and thus feel at home with this project.

DESCRIPTION

Materials

A sheet of drawing paper and colored markers, pencils or crayons.

Therapist: I have an idea for a picture I'd like you to draw for me to help me remember who is in your family and how they all get along. We start by folding the paper in half (for children who are living with more than one family, as in divorce, foster care, etc.). Draw each family group on one-half of the paper. Stick figures are fine, and let's put names under each one so I can remember. (The child should put him- or herself in whichever group he or she chooses.)

Child: (Draws stick figures. Most children are willing to do this to help the therapist who is "confused" and when they are not asked to draw representational figures.)

Therapist: Great. Okay, I'm getting a better idea of who is who. Now, pick a color that stands for people getting along really well.

Child: (Chooses whatever color he or she wishes, say, yellow.)

Therapist: That's a good color for "getting along." Let's start a key at the bottom.

Child: (Makes a key and puts in yellow. The therapist can do the writing if that's an issue.)

Therapist: Okay, now draw a yellow line between all of the people you think get along well, both in each family and between families.

Child: (Draws and may comment.)

The therapist proceeds to ask the child to pick colors to represent "so-so getting along," "not getting along," and, if needed, a color for people who fight a lot or really dislike each other, to draw colored lines between the relevant figures, and to put the colors in the key. This process may result in the child making comments about the interactions such as, "Me and my stepbrother get along 'so-so' most of the time, but he won't let me use his stuff and really blows up if I do." The therapist can encourage the child to be creative about how he or she wants to represent these interactions, for example, by using more than one color and line, a dotted line, and so forth. This process creates an opportunity for some exploration of the child's feelings about the relationship, how he or she copes with it, how he wishes it could be, and so forth. If spontaneous comments are not forthcoming during the drawing process, the therapist can initiate conversation at the end, asking questions such as, "Have these two people always gotten along 'so-so,' or was there a time when it was better (or worse)?" "Who do you wish would get along better?" and "What do you do when these two people fight?"

APPLICATIONS

This technique is useful in a variety of child treatment circumstances. It is most clearly applicable when a child has a large or complex family situation that is difficult emotionally for the child to discuss. Divorce and foster home situations lend themselves readily to this project, and it can be modified to be used with children in homes of intact families when there is a need to assist the child in talking about family relationships.

38

The Book of Feelings

Neresa B. Minatrea and Susan H. James

INTRODUCTION

Children and adolescents commonly find it difficult to discuss their feelings, attitudes, or factual events surrounding current or past emotional, physical, or sexual abuse. Traditional talk therapy often meets resistance due to intentional or unintentional reasons. An alternative technique involves asking the child or adolescent to draw pictures about his or her life. The therapist compiles the drawings into a Book of Feelings. This method provides a possible avenue for the therapist and the client to circumvent counseling interfering behaviors and explore previously silent feelings about difficult events and life patterns. Furthermore, the Book of Feelings provides a method for assessment, a focus for family sessions, and a tangible product from the counseling sessions.

RATIONALE

Traditional talk therapy usually involves a client's release of thoughts, ideas, and feelings, which lead to problem solving or increased self-esteem. Drawing one's story moves the discussion from a cognitive realm to an emotional arena. This technique can be ideal for a child who has limited verbal skills or a child whose cultural background is such that feelings are rarely expressed. A shy child may lack the experience to adequately express his or her feelings or may feel embarrassed when using certain words. Another child or teen may be reluctant to disclose information because he or she fears punishment for him- or herself, family members, or friends. One child may feel disloyal if he or she tells about family problems. When the child or adolescent expresses feelings of resistance, fear, repulsion, or apprehension in the Book of Feelings, then the work of therapy can proceed. Perhaps another child or adolescent has verbally disclosed factual history of his or her abuse with little or no emotions. Drawing the child's story frees the individual to express feelings, themes, attitudes, or information, while providing a medium for the therapists to pursue otherwise unexplored territory. The pleasure of expression through drawing lowers defenses.

DESCRIPTION

The therapist provides markers, pencils, crayons and 8½ by 10-inch white paper for the session. The therapist and child or adolescent sit side by side at a table during the session. The therapist shows the client a three-ring notebook with tabs for each (age appropriate) feeling word. Between the tabs are clear plastic page covers. The therapist explains the task.

Therapist: Today I would like you to draw a picture about any feeling in the book. Afterward, we will place your picture in a plastic cover and start to make a Book of Feelings.

The therapist observes the drawing without interfering or guiding. The therapist uses encouragement, tracking, and reflective listening.

Therapist: You are putting a lot of effort into the picture. I see you are using the same color for all the parts of your picture. It seems you are happy when drawing your family's picnic.

After a brief time of 10 to 15 minutes, the therapist begins the processing part of the session. The therapist uses open-ended questions, attending, and basic listening skills such as reflective listening, paraphrasing, and summarizing.

Therapist: Tell me about your picture.

Child: It is a picture of us eating dinner. Here is Mom, my brother, and sister, and Ted.

Therapist: Tell me about Ted?

Child: Ted is Mom's boyfriend. He lives with us.

Therapist: You sighed when you said Ted's name; you seem sad.

The remainder of the session time is focused on the child or adolescent's picture exploring his or her emotions, information, themes, and so on. Additionally, the therapist may ask the client to draw a portion of the picture outlining more detail.

Therapist: I cannot see (you, Ted, Mom, sister, brother) at the table. I would like you to draw (you, Ted, Mom, sister, brother) on this new piece of paper.

Child: (Draws new picture in larger detail.)

Therapist: Tell me what you see. What are they saying? What do you want them to say?

The therapist helps the client date and narrate each picture by writing down the explanation. These comments can be placed on sticky labels, which can then be transferred to the picture or an adjoining page. Then the therapist asks the child about his or her feelings in the picture. The child or adolescent can decide the feeling chapter in which the picture will be placed. If the child has two strong feelings, such as anger and jealousy, the picture can be copied and placed in both chapters. This procedure helps a client understand it is okay to have more than one feeling at the same time. Each chapter helps the child accept all emotions, both pleasant and unpleasant. The therapist and client can see which emotions are easily expressed and which ones have been avoided. Eventually, the client moves toward expressing feelings for each chapter and accepting all parts of his or her personality and its experiences. Therapists can also ask clients to draw a variety of pictures. These pictures may move from general ideas to more specific ones. Some suggestions are:

Draw anything you wish.

Draw some imaginary people and tell a story about them.

Draw your family doing something.

Draw a dream that scared you this week.

Draw something about the abuse.

Children often project their emotions, experiences, and ways of thinking in their drawings and stories. Eventually the child can own the projections as his own. Many children will enjoy looking at their Book of Feelings. Some may fixate on a page of the book for a long time, indicating something important to themselves.

Therapist: You have looked at that picture for a long time. It seems very important to you.

Child: I wish my family were different. I don't like having stepbrothers.

Several possibilities exist for future work using the child's or adolescent's Book of Feelings. The individual discusses parts or the entire Book of Feelings with family members or significant individuals in his or her life. Parents or guardians can be taught to use feeling pictures with children as a way of enhancing communication.

APPLICATIONS

The possibilities for application can be as creative and immeasurable as the drawings. This chapter's authors particularly find drawing beneficial when working with emotional, physical, and sexual abuse, however the same procedure could be used with children facing issues of loss due to death, divorce, stepfamilies, foster care, parents in prison, trauma, and so on. Any child or adolescent participating in counseling may benefit from keeping a Book of Feelings. Therapists will find that the Book of Feelings serves as an excellent assessment tool because it documents feelings and thoughts over a course of time. Drawing facilitates emotional catharsis and provides a means of nonverbal communication. The Book of Feelings helps the therapist understand a child's world.

Section Two

Puppets

39

Silent Puppet

Sylvia Fisher

INTRODUCTION

Puppets take all forms, shapes, sizes, and colors. Puppets are wonderfully creative in allowing children to act a drama or express an interaction. The child can become a different person through the puppet or watch what happens to the puppet. This medium is an age-old technique that is part of our collective unconscious, however we have creative license to alter the play. This puppet has no voice.

RATIONALE

Common themes in puppet play often have to do with the good/small triumphing over evil; fears being overcome; aggression being reversed onto the aggressor. Emotions are usually intense, especially in family dramas. If the play becomes too close to a real situation for the child, the play may end suddenly, or the focus will shift.

When children engage in puppet play, they often have an imagined scenario complete with voices and other puppet players. Some children become frustrated when the other puppeteer doesn't know the "right" lines or responds with the unexpected. For children whose self-esteem is fragile, the outcome often is disappointing whether the child is playing alone or with the therapist. Some children respond more concretely to what the puppet actually represents (such as a specific animal). I have found that some children are easily distracted by the external, so I have eliminated one element: the voice.

DESCRIPTION

I have a long (approximately 18-inch) puppet that fits over my entire hand and arm to my elbow. This is a furry critter with large eyes, a red vinyl mouth that opens, arms that Velcro together at the hands, and legs that Velcro at the feet. It looks like a cross between a Dr. Seuss character and a Muppet. When I put my arm in the puppet, I also place the arms around my neck. The puppet has a look of curiosity and surprise. I have been told by children and adults that it looks life-like, but not like anything identifiable.

I bring this puppet to my school-based counseling groups and the children engage in conversations with it. They don't see me carry it into the therapy room, but when they ask me where it is I take it out of a plastic grocery bag. The children are often very upset with me and are concerned because it can't "breathe."

I invite a child to name it (Hairy is the most common) and I explain that the puppet will "talk" only to me. Children readily accept the reality I have defined. The children can now engage with the puppet while I make the responsive movements. The puppet "talks" in my ear and I communicate what it says to the child. The child is not distracted by my voice or tone as the puppet, and the interaction is away from my face when the child speaks. I can make therapeutic interventions and responses in my own words through what the puppet "tells" me. Because the message comes from the puppet, the relationship between the child and the therapist remains intact.

APPLICATIONS

It is helpful to practice with a puppet in front of a mirror to perfect the moves in the neck and mouth for a more realistic response. This technique encourages children to interact verbally while relating through an animated puppet, with the therapist being the animator. This is particularly helpful with shy children, shamed children, and children who have difficulty speaking directly to adults. Aggressive children can be calmed by communicating with an object that interacts quietly. Children often relate more easily to toys, stuffed animals, and cartoon figures. Using a puppet in this fashion blends the child's comfort level with the therapist's nonintrusive interventions. Both the child and the therapist can have creative fun with a silent puppet.

40

Using a Puppet Show and Photography Together: A Healing Technique

Vivian Gentz

INTRODUCTION

Almost all children enjoy working with puppets and will have a good time giving a puppet show. Because of this, puppets are very effective tools in the treatment of children. Conflicts, feelings, and the relationship issues of children can all be given a safe environment for expression using puppets. Children also experience a sense of control with puppets; this control aids in the mastery of acceptance or letting go of feelings and thoughts that may be causing distress in their lives.

The addition of photographs in the therapeutic use of puppets provides a visual cue, which reinforces and, I believe, amplifies the work accomplished by the child in a puppet show. I use this technique with children ages 5 and older. It appears that children who enjoy this medium or who need some distance between themselves and the problem are good candidates for this technique.

RATIONALE

Children reveal their problem, work through issues, and find new solutions through play. With puppets children can externalize thoughts, feelings, and ways of relating to others. As they engage in this externalizing process, their fear of expressing feelings and thoughts about their reality seems to decrease. With this comfort comes a greater sense of control to pursue a resolution.

Children are capable of projecting themselves psychologically into the drama of the puppet show. They act, think, and feel as if the puppets are alive. A child can be transformed from shy and withdrawn to outspoken and engaged with the aid of a puppet. The child can find his or her "voice."

Puppets provide a safety net for the child. The puppet does the talking and the acting. The story that is told in a puppet show serves as a visual representation of the metaphor that the child can take home. At home, the photograph becomes a way for the child to consciously review the session or to unconsciously revive a visual cue of the therapeutic work. In this way, the therapeutic work continues outside the office and into the child's life and home.

DESCRIPTION

The therapist introduces the idea of a puppet show to the child. If the child decides to perform a show, he or she chooses the audience. The audience can be imaginary, or it can include the therapist only, or it can include some family member(s). Whether this technique is used with a child alone or with a child and others does not seem to reduce the positive effects. The child chooses the puppets for the show from an assortment of puppets and stuffed animals. The child decides on the lighting (spotlight, overhead lights, etc.), and then has a few minutes to think about the story.

The therapist introduces the puppeteer and the show to the audience (real or imaginary), and the child begins the show (which is the therapeutic work). During the puppet show, a therapist can intervene by asking questions. Some children enjoy this interaction, and it is a way to increase the therapeutic value of the process. Other children appear to want to do the show without interruption and this should be respected.

After the puppet show is completed, a photograph is taken of the child with the puppets. Subsequent to the first photograph, it has been my experience that the next time the child will describe what picture is wanted and how he or she wants the photograph staged. Sometimes the child will want more than one picture. This often becomes a negotiation which, of course, is another therapeutic opportunity.

The photograph is dated and numbered by the therapist and given a title by the child. The picture is pasted to a poster board and the child draws a frame around the picture and decorates it. This decorating usually happens at home due to time constraints. The child takes the picture home and displays it in a place where it will be seen often.

The title given the photograph also provides the language for the therapeutic visual cue. One child gave his picture the title "A Problem with Anger and a Solution Is Found." In his show a young lamb found a way to voice hurts and make requests rather than holding issues in until having a big blow up. His picture was of two puppets next to each other holding a flower between them.

APPLICATIONS

This technique works well with many issues. It appears especially helpful for children who have difficulty expressing themselves, who need a buffer between themselves and the issues, or children who have relationship issues.

CASE EXAMPLE

The client was a depressed 8-year-old child. A death had occurred in the family three years prior to the beginning of treatment. For the intervening three years, the mother had been grieving intensely and had been emotionally unavailable to the child. I was working in a nondirective way and the child wanted his mother in the session. She was invited in and the child proceeded to put on a puppet show about a monkey that could not find his mother. The monkey went to many different puppets asking if anyone had seen his mother. No one had seen her. Some puppets said, "We think she is lost." This statement visibly affected the mother. At this point the boy told his mother to pick a puppet. She chose a kangaroo. The monkey said to the kangaroo, "Have you seen my Mom?" and the kangaroo said, "Here I am." The monkey responded with great joy in his voice, "I found her; I found her." The child then had the monkey tell all the other animals that he found the kangaroo. He then went back to the kangaroo and they had a talk.

I took a picture of the two of them with their puppets. The picture was entitled "The Monkey Finds His Mom." The power of this session was the child's ability, through the puppet, to voice his distress at missing his mother while she had been grieving. The mother, with the use of a puppet, was able to speak to this distress and reaffirm that she was still in his life. The picture framed the meeting for the two of them.

In a follow-up I discovered that the mother had wisely purchased monkey and kangaroo puppets. She reported that at times the child wanted the two of them to talk with puppets. She read this action as a way for her child to say it was important that they talk. The photograph was a visual reminder of a healing process that began in a therapeutic session and continued on into the child's home and life.

CONCLUSION

I have learned a great deal from children with this technique. They are very creative in how they can use the puppets together with the visual information from the photographs to help themselves. This technique continues to evolve with the help and hard work of brave children and their families. When therapists are able to witness such a process, children and families are able to grow and change.

41

Parent as Guest Actor or Actress

Jennifer Baggerly

INTRODUCTION

During the later stages of play therapy, many children demonstrate fantasy play through puppets, sand play, or dramatic play (Landreth, 1991). During this fantasy play, children often repeat a story line, indicating a play theme, which reveals significant perceptions, experiences, or traumas of the child (Terr, 1983). In some cases, children may need their parent to witness their story (Allan, 1988). Some children simply want their parent(s) to see their perspective of the situation or they may need their parent(s) to bring resolution to their story. If children request their parent(s) to come to the playroom, then the play therapist facilitates this request by inviting parent(s) to be a "guest" in a play session. The child becomes the director and assigns the parent a role of either audience or actor/actress. By allowing the child to direct the play, the child becomes empowered to determine the outcome of the scenario, thereby bringing about his or her desired resolution.

RATIONALE

Parents are often part of the ongoing healing process after their child has experienced trauma. For example, parents whose children were sexually abused participated in filial therapy and received training and support to conduct weekly play sessions with their children (Costas and Landreth, 1999). Parents significantly increased their empathy and acceptance toward their children while their children's behavioral problems and anxiety tended to decrease when compared to parents and children in the control group.

Given that parents' relationship with their children continues long after play therapy is over, play therapists need methods that will increase parents' supportive interactions with their children. The Parent as Guest Actor or Actress technique will deepen parents' understanding of their children's perception and needs. As a result, parents' empathy toward their children may increase. This technique will also assist the play therapist in understanding children's play scenarios and themes. Because parents have more in-depth knowledge of their children, they may give the play therapist helpful information or a perspective within the "play story" that the therapist may never have recognized without the parents' interpretation.

DESCRIPTION

The play therapist allows the child to lead and offers facilitative responses, such as reflection of content, reflection of feelings, and building of self-esteem. When the child repeats a storyline with puppets, toys, or stage play, the therapist verbalizes the theme using the child's words. For example, consider the following dialogue of a 7-year-old girl who was receiving play therapy after being sexually abused by a stranger. Prior to treatment, the girl was questioned by police during an investigation, which confirmed the abuse. During the session, the girl placed a black hat on her head and a bandana around her neck, placed the handcuffs on the table, and made the following statements.

Child: There was a bad guy running around. The girl was sitting here, and the police thought she was the bad guy and arrested her.

Therapist: The girl was mistaken for a bad guy and sent to jail. The girl looks scared.

Child: She kept saying she wasn't the bad guy, but no one helped her.

Therapist: The girl feels all alone and wants someone to rescue her.

Child: But no one did.

After several sessions of repeating the storyline, children may ask for their parent(s) or someone else to join them in the playroom. If not, the therapist may tentatively ask children if they would like someone else to visit the playroom with them. Children then have the power to either say no, indicating they are not ready for resolution, or they may say yes and specifically name *who they need to be in the play session.*

Therapist: Vicki, if you would like someone to visit the playroom with you, you may invite her or him next time.

Child: I want my mom to come.

The therapist briefs the parent about general themes appearing in the child's play and instructs the parent to follow the child's lead.

Therapist: Mrs. Smith, Vicki would like you to come to the playroom with her next session. This may be a time when she needs you near her or wants you to see something. Lately, a general theme in her play seems to be that she feels misunderstood and needs to be rescued. The important thing for next session is to let her be in the lead, let her direct you, and listen with your eyes and ears. If she asks you to be in a play story, whisper to her, "What should I say or do?"

During the next session, the therapist provides a chair for the parent and proceeds as usual. The child directs the play and the pace, while the therapist reflects feelings, content, and underlying meaning.

Child: Mom, you sit over here and put this jewelry on. A bad guy is running around. The girl was sitting here and the police come and arrest her because they think she is the bad guy.

Therapist: The girl is mistaken for the bad guy. She looks scared. This time there is someone else there.

Child: Now, I'm the judge. Lady, did you see the bad guy running around (to Mom).

Mom: What should I say?

Child: Just say, "Yes, but the girl wasn't the bad guy."

Mom: Yes, I saw the bad guy, but the girl wasn't the bad guy.

Child: The police said this girl, Vicki, was the bad guy.

Mom: That's not the bad guy. That girl's real name is Victoria.

Child: (Smiles broadly.)

Therapist: The girl's so happy! The lady knew the girl's real name and rescued her. The little girl's given name was actually "Victoria" and her mother made the name connection, facilitating a greater healing through the play story.

APPLICATIONS

The Parent as Guest Actor or Actress technique can be used in the later stages of play therapy when the child enters fantasy play and requests his or her parent to come to the playroom. This is particularly helpful for children who have experienced trauma when their parents were not present or not emotionally available, such as in occurrences of sexual abuse, domestic violence, community violence, or natural disaster.

Application of this technique is appropriate for counselors in both mental health agencies and school settings. School counselors may also apply this technique with students' teachers to gain an understanding of classroom dynamics such as punitive teaching methods, peer interactions such as bullying, or academic challenges such as reading difficulties.

Parents and children from culturally diverse populations will also benefit from application of this technique. Struggles with acculturation or racism may be revealed during the play session. Because the parent and child are more culturally similar than are the play therapist and child, the play therapist may gain new awareness of cultural values, beliefs, or rituals that will enhance the child's healing process.

References

Allan, J. (1988). *Inscapes of the Child's World: Jungian Counseling in Schools and Clinics*. Dallas: Spring Publications.

Costas, M. and Landreth, G. (1999). Filial therapy with nonoffending parents of children who have been sexually abused. *International Journal of Play Therapy* 8(1), 43–66.

Landreth, G. (1991). *Play Therapy: The Art of the Relationship*. Muncie, IN: Accelerated Development.

Terr, L. (1983). Play therapy and psychic trauma: A preliminary report. In C. Schaefer and K. O'Connor (Eds.). *Handbook of Play Therapy*. New York: John Wiley and Sons.

42

Problem-solving Play Therapy

Susan M. Swearer

INTRODUCTION

A common issue in conducting therapy with children is that although they may perceive that there is a problem or problems in their lives, they often are ill-equipped to think about and verbalize the actual problem and generate realistic solutions. Therefore, problem-solving play therapy is designed to help children learn effective steps to solve their problems. Problem solving helps children take control over the problematic situation and empowers children to think of solutions to their problems. A cognitive-behavioral approach to teaching these steps through the use of puppets, dolls, and other play therapy materials is used (Knell, 1993). The steps are taught through the acronym "POWER." The five steps are:

1. *P*roblem?
2. *O*ptions?
3. *W*hich option is best?
4. *E*xecute the option.
5. *R*ate. Did it work?

RATIONALE

Problem-solving skills are designed to help children improve their means-end thinking, impulse control, and to engage in systematic problem solving (Braswell and Bloomquist, 1991). Problem-solving skills have been used with children experiencing both externalizing disorders such as attention deficit/hyperactivity disorder (Braswell and Bloomquist, 1991) and conduct disorder (Horne and Sayger, 1990), and internalizing disorders such as depression (Stark, 1990) and anxiety (Kendall, 1992). The problem-solving strategy is one that has been widely utilized in the treatment literature on children and adolescents. The application of problem solving to play therapy allows children to practice and enact solutions to problems that they may be experiencing. Problem-solving play therapy encourages children to use the play materials to enact problems that they may encounter in their daily lives.

DESCRIPTION

The therapist introduces the acronym "POWER" using puppets, dolls, or other play materials that the child chooses. The acronym "POWER" and the steps are listed on an index card that the child can see. This process can be introduced to the child as described:

Therapist: We are going to put on a puppet show with these puppets. These puppets are having a problem and we're going to help them figure out what to do. How does that sound?

Child: Okay.

Therapist: This puppet (female character) is having a problem because her friend (female character) won't talk to her. She wonders what the problem is and says, "This is a good time to use my POWER." What is the first step that the puppet says?

Child: She wonders what the problem is.

Therapist: Great! She says, "What's the problem?" It seems like the problem is that my friend won't talk to me when I ask her a question. What is the next step the puppet can ask herself?

Child: What are my options?

Therapist: Great! What are my options? Well, I could ask my friend what's wrong. Or, I could ask my friend if she wants to eat lunch with me. I could leave her alone because maybe she wants to be left alone. Or, I could ask the teacher what to do. What is the next step the puppet should do?

Child: She should ask herself, "Which option is best?"

Therapist: Great! Which option do you think the puppet should choose?

Child: I think she should leave her friend alone for a little while and then go and ask her if everything is okay.

Therapist: What's the next step the puppet should do?

Child: She should execute her option.

Therapist: The puppet is leaving her friend alone and then goes up to her and asks her if she's okay. What do you think will happen?

Child: I think her friend will talk with her because she gave her some space and now she's feeling better.

Therapist: So, what's the last step that the puppet should do?

Child: Rate the option and see how it worked.

Therapist: Do you think it will work?

Child: Yep, because now they're friends again.

APPLICATIONS

Problem solving can be applied to most situations in a child's life. Problems can be social in nature (i.e., problems with peers, teachers, or parents) and problems can be internal in nature (i.e., feelings of sadness, frustration, anger, or disappointment). Problem solving can be used when the child anticipates that a problem may occur or in response to a problem that has occurred. Children can be taught the five problem-solving steps in play therapy through a more directive modality through which the therapist prompts the child to describe the five POWER steps (as delineated previously). Through practice and repetition, children internalize the steps. The goal is to have children use the steps as they are enacting problems with the play materials or the therapist. We want children to be able to cue themselves by stating, "This might be a good time to use my POWER" and then use the five problem-solving steps to engage in solution-oriented thinking and behaving.

References

Braswell, L. and Bloomquist, M. L. (1991). *Cognitive-Behavioral Therapy with ADHD Children: Child, Family, and School Interventions*. New York: The Guilford Press.

Horne, A. M. and Sayger, T. V. (1990). *Treating Conduct and Oppositional Defiant Disorders in Children*. New York: Pergamon Press.

Kendall, P. C. (1992). *Anxiety Disorders in Youth: Cognitive-Behavioral Interventions*. Needham Heights, MA: Allyn and Bacon.

Knell, S. M. (1993). *Cognitive-Behavioral Play Therapy*. Northvale, NJ: Jason Aronson Inc.

Stark, K. D. (1990). *Childhood Depression: School-Based Intervention*. New York: The Guilford Press.

Section Three

Storytelling

43

The Talking Stick Totem: A Family Play Therapy Technique for Teaching Listening, Witnessing, and Speaking Your Truth

Deborah Armstrong Hickey

INTRODUCTION

The Talking Stick is an ancient tool that has been used by many indigenous communities around the world, Aboriginal and Native American in particular. The Talking Stick has been used for decision making in groups; expressing grievances in such a way that all voices are honored and listening is privileged; and as a ritualized way for a community to entertain themselves through storytelling.

In the Aboriginal tradition the Talking Stick was primarily a tool for healing relationships through learning to listen to others and to speak your truth (Forest and Pearpoint, 2000). Native Americans used the Talking Stick in a similar manner, usually in a council meeting, and according to the Indigenous American tradition, the stick was "imbued with spiritual qualities, that called up the spirit of their ancestors to guide them in making good decisions" (Fujioka, 2000).

In all of these traditions, the stick ensured that everyone within the community had an opportunity to speak their truth, without interruption, until completed, along with ensuring that the community in witness was listening. Everyone in the circle was valued and all voices were privileged.

There are and were rules about using the Talking Stick in that, "Whoever holds the Talking Stick has within his hands the power of words. Only he can speak while he holds the stick and the other council members must remain silent. The Eagle feather tied to the stick gives him the courage and wisdom to speak truthfully and wisely. The rabbit fur on the end of the stick reminds him that his words must come from his heart" (Locust, 1998).

RATIONALE

A common challenge in working with families is ensuring that everyone has an opportunity to speak and be heard, along with influencing those who are not speaking to listen and refrain from interrupting the person who is speaking. The Talking Stick is an excellent method to use when conducting a family play therapy session.

Younger children, in particular, can benefit from the concrete cue that a Talking Stick provides in learning to be silent and listen to others, *and* other family members benefit from the unspoken message that the Talking Stick embodies—that every voice is important and that everyone deserves to be heard.

The manner in which the Talking Stick is used also introduces a ritual-like structure for coming together and sharing in a way that is deeply respectful. Creating a Talking Stick can enhance the process of using this technique in family play therapy also, with each individual adorning the stick with objects and symbols that represent themselves and how they wish to be in the family.

The Talking Stick can be used in a family play therapy session specifically to introduce a way to share with one another or it can be used intermittently when issues that have arisen in session require everyone's voice to be heard. The family can make a Talking Stick and use it in sessions, or take it home and use one that the therapist has in his or her office.

DESCRIPTION

The therapist may want to introduce the family to the use of a Talking Stick early on in family sessions as a way to set guidelines for ensuring that everyone has an opportunity to speak, and everyone who is not speaking knows that they are to listen and not interrupt. The therapist may introduce the Talking Stick through a story or just simply explaining it as "a tool for ensuring that everyone has an equal opportunity to listen and be listened to."

Although it is important that the therapist have a Talking Stick in his or her office (can be bought or made), it is often fun for families to create one for themselves in a session. The therapist should have a wide variety of materials, preferably those from nature (such as stones and leaves), glue, and several sticks for the family to choose from. If possible, making sure that there is a feather (the courage and wisdom to speak truthfully as an eagle) and some soft fur (the holding an open heart and speaking from the heart as a rabbit might) enrich the symbolism of the stick. Families can also be invited to find their own stick and bring objects that represent themselves individually on the stick. This is a wonderful way to personalize the stick.

It will likely take the family an entire session to make their Talking Stick. The therapist can observe the manner in which decisions are made, who listens, who talks, and can reflect on these observations to the family in preparation for their using the Talking Stick. An example might be, "I notice that when Dawn was talking, no one was listening. It'll be important for everyone to listen to her when she has the stick."

In session the therapist can routinely bring the Talking Stick out when the family begins to share together. The therapist can also bring it out when it seems as if essential issues are being shared, family members are interrupting and not listening, or the therapist has the impression that a family member wants to be heard and for some reason *isn't* being heard. It is also important to note that sharing is entirely a choice, though listening is required. The therapist can teach about using "I" messages and help the family to communicate assertively as they become familiar with using the Talking Stick.

APPLICATIONS

This technique can be used with families, couples, and groups. This technique can be introduced as a family begins the process of therapy, although the therapist may choose to wait until they have some understanding of the family's more typical style of communication. Each individual therapist should determine any kind of limit setting he or she might prefer if a family does not respect the guidelines of using the Talking Stick. It is, however, recommended that the Talking Stick be removed when the guidelines are not followed (interruptions in particular).

References

Forest, M. and Pearpoint, J. (2000). *The Talking Stick Reflections: An Exercise in Listening*. www.inclusion.com/tools.2000.

Fujioka, Kimberly. The Internet TESL Journal. *The Talking Stick: An American Indian Tradition in the ESL Classroom*. Vol. IV. No. 9, September 1998.

Locust, C. (1998). *The Talking Stick*. www.acaciart.com/stories/archives.2000.

Talking Stick: Journal of the Native American Educational Trust. (1997, 2000.)

44

The Stretching Story

Jeffrey S. Ashby, Shane Blasko, Linda Pak Bruner, and Jim Martin

INTRODUCTION

The Stretching Story combines movement with shared storytelling to engage a child in therapy. In a nutshell, it involves the play therapist and the child taking turns telling parts of a story and simultaneously acting it out. It is a flexible technique amenable to a variety of theoretical approaches. Sharing this activity can aid the therapist in making a connection with the child, while the enactment process provides a safe therapeutic distance between the child and the material of the emerging narrative. Children can frequently disclose uncomfortable feelings or experiences readily through the Stretching Story technique.

RATIONALE

Engaging a child in therapy is a common goal for play therapists. The Stretching Story can foster the development of a therapeutic relationship between the play therapist and the child. The process of the therapist and the child doing the same movements at the same time and sharing the storytelling facilitate a sense of connection. The Stretching Story also encourages the child to communicate freely, while focusing on the tasks of telling the story and acting out the movements of the character(s). The physical process of enacting the story appears to be less threatening than simply asking the child to tell a story. The distraction provided by the enactment may lower a child's inhibition and reduce any tendency to censor the story he or she is telling. The technique's open-ended format invites the child to create personally meaningful storylines. The content of these stories often reflects the child's perception of significant relationships and important underlying issues in his or her life. Play therapists further benefit from the open-ended format because it provides sufficient flexibility to adapt the activity to a variety of theoretical orientations.

The therapist is presented with numerous opportunities to model a variety of appropriate behaviors, responses, and interactional styles. Sharing the story back and forth models appropriate turn-taking behavior and fosters power-sharing between the child and the therapist. Humor and fun encourage the child to engage in the process. As the therapist dramatically or humorously acts out the narrative, the child sometimes feels less self-conscious about enacting his or her part of the story. Such behavior may lessen the power differential in the relationship and deepen the therapeutic alliance.

DESCRIPTION

This technique works best when the child and play therapist stand facing one another. The therapist begins by explaining to the child that they are going to take turns telling a story together, which they will act out as they go. He or she explains that the person doing the talking also decides how to act out that part of the story, while the person doing the listening copies the actions of the talker. The therapist begins the story, physically miming the action, while the child mimics the therapist's movements. After a few lines, the therapist passes the story to the child, using a transitional phrase such as, "and then . . . ," which allows the child to pick up the thread and continue the story. The story is passed back and forth until it reaches its conclusion. The play therapist can use his or her storytelling turn to change subject matter, move the plot forward, incorporate socially appropriate problem-solving strategies, model social skills, or end the story on a positive note.

The following is an example of how a Stretching Story might begin:

Therapist: We're going to tell a stretching story. I'll start the story and act out what I'm saying. While I'm telling my part of the story, you do what I do, and then we'll switch. When you're telling your part of the story, I'll do what you do. I'll pass the story to you by saying "and then . . ." When you want me to tell the story again, you can pass the story back to me by saying "and then." Let's give it a try.

Therapist: One morning a little mouse woke up, yawned, and stretched his little arms way over his head. *(The therapist pretends to yawn mightily. As the child pretends to yawn, the therapist reaches high over his or her head and spreads his or her arms wide in a stretching motion; the child stretches too).* And then he rubbed his eyes, got out of bed, and went to brush his teeth. *(The therapist mimes these movements and allows the child to mimic each of the behaviors before moving on with the story).* And then . . .

Child: And then he got dressed and grabbed his skateboard and ran outside. *(The child mimes getting dressed, picking something off of the ground, and running in place; the therapist enthusiastically copies the child's actions).* And then . . .

They continue to pass the story back and forth. If the child forgets to pass the story back, the therapist can encourage appropriate turn-taking and power-sharing by asking in an exaggerated stage whisper, "When is it my turn?"

APPLICATIONS

This technique can be useful with children of any age. In the early stages of therapy, it can help to engage the child in the therapeutic relationship. It encourages the child to communicate verbally with the therapist in a manner that is fun. Once a therapeutic relationship is established, the technique can be used to facilitate deeper self-disclosure.

If the therapist and the child have used this activity before, the therapist can suggest that the child begin the story this time. This can be used as a vehicle to help the child introduce and explore current issues.

This activity can also be used in play therapy groups, with participants standing in a circle facing each other. The story is passed around the circle with all of the members mimicking the actions of the storyteller. Used in this group format, the activity can enhance a child's sense of appropriate empowerment and foster a sense of connection with other group members through universality.

45

Working with a Child's Dream

Melissa V. Bush

INTRODUCTION

Telling a dream is one way of learning about the inner and outer worlds of a child. Without any prompting, a child may spontaneously tell the therapist a dream during a session. The therapist should be receptive to such an event and not be fearful that dreamwork with a child is too complicated and scary. Dreams after all are normal events experienced by all humans and are nature's way of helping us deal with events of the day. Even though dreams are nightly events, many people don't remember dreaming. People need help in learning to catch a dream by developing a mindset to write the content in a journal each morning. Usually, this needs to happen before the dreamer steps out of bed because a dream is illusive and will disappear from memory. The child may be encouraged to write down a dream to be shared with the family at the breakfast table helping conversation skills or writing the dream for writing skills. The most important benefit is to help the child slow down and become more conscious in this hurried and stressful world we live in.

RATIONALE

Paying attention to a dream is an important way for the therapist to understand the innermost feelings of a child. Dreams often tell what is really going on inside of a child. Because dreams come while a child is sleeping, they may represent unguarded emotions not screened by the conscious mind. For example, when a child dreams of grizzly bears it may be obvious that bears represent an argumentative family with loud growls. Dreaming of a garden with hundreds of different flowers may be a healing dream that follows a trauma that has been worked through. Dreams can be scary (nightmares) or humorous, remedial or simply creatively expressing the day's events. Only the dreamer knows for sure. Often, it is not necessary to fully understand a dream because the child is experiencing the dream naturally and is engaged in a healing process whether the therapist analyzes the dream or not. It is best not to interfere with the process and follow the child as a kind, safe, listening ear.

DESCRIPTION

The child tells the therapist the dream. This may be spontaneous or in response to a request. Do you have a dream to share? The therapist is attentive and listens to the dream. The therapist may ask for clarification on some points and may ask a few questions. How many trees did you say you saw in the forest? What feelings did you have in the forest? Some possible responses are: What does the dream mean to you? Were you scared? If affect is readily displayed, then the therapist may wish to reflect the child's feeling, such as "The forest felt really scary."

The therapist offers the child an activity. The activity chosen gives the child personal space to explore the dream for meaning or to delight in appreciation of the dream. Sandtray, art, journaling, or sculpting clay are a few examples of an activity.

CASE EXAMPLE

A 12-year-old girl dreamed of a scary man dressed in black who was laughing and laughing at her. After telling the dream, the girl started crying. The therapist simply reflected her feelings by saying this dream was scary for her. This girl then chose the sandbox to work on her feelings, and she made a tray with one little lamb placed in the middle of the box. She did not comment on the dream itself, but hypothesized that the nightmare showed the magnitude of her fear and that she felt hopeless about any relief. Because her father had died in an unexpected accident, the therapist wondered if she felt vulnerable, scared of death, or fearful of losing her mother.

The therapist witnessed the picture in the sandtray and asked the girl what her picture meant. This little girl said that she was the lamb and that she was scared and alone. The therapist may reflect the child's feeling, take a picture of the scene, and invite the child to come again to share more feelings. The therapist should be careful not to interpret the sandtray but to accept it as a whole with no judgment.

The therapist may hypothesize some ideas about the girl's situation:

1. The child is scared, alone, and lacking support.
2. The child is grieving her father's death, which occurred one year ago.
3. The mother had just started dating, which may have triggered abandonment issues. This explains why the child may have felt like a vulnerable little lamb, scared she could lose her mother as well.
4. The child will need to grieve, feel comfort from her mother, learn to relax and reconnect with her peer group, and find her life again.

Dreams may set the emotional tone for therapy by highlighting the most basic issue. If parents or caretakers are available, they may be invited to participate in the session learning parenting skills that would make a difference. For example, this mother learned to comfort her child instead of getting angry when it was time for her to go out for the evening. Comforting and discussing feelings as a family are important during the grieving process.

Future sessions will be determined by tracking the child's healing process in the playroom. Tracking is important because it allows the child to share what he or she felt each time and gives the child an opportunity to display externally what is going on. The therapist serves as a witness, and as sessions continue, the parent(s) are supported and taught ways to deal with the healing process for the whole family and not just for the child. Working with dreams may also be used as a creative means to express ideas and feelings with art, sand, creative movement, or sculpting.

46

Sharing Beauty To Enliven the Spirit

Vivian Gentz

INTRODUCTION

I have been treating families, including children, for more than 20 years. In that time I have come to appreciate both the complexity and the simplicity of the healing process that I have witnessed in clients. This article is not about the complexity of healing—it is limited to the simplicity of using beauty as one ingredient in healing the soul so that the human spirit is more accessible for living and growth.

Children appreciate beauty and they enjoy sharing what they consider to be beautiful with others. As I have watched children notice and share beauty over the years, I am always in awe as I see eyes that were dull begin to sparkle, faces that were sad acquire a smile, and the spirit of a child begin to blossom. The Sharing Beautiful Things technique has a significant place in the healing process.

RATIONALE

In his book *Care of the Soul,* Thomas Moore offers the idea that our particular society seems to believe that we "can't live without technology, but we can live without beauty." He contends that as we move further toward this belief we lose our understanding of what the soul really needs. He continues to say, "The soul is nurtured by beauty. What food is to the body, . . . pleasing images are to the soul" (p. 278).

The January/February 2001 issue of the *Networker* magazine (pp. 31–35) included an article entitled "Beauty Resurrected—Awakening Wonder in the Consulting Room" by Michael Ventura. He offers the idea that "beauty has not still been sufficiently recognized as both a healing balm and a necessity" (p. 33). In a workshop I attended, Mark Barnes, Ph.D., an international play therapist, suggested that healing does not occur around words. He feels that healing occurs below the jaw. Drawing a child's attention to a visual experience with the Sharing Beautiful Things technique can stimulate this kind of healing. Children can usually point out what they consider beautiful. Their art reflects this beauty—rainbows, flowers, the sun, trees, birds, animals, and so forth. The Sharing Beautiful Things technique draws on this natural ability of children.

DESCRIPTION

The therapist introduces the idea of sharing beautiful things by telling a story such as *The Crystal Ball* by Gerda Marie Scheidl. This is the story of a giant and a town healed by the gift of a beautiful crystal ball. The therapist can then show the child several kaleidoscopes to choose from and ask the child to look into the kaleidoscope and find an image he or she thinks is beautiful and then share it with the therapist. When the image is shared, the therapist can make simple comments such as "You found a beautiful one" and make eye contact if possible. Then the therapist finds a beautiful image in the kaleidoscope and shares the beauty with the child. The process moves back and forth in this way.

Another version of this technique is to go for a walk with a child and have similar exchanges. The therapist and the child can see and breathe in the beauty of a tree, a flower, and so on. After a walk, a child may have a picture taken of him- or herself with something beautiful found on the walk. Then the child can take the picture home. He or she can draw a picture and make a book of a beautiful thing seen on the walk. Sometimes I suggest a child notice beautiful things during the week and tell me about them the next week or share the beauty with someone else between our visits.

APPLICATIONS

This technique can work well as a way of establishing rapport and increasing engagement. Children aged 4 and older seem to enjoy this technique. Anxious children can use this to calm down, and depressed children can use it to expand a bleak world. It can be helpful in shifting negative parent-child interaction patterns in the direction of more positive engagement. I often utilize this method at the end of a grieving process. Beauty helps to heal the heart and soul, and with healing, the spirit of the child emerges.

CASE EXAMPLE

The client was a depressed 7 year old who had experienced domestic violence in his home. He was struggling with identifying with the aggressor and acting out in anger with family members and peers. After expressing anger, he would often cry. His caretaker was beginning to describe him in negative terms such as *angry, defiant,* and *uncooperative*. In his play, this boy expressed a world of hurt and mistrust. He worked to gain control over the experiences locked in his body that told of a home life filled with fear.

I utilized the Sharing Beautiful Things technique to help him calm down and to get him engaged with others in a positive way. After beginning this technique, I used it thereafter for five minutes during every session. Sometimes he would ask to take a walk and look for beautiful things.

When I incorporated the technique with his parent present, I used the kaleidoscope. They shared beautiful images and a shift within this child began, which opened him to a more positive engagement with his parent and helped his mother to view him as a vulnerable boy. This child looked forward to the kaleidoscope-sharing with his parent. It was noteworthy to me that this mother became teary when her son first showed her an image. Often this happens as the parent softens when a sparkle is seen in the child's eye. The parents are touched and the child's spirit emerges.

CONCLUSION

This technique is one way to open a space so that children can begin to experience the beauty in life and heal their hurts. When beauty is seen, heard, felt, and touched, the body takes in life's natural healing force. If I felt sad as a child, my mother would suggest we go for a walk and that I feel the air on my face, see the beauty of the trees and flowers, let my feet connect with the earth, and she told me that I would feel better. To this day it works for me. Beauty feeds the soul.

References

Moore, T. (1992). *Care of the Soul.* New York: HarperCollins.

Scherdl, G. M. (1993). *The Crystal Ball.* New York: North-South.

Ventura, M. (2001, January/February). Beauty Resurrected—Awakening Wonder in the Consulting Room. *Family Therapy Networker,* 31–35.

47

Where Am I? The Effects of Immigration on Children

Diana P. Malca

INTRODUCTION

Each one of us has met at least one person who is not a native in this country. The following article teaches how to develop a personalized story for children who have emigrated and are in the process of acculturating and adapting. People have left their families, homes, business, and culture—almost always—for the sake of safety and better opportunities. Migration does not always entail moving from one country to another; it can also include moving within the same country and sometimes even within the same city or state.

Thousands of people migrate from day to day. Among them are thousands of children. The effect and impact it has on children is extensive.

RATIONALE

Home—Where It All Begins

The support commences at home and carries through to counselors and educators. The latter have a central role in helping children achieve a smooth adaptation. Successful adaptation to a new country requires certain prerequisites of the family. The primary and most important condition is the support and understanding of the people in touch with an immigrant child.

The Effect of Immigration on Children

Loss is the principal concept of immigration. Immigration does not entail a single loss. As previously mentioned, a culture, language, rites, as well as friends, families, and home are part of the "package deal." Normal reactions to loss include pain, sadness, fear, anger, excitement, acceptance, and for some children some age regression (reassuming developmental stages, such as toilet training, sleeping with parents, wanting to be fed, etc.).

DESCRIPTION

The Story: "Grand"

The following story was written for a very special child. He recently migrated from Colombia due to the political situation and lack of safety. This child has endured great losses: leaving his family, friends, environment, language, culture, and home.

The introduction of the story sets the stage to introduce the child. In the following story the airplane represents the child. The character is chosen according to the child's favorite toys, animals, or characters. For example, if a child's favorite animal is the horse, then the main character of the story is a horse. The name of the character is chosen by a certain quality the child has that begins with the same letter as his or her name.

The middle of the story represents the conflict or problem the child is dealing with. In the story, the storm represents the danger and the circumstances of escape that the family went through. The weird noises are the language.

The end of the story brings the resolution, how the solution was accomplished and its outcome. In the following story this was achieved through introducing the capacity that all humans have to communicate regardless of language barriers. The story is effective when it is concise and concrete.

"Grand"

Not long ago, in a nearby land, there was a town. This town was very beautiful because it was surrounded by mountains and crossed by a river. The mountains were seen from anywhere in town, and the stream of the river was heard from any place in the valley. A small airport was located on the outskirts of the valley. In the airport there were many airplanes that were all cared for by the airport personnel. The people who worked there gave names to the airplanes according to their capacities. "Grand" was a small plane that was white and had green stripes around it. Inside it was red and the chairs not only were beautiful but they were very comfortable. The people who flew on this plane felt safe and relaxed inside. "Grand" really knew how to fly and maneuver his engine. Often he would help other planes in difficult tasks, such as flying over rocky mountains and landing in small places. "Grand" was named for his ability to excel himself as a small aircraft. One Day, a big storm was approaching town. Most citizens found shelter and a place to hide. Even the airplanes were secured under a roof that was protective from the lightning and striking thunders. However, this storm was known to be a long one—at least for twenty-four consecutive full moons. The people and the airplanes were feeling bored and angry for having to be locked up for so long. The airplanes wanted to fly and see the blue sky; the people wanted to leave their shelters to see their families and friends. The people in the small valley were feeling discouraged and sad.

As the storm was gaining strength, the management of the airport called it an emergency situation and it was treated as such. The airplanes were to transfer to another country where they could be safer. "Grand" was among the chosen ones to move to a new place. A bigger place, without so many storms. . . .

"Grand" moved to a new airport that was as big as his town. The signs were written in a foreign language and it was almost impossible to understand where he should go. In this new city, there were neither mountains nor little airplanes, or so it seemed that way.

"Grand" felt lonely and terribly scared. His fear was seen through his rough flying and risk-taking. He would fly as high as he could and then land so rapidly that it would stop anyone's breathing for a few moments. "Grand" also felt angry for being forced to leave his airport. The other airplanes would communicate with each other in strange sounds that were unintelligible.

One day on a routine flight, "Grand" saw that a small aircraft was coughing smoke in the air. "Grand" alerted the authorities by making signs in the air. He flew up and down, made wide loops in the air, and then sank as if falling. The authorities noticed that this was a cry for help. They flew closely to the small aircraft and were able to help him land safely. People in the airport were impressed and happy to notice that language was not a barrier to help someone in need.

As time passed by, "Grand" learned to make the "weird" noises and connect with others. He also noticed that he was not the only small aircraft from a faraway country. Many others were coming to this airport to make it a new home far from the danger that storms brought to their countries.

"Grand" and his new friends learned that they can always remember their country and feel that they now belong to two countries instead of one. They taught each other things from their own country and learned to fly with each other, blending in the sky.

Just like the clouds blend so perfectly with the sky . . . always moving on. . . .

APPLICATIONS

A story is powerful when it is personalized so that it fits the child's individual needs. Following the guidelines, counselors, in conjunction with parents, may apply their own stories to their children according to their history and needs.

This technique may be applied to an array of presenting problems, whether it is anxiety, depression, or self-esteem issues. The story should be specifically tailored for the child with his own story—only metaphorically told.

48

The Door to a Special Place

Tracy C. Leinbaugh

INTRODUCTION

Children enjoy fantasy for the entertainment value and because it arouses their curiosity. They also enjoy attention and will often talk freely, combining fantasy and reality to tell a story, when provided encouragement and the undivided attention of a trusted adult. Children's stories may be used not only to stimulate their imagination, but also to develop the intellect and to clarify emotions. Because children lack the formal thinking skills and verbal skills of adults, they can communicate their thoughts, feelings, and expectations by acting out their fantasies (Thompson and Rudolph, 2000). Story plots and characters have been found to parallel events in children's lives (Kestenbaum, 1985). When attuned to their anxieties and aspirations, children's stories give full recognition to their difficulties, suggesting solutions and promoting confidence (Bettleheim, 1975).

RATIONALE

Children, much more than adults, live in the present. Fantasy and storytelling can act as a vehicle to bring past experiences into the present in a nonthreatening manner, provided the opportunity for the child to explore and develop more adaptive coping abilities. Children's stories can help them cope with feelings, thoughts, and behaviors they are not ready to discuss directly with the counselor.

DESCRIPTION

A picture of a wooden door set in a stone wall is hung on the inside of the office door or someplace on the wall where it can be easily seen (see figure 48.1). It can be merely a line-drawing on white paper, but a more colorful, elaborate picture may be more helpful in exciting the child and stimulating his or her imagination.

The picture can be drawn with colored pencils, markers, or crayons, or painted on the unwaxed side of a large piece of butcher paper. It may be more helpful to the child who is resistant or has difficulty with the process of imagining that he or she is going through a door to another place if the drawing more closely approximates the size of a real door. Drawing the wall in which the door is located partially covered with ivy and partially hidden by large shrubs lends an air of secrecy to it. The door is drawn partially open, inviting the child to open it wider and enter in order to see what is behind it.

The therapist shows the child the door to a special place and explains to the child that this is a very special place that is different for every person. It can be inside or out, large or small, populated by various animals and creatures, filled with magic and adventure, or peaceful and quiet. One never knows until one steps inside.

The therapist then invites the child to draw a picture of him- or herself that can be pinned or otherwise attached to the door. The self-portrait becomes the character who enters the secret place, if the child chooses. In this way the fantasy can be extended for additional counseling sessions, with the character removed from the door and folded or rolled up and stored safely until the next time. This way the character is not left in possibly dangerous situations in the story, which may increase the child's anxiety, but is always protected.

In addition, the child can add accessories to the character if he or she feels something is needed, increasing the child's feeling of control.

The character, once attached to the door, is invited to enter the secret place and describe what he or she sees. Then the child, as the character, is invited to walk around and explore and tell the therapist his or her experiences.

Figure 48.1

At the end of the time allotted for the storytelling, the child is informed that he or she must leave the special place, but the invitation is extended to return at a later session if desired. This brings a sense of closure to the story, which will alleviate anxiety that may have been created and increase a sense of control and mastery over the situation.

APPLICATIONS

This technique can be useful for children who have experienced events that have generated feelings that the child is unable or unwilling to express. It is particularly helpful in facilitating a sense of control and mastery in children who are fearful and withdrawn, because they can develop more adaptive behavior without the anxiety of direct confrontation.

The counselor using short-term counseling may facilitate the process by using the following four steps: (1) define the problem, (2) explore what was done by the character to solve it, (3) explore new things that could be done to solve it, (4) encourage the child to have the character try one of the new strategies. This technique may effect behavior change in a short period of time.

References

Bettleheim, B. (1975). *The Uses of Enchantment: The Meaning and Importance of Fairy Tales*. New York: Random House.

Kestenbaum, C. J. (1985). The creative process in child psychotherapy. *American Journal of Psychotherapy* 39, 479–489.

Thompson, C. L. and Rudolph, L. B. (2000). *Counseling Children (5th ed.)*. Belmont, CA: Brooks/Cole.

49

The Dramatic Retelling of Stories in Play Therapy

Shelley A. Jackson

INTRODUCTION

Since 1916 when Samuel Crothers created the term *bibliotherapy*, books have been used therapeutically (Pardeck, 1994). *Webster's Third New International Dictionary of the English Language* (1961) defined *bibliotherapy* as "guidance in the solution of personal problems through directed reading." Counselors often use children's literature to help clients in therapeutic ways. For example, counselors may use bibliotherapy: (1) to provide information about problems, (2) to provide insight into problems, (3) to stimulate discussion about problems, (4) to communicate new values and attitudes, (5) to create an awareness that others have dealt with similar problems, and (6) to provide solutions to problems (Pardeck, 1994). The dramatic retelling of stories is a bibliotherapy technique that can be incorporated into play therapy. The dramatic retelling of stories can provide an avenue for the play therapist to explore various feelings and emotions, to explore possible solutions to problems, and to explore alternative ways of being with the child.

RATIONALE

Literary critics and theorists agree that literature contains thousands of years of stories and emotions about families and society and, therefore, can be a useful therapeutic tool. These formalized and consensual assumptions of everyday family life contained in children's literature are invaluable to the play therapist. Children's literature becomes a helpful tool for the play therapist to explore and demonstrate alternative ways of being with and relating to children. The dramatic retelling of stories allows children the opportunity to role play and investigate how things can be different in the characters' lives as well as their own lives. While retelling the story, through play activities children can be encouraged to try on new behaviors, to explore possible new endings, to find other solutions, and to become the heroes of their own stories.

DESCRIPTION

The dramatic retelling session begins with the shared reading of a children's book by the therapist and the child. Look for books that match the child's interests and developmental age. Annotated bibliographies may be helpful when beginning the dramatic retelling of stories. Annotated bibliographies provide detailed descriptions of books appropriate to address specific problems. Pardeck and Markward (1995), for example, provide therapists with annotated bibliographies for the following topics: alcohol and drugs, anger and other emotions, attitudes and values, child abuse, family breakdown, family struggles, fear and fantasy, peers and school, self-image and sex roles, sex education, and special developmental needs. After reading the book with the child introduce one of the following dramatic retelling activities:

1. Have the child take the part of a character in the book and role play a favorite scene.
2. Ask the child to write or record on a cassette a different ending for the story and then draw pictures to illustrate the story.
3. Ask the child to write a letter to one of the characters in the book and talk about how they are alike and different.
4. Have the child make puppets and act out a favorite part of the story.

5. Provide clothing and props that fit the theme of the book and observe the plot unfold as the child plays.
6. Ask the child to write a song or poem that the character would sing.

Next, connect the child's general real-life experience to the book by helping the child make connections between his or her behavior, actions, and feelings with the characters in the book. The following specific questions may be asked:

1. Do you ever feel or wish that you were like that?
2. If you were that character, what would you do (think, wish for)?
3. What do you do when you feel like the character in the book?
4. Do you wish you could act that way?
5. Tell me about a time when you felt that way.

APPLICATIONS

This technique is helpful with all children, but especially with shy or disruptive children. Often these children have been labeled early in their school career and have a designated reputation to live up to. The dramatic retelling of stories can be especially helpful for these children because it facilitates the creation of alternative stories, helping them experience themselves in more positive ways.

CASE EXAMPLE

Sergio was referred to counseling by his first-grade teacher, who was concerned because of Sergio's lack of participation in class activities. The teacher stated that Sergio often refused to participate in activities and would often retreat to his seat and put his head down. Sergio lived with both his mother and father and a 10-year-old brother. Sergio came to the playroom apprehensively and when instructed that he "could do almost anything in the playroom" chose to sit at the small table and stated that he didn't know what to do. During these first sessions with Sergio, the counselor struggled to establish a relationship with him by being nondirective and reflecting his apprehension of the playroom and the therapist. Sergio appeared a frightened, lonely child who was unable to make even the simplest decision. During the fourth session, the book *Donna O'Neeshuck Was Chased by Some Cows* by Bill Grossman was introduced in which Donna, a young girl, is chased through a town by cows, moose, geese, sows, and a host of others. Donna finally stops and turns around to face the animals and discovers that they are all chasing her for a pat on the head. After reading the book with Sergio, I asked him to use puppets to retell the story. He then wrote a letter to Donna about how he and she were alike. On a large piece of paper, Sergio wrote, "I would run away." Sergio and I discussed what Donna had learned about the animals when she stopped and turned around. I asked Sergio if we could act that out. He agreed and wanted to be Donna and I was to play the animals. He told me to chase him around the room, and when he stopped and turned around he told me to pat him on the head. Using the dramatic retelling of stories with Sergio in play therapy facilitated his engagement and participation in the therapy process and allowed him the opportunity to discover a new ending to his own fear.

Play therapists can encourage the use of bibliotherapy and the dramatic retelling of stories by having literature and creative art materials available for clients. Using familiar literature the therapist may reorient and re-educate the child. Careful selection and presentation of books is extremely important. The dramatic retelling of stories provides the play therapist with a powerful tool to use with children.

References

Grossman, B. A. (1991). *Donna O'Neeshuck Was Chased by Some Cows*. New York: HarperCollins.

Pardeck, J. T. (1994). Using literature to help adolescents cope with problems. *Adolescence* 29, 421–427.

Pardeck, J. T. and Markward, M. J. (1995). Bibliotherapy: Using books to help children deal with problems. *Early Child Development and Care* 106, 75–90.

Webster's Third New International Dictionary of the English Language. (1961).

50

Mutual Storytelling, Adlerian Style

Terry Kottman

INTRODUCTION

Mutual storytelling was originally introduced by Gardner (1986). In Gardner's version of the technique, the therapist asks the child to tell a story (with a beginning, a middle, and an end). The therapist listens to the story using a psychodynamic framework to conceptualize the client and his or her situation as metaphorically represented in the narrative. The therapist then retells the story using the same characters, setting, and problem situations as the original story, but with a different ending that would represent a more psychodynamically balanced worldview and problem resolution.

I have adapted and extended Gardner's technique, focusing on using storytelling in play therapy and using an Adlerian conceptualization of the story (Kottman, 1995; Kottman and Stiles, 1990; Stiles and Kottman, 1990). I ask the child to use dolls, puppets, or other play materials to tell a story, pretending that the play materials can talk.

As I listen to the story, I conceptualize the child and his or her problem situation from an Adlerian perspective, using concepts such as goals of misbehavior (Dinkmeyer and McKay, 1989; Dreikurs and Soltz, 1964; Kottman, 1995) and the Crucial Cs (Kottman, 1999; Lew and Bettner, 1996,

1998). According to Adlerian theory, all behavior is purposive. Adlerians believe that children who are misbehaving are striving toward four main goals of misbehavior—attention, power, revenge, and proving inadequacy. In order to understand the child's goals of misbehavior, Adlerians consider the child's behavior, the reaction of significant adults to that behavior, and the child's reaction to correction. By understanding the goal of the child's misbehavior, the therapist can tailor interventions with the child and recommendations to the parent(s) based on moving the child toward more positive goals of behavior—the Crucial Cs (connect, count, capable, and courage) (Lew and Bettner, 1996, 1998). Lew and Bettner (1996, 1998) believe that in order to thrive all children must connect with other people, feel as though they count and are significant, feel capable, and show courage in the way they deal with life's problems. By examining how a child manifests each of these positive goals, the play therapist can begin to make a plan for increasing those that are lacking and emphasizing those that are assets for the child (Kottman, 1999).

As I retell the child's story, I work toward a resolution of the story situation that represents more socially appropriate problem-solving skills and a more positive view of self, others, and the world that was present in the child's original story. Although this version of mutual storytelling is consistent with the theoretical underpinnings of Adlerian play therapy (Kottman, 1995), it can also be utilized effectively by any play therapist comfortable with occasional directive techniques.

RATIONALE

One maxim of Adlerian play therapy is that children's play, artwork, and stories can be understood metaphorically (Kottman, 1995). The mutual storytelling technique allows the play therapist to listen to a child's story metaphorically. The story may illustrate the child's lifestyle (the child's orientation to life, based on his or her perception of self, others, and the world), various issues in the child's life, or the child's relationships with significant others. The child's story can enhance the play therapist's understanding of the child and his or her situation. The retelling process allows the play therapist to emphasize the child's strengths and to positively influence the child's perception of self, others, and the world and teach constructive problem-solving skills by retelling the child's story.

DESCRIPTION

1. The play therapist asks the child to choose some toys (puppets, plastic or stuffed animals, dolls, etc.), pretend they can talk, and tell a story. It is often helpful to suggest that the story have a beginning, a middle, and an end.

2. The play therapist listens to the story metaphorically. As mentioned previously, the story may illustrate the child's lifestyle, various issues in the child's life, or the child's relationships with significant others. In listening to the child's story, the therapist may want to consider the following questions:

   How do the actions of the characters in the story fit with what you already know about the client?

   How does the situation in the story resemble situations the client normally encounters?

   Which character(s) in the story represent the client?

   What are the behaviors of the character who represents the client?

   How do those behaviors fit with your conceptualization of the client's goals of misbehavior? (For example, is the character getting into power struggles, fights, or arguments as would a person whose goal is power? Is the character acting as a clown or being oversolicitous of feedback or attention from others as would a person whose goal is attention?)

   How does the character who represents the client feel in the story? (For example, has the character been hurt badly by others and does he or she feel a need for revenge as would a person whose goal is revenge?)

   How do any adults in the story feel? (For example, are adults annoyed by the character, which would indicate that the goal of misbehavior is attention or are they angry with the character, which would indicate that the goal is power?)

   How would you (as an adult) feel if you had a similar interaction with the character who represents the client? How would most adults feel/react to the character's behavior?

If there is some kind of correction or consequence for negative behavior in the story, how does the character who represents the child react when corrected? (For example, does the character just give up as would a person whose goal is proving inadequacy?)

How does the character that represents the child manifest the Crucial Cs? How does the character connect with others? How does the character demonstrate that he or she counts and is significant? How does the character deal with the issue of being capable? How does the character demonstrate courage or lack of courage in the story?

3. After listening to the child's story, the play therapist retells the story using the same characters, setting, and beginning as the child's story, however the play therapist may choose to change portions of the middle or ending of the story. The altered portions of the story can illustrate (a) more appropriate resolution of the story conflict; (b) alternative ways of viewing self, the world, and others; (c) different ways of building relationships and getting along with others; and (d) varied interpretations of personal issues that may be interfering with the child's ability to function. As the play therapist thinks about the retelling of the story, he or she may want to consider the following questions:

   Which character(s) would you leave in? Why?

   Would you add any character(s)? What traits would you incorporate in any added character(s)? What do those character(s) have to teach this client?

   What positive characteristics/traits/skills would you want to encourage in your client through this story?

   Which of the Crucial Cs would you want to stress in the story—either as a strength of certain characters or as a positive goal for one or more characters to strive to enhance?

   Do you want to incorporate some kind of consequences for negative behaviors in the story? If so, what kind of consequences?

   Do you want to incorporate some kind of positive consequences for positive behaviors in the story? If so, what kind of consequences?

What method of conflict resolution or problem-solving strategy would you like to illustrate in the retelling? How could you resolve the conflict in an appropriate and realistic way?

How can you incorporate more positive ways for the main character that represents the child to view self, the world, and others?

How can you illustrate more appropriate ways of building relationships and getting along with others?

How can you illustrate a variety of interpretations of personal issues that may be interfering with the child's ability to function?

APPLICATIONS

This technique works best with children who already have a relationship with the play therapist and are working on making changes in their attitudes toward themselves, others, and the world and learning new behaviors. It seems to work best with "older" play therapy clients—those 7 or older. In my experience, it has been an effective technique with a wide range of children with a variety of presenting problems—especially those with behavior difficulties, self-esteem issues, social skills deficits, and attention deficit problems.

References

Dinkmeyer, D. and McKay, G. (1989). *The Parent's Handbook: Systematic Training for Effective Parenting (STEP)* (3rd ed.). Circle Pines, MN: American Guidance Service.

Dreikurs, R. and Soltz, V. (1964). *Children: The Challenge.* New York: Hawthorne/Dutton.

Gardner, R. A. (1986). *The Psychotherapeutic Techniques of Richard A. Gardner.* New Jersey: Creative Therapeutics.

Kottman, T. (1995). *Partners in Play: An Adlerian Approach to Play Therapy.* Alexandria, VA: American Counseling Association.

———. (1999). Using the Crucial Cs in Adlerian Play Therapy. *Individual Psychology* 55, 289–297.

Kottman, T. and Stiles, K. (1990). The mutual storytelling technique: An Adlerian application in child therapy. *Journal of Individual Psychology* 46, 148–156.

Lew, A. and Bettner, B. L. (1996). *A parent's guide to motivating children*. Newton Center, MA: Connexions.

———. (1998). *Responsibility in the Classroom*. Newton Center, MA: Connexions.

Stiles, K. and Kottman, T. (1990). Mutual storytelling: An alternative intervention for depressed children. *The School Counselor* 38, 36–46.

Section Four

Group

51

"I'm Sick of . . ." Eggs

Paris Goodyear-Brown

INTRODUCTION

This technique was created in a school-based group-treatment setting to help elementary school-age children relieve some of the tension/frustration caused by test-taking. Although this technique was generated for a specific problem, it works effectively for helping clients achieve catharsis of angry/frustrated feelings in any number of situations.

RATIONALE

Many of the children that we see for mental health issues (ADHD, ODD, grief and loss, depression, etc.) also have co-morbid educational/academic deficits. Many of our clients carry a special education label and get very little boost to their self-esteem from academic achievements. Every year our state requires children to take a week-long standardized achievement test. The clients who have attention problems or difficulty sitting still are required to pay attention and sit quietly for several hours each morning for an entire week. The behavior problems in our school typically go up during this week and the most difficult clients are repeatedly sent to the office. Oftentimes this is to avoid taking the test.

Other times, it is simply because the test-taking situation highlights their inadequate skills in academic/cognitive areas as in behavioral areas. These children need an outlet for their frustration. Perhaps if they are able to blow off some steam after each testing session, they will be better able to focus on the next one. It has been shown that aggression or venting that is unfocused usually just gives rise to further aggression; it is positively reinforcing. However, focused or channeled catharsis of feeling (which may often release anger) serves to decrease the child's stress level and relieve the necessity of acting out in other ways. Therefore, giving children concrete objects to focus on when releasing their anger can be therapeutic.

DESCRIPTION

This technique will be messy but will release some anger. The group should discuss the special nature of the therapy room and the difference between what is allowable in the playroom and what is allowable in the classroom prior to attempting the activity. My groups have always understood that different rules apply in the therapy space than in the classroom. If you explain this carefully, and remind the clients overtly about the boundaries of the playroom, you will significantly decrease the likelihood that clients will engage in destructive behavior in the classroom as a result of the therapeutic catharsis.

This technique can be used inside or outside. If you do it inside, you will need to put plastic sheeting up to protect the walls from the eggs. I begin by talking with the children about the testing and I ask each of them to tell me one thing that they are "sick of" regarding the testing. Some responses have been, "I'm sick of sitting," "I'm sick of holding a pencil," "I'm sick of filling in holes," "I'm sick of guessing," and "I'm sick of getting the wrong answer." I have each child pick an egg out of the carton and gently write his or her "I'm sick of" statement on the egg. Then the group watches, as one by one, each child makes his or her "I'm sick of" statement out loud and throws his or her egg as hard as he or she can. The "splat" sound is very satisfying and my clients always grin afterward. Moreover, they are more relaxed for the next day of testing.

APPLICATIONS

This technique can be used either individually or in a group setting. It can be used to deal with test anxiety or a child's frustration related to poor academic achievement. This particular technique can be modified to deal with almost any feeling or situation in which catharsis of anger, frustration, fear, shame, or embarrassment is needed. Moreover, therapists could help clients generate "I'm sick of" statements based on one of a multitude of presenting problems. For example, if a therapist is seeing a client whose parents have just been divorced, he or she could generate statements such as "I'm sick of my parents bad mouthing each other!" or "I'm sick of going back and forth between houses!" These could be written on different eggs, and then smashed as an outward expression of the child's inward frustration.

52

Jenga Tower Challenge

Heidi Gerard Kaduson

INTRODUCTION

Social skills are not easily taught to children in the latency-age category. Many of the children know what to do intellectually, but when it comes to actually doing it, they lack the ability to stop and think before acting. Even when they do begin to use social skills that they have learned, they still find it difficult to fit into groups and join comfortably in many situations. From the early grades, these children are identified by their peers as different, rejected, or ignored. One of the most difficult behaviors to manage is being teased. Adults as well as children find it very hard to ignore any behavior that bothers them. In order to teach children how to ignore teasing, they must explore and develop their own strategies.

RATIONALE

In many cases, children with social skills' deficits also have other difficulties (Attention Deficit Hyperactivity Disorder, learning disabilities, Asperger's Syndrome). Along with those difficulties there may be processing problems as well. With that as a foundation, these children are more likely to be teased. In the earliest years of education, these children often have adults to help them out. Once the child is identified as someone who reacts to teasing, he or she is more likely to be a target in future years. People who were teased as children remember it throughout their lives. It is a very difficult position to be in. Telling the children to just ignore the teasing will not work; we can't teach them what to do, they have to learn how to handle the situation themselves.

DESCRIPTION

This group technique requires the game of Jenga™ (Milton Bradley). The children are most likely familiar with this game, but for this technique the rules will differ. To play the Jenga Tower Challenge, the children are instructed that the goal of each participant (the "builder") will be to build the Jenga tower all by himself. The leader of the group informs the builder before he or she begins that the entire group, including the leader, will try to distract him or her by pretending to be "teasers" and taunting him with teasing comments. The leader can ask the builder to share with the group some "good teasing statements" that he or she has heard. This will give the child some control over the experience. Then the builder is told that he or she will have two minutes to build the tower by laying three blocks down, and then another three in the other direction so that the tower will be sturdy. During the time that the child is building the tower, the rest of the group (including the leader) will be taunting and teasing the builder. The builder is told that it will be pretend teasing and that all of the group will try to distract the builder so that he or she can't finish the tower. Because of his or her desire to make the tower, the child will use his or her own resources in order to "ignore" the taunting done by the rest of the group. The taunts should be led by the leader so that the children know what to say. Simple taunts may include "You can't build anything," "Who told you that you could do that?" "Big deal, so you put two blocks together," "Anyone can do that; you're nothing special," and so on.

In most cases, the builder will finish the tower. If a child begins to become too affected by the teasing and is unable to build, the leader should immediately stop the game and process the child's experience, reinforcing that this is pretend teasing and not real. After the child completes the tower, the leader asks him or her if he or she heard anything that was being said. If he or she did, then the leader would ask him or her how he or she concentrated in order to build the tower even though he or she was being teased. The child will report his or her own way of ignoring or dealing with the teasing. Each child takes a turn to build the tower. When everyone has finished being the builder, the leader lists all of the different strategies used by the group to ignore the teasing. Discussion is held about the different ways to illustrate that we all have different ways of handling good and bad information. Then the leader tells each member to remember his or her own way of making the tower and ignoring, and when the child next gets teased to "build the tower."

APPLICATIONS

The Jenga Tower Challenge can be used in groups for social skills or other groups where the issue of teasing becomes an important factor. It helps children who have deficits in this area to learn their own strategies. Although it also can be played on an individual basis, the therapist would be the only one "teasing," which is not effective and risks the therapist/client relationship.

53

Feelings Charades

Cynthia Reynolds

INTRODUCTION

Feelings Charades is an excellent technique to facilitate the emotional education of children. It can be used as prevention for the emotional well-being of children, as an intervention for children experiencing emotional difficulties, or as remediation for children who appear to be lagging in emotional development. Because this technique requires the child to be in the spotlight and the center of attention for a few minutes, it is intrinsically motivating. Games of charades or pantomime that involve body movement and facial expressions are fun and encourage creativity and spontaneity on the part of the child.

RATIONALE

This technique encourages awareness, recognition, and identification of feelings. It facilitates development of empathy and a sense of universality when used in a group situation. It also provides an opportunity for children to validate and appreciate each other as human beings with feelings.

DESCRIPTION

Selected feeling words are written or drawn on index cards. The number and complexity of feelings are varied according to the child's developmental level. (For example when working with a typical 5 to 6 year old, six cards might be used with the following feelings: happy, sad, mad, scared, worried, lonely. When working with a group of sixth graders 15 to 20 different feelings might be used.) The player who is chosen to be "it" selects one card and acts out the feeling silently. The other players are allowed three guesses to identify which feeling is being portrayed. If the feeling is not guessed accurately, the player who is "it" discloses the feeling to the group. After the feeling is guessed or disclosed, the player who is "it" must share a time he or she felt that way. The player who guesses correctly may be "it" next, or being "it" may be rotated among the remaining players.

APPLICATIONS

This technique is excellent for children who are resistant, closed, or unaware of feelings. It can be an excellent warm-up activity before working on deeper therapeutic issues. Feelings Charades has been used successfully with children from kindergarten through sixth grade individually, in small groups, and in classroom guidance activities.

In individual counseling, Feelings Charades can be used to develop therapeutic rapport with the child. The therapist can "stack the deck" by deciding which feelings are included in the game or the order in which the cards are drawn. Selected self-disclosure of feelings by the therapist similar to what the child is experiencing helps to facilitate a development of compassion and understanding. The therapist can depart from the game at any time for deeper therapeutic work as opportunities present themselves.

Feelings Charades can be used at any phase of the therapeutic process (as a warm-up, working stage, or closure activity) depending on which feelings are included in the game.

In a small group session, Feeling Charades can serve as a warm-up for sharing deeper emotional issues and help to establish a comfort level through acceptance of all feelings. It is also possible to tailor the game to a specific type of children's group such as divorce, social skills, ADHD, adoption, and so on. The therapist can select feelings common to children who have been through a specific issue to use in the game. The player who is "it" can be asked to share a time he or she felt angry about divorce, frustrated about ADHD, happy with friends, or curious about adoption, depending on the type of group.

An additional benefit of using this game in a small group is that feelings are modeled for children who are unaware of or unable to read nonverbal gestures and facial expressions. Children who state, "I have never felt that way" are asked to imagine a time that another child might have felt that way or a time they have witnessed another person displaying that emotion. In situations where members of the group have had a history of previous contact with each other, the other players can be recruited to help remember a time that they witnessed or imagined the child who is "it" experiencing a particular feeling. In a group setting, children often notice and appreciate similarities and differences of feelings. Group members may also be encouraged to act out feelings that have not been included on the index cards.

Feelings Charades can be incorporated into a development guidance lesson focused on emotional education that would be approximately 20 to 40 minutes long depending on the grade level. As an educational tool, it is helpful to provide students with a list of all the possible feelings included in the deck of cards on a sheet of paper or chalkboard. Students are better prepared and less likely to become "stuck" when called on if they have an idea of feelings they might draw from the deck. It is important that the facilitator set ground rules for appropriate behavior so that students do not make fun of others doing this activity. This activity is most successful when a standard of kindness and acceptance of feelings is established and followed. Outgoing children enjoy a chance to be "on stage," and shy children can participate with relative ease as the talking part is limited to sharing a time they felt that particular feeling. Most children come to appreciate that almost every person in their classroom has experienced most of the feelings on the cards and that there is a universality of human feelings. Children also learn that not every person reacts with the same feeling to similar situations. This activity promotes the development of empathy for others, thus reducing feelings of alienation.

An extension of this technique can be used to teach appropriate expression of feelings. After disclosing a time he or she felt a certain way, the student can be encouraged to decide if it is okay to share that feeling with others, and if so, what is an appropriate way to share it with others. Children can benefit from discussions regarding how to select the best time, place, and person to disclose feelings. This might be done through a role-play with the other class members.

54

"The Guessing Game"

Bob H. Milich

INTRODUCTION

The importance of peer groups in the personality development of children and adolescents has been well documented. The opportunities for children and adolescents to participate in group activities in their formative years are numerous and range from spontaneous groups that develop in neighborhoods and schoolyards to more structured and activity-oriented groups organized around sports and/or civic activities such as Little League baseball, Pop Warner football, AYSO soccer, and Boy and Girl Scouts to name just a few.

Regardless of the specific group activity that children and adolescents participate in, these group experiences provide myriad opportunities for children and adolescents to learn appropriate social skills, to develop a sense of mastery and competence, as an outlet for the expression of feelings and, perhaps most importantly, contribute to the development of a positive sense of self. In fact, there are those who believe that peer group influences are so extraordinarily powerful and far reaching that "The best early predictor of adult adaptation is not IQ or school grades or classroom behavior but rather the adequacy with which children and adolescents get along with their contemporaries" (Hartup, 1993).

The psychotherapy literature is rich with descriptions of the therapeutic use of children's groups and their ameliorative power. Beginning with Slavson's (1943) innovative work in the 1940s with Activity Group therapy, a variety of group interventions have been developed and utilized successfully with children and adolescents (Redl, 1944; Ginott, 1961; Schiffer, 1969; Schiedlinger, 1960; and Axline, 1947). In addition, the literature describes a variety of group interventions ranging from short- and long-term behavioral groups to psychoeducational and support groups. Although these approaches differ in a number of ways, they have in common the goal of enhancing or improving the functioning of the members.

I have developed a group model in my private practice that I call Developmental Social Skills groups, which is an amalgam of many of the different approaches described in the literature: sometimes activity oriented, sometimes problem centered, sometimes supportive, sometimes confrontational, sometimes social skills focused, but always with the ultimate goal of helping members become more effective at relating to peers and, not coincidently, improving their self-esteem.

Many of the children and adolescents who participate in my groups have in common a deficiency in their ability to effectively socialize with peers. Many have a sense of themselves as socially inadequate and often are rejected, teased, or bullied by peers and thought of as weird, odd, different, or unacceptable. Some of these youngsters engender hostility and/or exasperation and are perceived by peers as abrasive or "annoying." All have significant problems making and/or keeping friends and, sadly, their self-esteem suffers immeasurably.

The Developmental Social Skills groups that I lead are designed to help members successfully address their social deficits and liabilities, provide membership in a positive social milieu, and, as a result of these experiences improve their self-feelings of well-being. To this end, group members engage in a number of activities that promote self-disclosure and provide useful feedback to other group members.

RATIONALE

The Guessing Game is an extremely effective intervention for several reasons. First, it is flexible in that the question which the therapist poses can be adapted and tailored to the age, sophistication, and cohesiveness of both the group members and the group itself. For example, an exercise involving, say, animals is an effective icebreaker in the early stages of group development. In this exercise, members are asked to write down the animal that they believe best describes them and the other group members subsequently guess the identity of the member who chose a particular animal. Variations of this such as guessing colors, foods, or numbers that reflect how members feel are other examples of this type of intervention.

As the level of intimacy and cohesiveness increases in the group, the type of questions used in the Guessing Game often reflects this. Questions such as "What is your biggest worry, problem, concern?" or "Other kids think that I am ________ but I really am ________," or using the category Adjectives, where group members are asked to select three or four adjectives that best describe them typically elicit information about how group members feel about themselves and deepens the level of intimacy and trust among group members.

One of the particularly useful aspects of this exercise is that not only do respondents reveal aspects of how they feel about themselves and associated self-esteem issues but that it provides group members with myriad opportunities for receiving feedback from peers. For example, to 8-year-old Jonathon who revealed that he felt like a tiger in the Animals Guessing Game, several other group members chose him because he looked "mad." To 14-year-old Alex, who described himself as "really mad," "turned off," and "isolated" in the Adjectives Guessing Game, group members easily recognized his self-description because as one group member put it: "You're always talking about blowing things up." To 12-year-old Tommy, whose response to the question of what do group members see themselves doing in 20 years, was "to be a doctor, probably a pediatrician" other group members easily identified his response because, according to one, he was "smart, nice, and helpful."

DESCRIPTION

The Guessing Game is a very simple and straightforward exercise and requires only index cards and pens or pencils to be distributed to the group members. Once materials are distributed to the participants (two index cards and pens or pencils), they are told that they will be asked to respond to a question posed by the therapist by writing their responses on one of the index cards.

Participants are also informed that their responses will be collected and read aloud, one at a time, and that they will be required to use the second index card to write the name of other group members based upon their "guess" as to how other group members responded to the question posed by the therapist. This makes for a lively interchange especially as participants reveal why they matched the responses to each group member. Sometimes, especially with younger children, tangible rewards such as prizes or stickers for the "best guesser" (or the group member with the most correct responses) provide additional motivation.

APPLICATIONS

The Guessing Game is a versatile, engaging, and compelling intervention that promotes meaningful interaction in therapy groups with children and adolescents. It is useful with a variety of populations and facilitates interpersonal growth and the acquisition of appropriate social skills because it encourages self-disclosure and allows for the provision of useful feedback in a nonthreatening milieu.

References

Axline, V. (1947). *Play Therapy*. Boston: Houghton-Miflin.

Ginott, H. (1961). *Group Psychotherapy with Children*. New York: McGraw-Hill.

Hartup, W. (1993). Adolescents and their Friends. *New Directions for Child Developments* 60:3–32.

Redl, F. (1944). Diagnostic Group Work. *American Journal of Orthopsychiatry* 14:53–67.

Schiedlinger, S. (1960). Experimental Group Treatment of Severely Deprived Latency-Age Children. *American Journal of Orthopsychiatry* 30:356–368.

Schiffer, M. (1969). *The Therapeutic Play Group*. New York: Grune & Stratton.

Slavson, S. (1943). *An Introduction to Group Therapy*. New York: International Universities Press.

55

The Toilet Paper Game

Norma Y. Leben

INTRODUCTION

What makes a game creative is to use material that is readily available in a child's environment. A roll of toilet paper is as basic as you can get. With this common household object, your group players will disclose their interests, talents, hobbies, and strengths. The task of the therapist is to give each player a moment to discover his or her merits, which form the base of his or her self-esteem.

RATIONALE

Children need self-esteem like they need air. Of all the emotional nutrients we try to pump into our young clients, the ingredients needed to produce healthy self-esteem are constantly in demand. Children with low self-esteem do not improve by paper and pencil exercises, or by talking. Playing games seems to be the best media to experience positive feelings about oneself.

DESCRIPTION

Material: A roll of two-ply toilet paper.

1. The therapist passes the roll of toilet paper around the group and instructs each child to pull off "a handful of toilet paper." Each child's amount may vary.
2. Next, each child will separate his or her handful of toilet paper into individual squares and stack them into their own stack of squares.
3. Surprise the children by instructing them to say one nice thing about themselves with each sheet of toilet paper! The therapist can participate in the game too and model how this is done, for example, "I am a good cook." Going around in a circle, each player takes one square of toilet paper, says one positive thing about him- or herself, and moves the sheet over one at a time to form a new pile. This continues until all the players have used all their sheets of toilet paper. The more toilet paper players begin with, the more self-compliments they must give themselves.

Figure 55.1

DISCUSSION

The therapist leads a discussion on how the children felt about giving themselves so many compliments. Was it bragging or sharing? Were they happy and proud of discovering all those wonderful things about themselves? Did they have enough squares to express themselves? How did they feel about the game? One time, one of the players took a huge handful of toilet paper. Exaggeration was one of his flaws. He quickly ran out of things to say. Even though he was not popular in this group, the other children gave him many suggestions (just so that they could finish the game). After the game, he thanked the group for their help. Without them, he would never have known that he had that many merits. He also said that he had learned to use less toilet paper! Another time, a 14-year-old biracial child, nicknamed the Amazon Rainbow Bird, shared after the game that "I've never thought that out of such a common object, I could find so many uncommon things about myself." (Tips: For the shy players who take only one or two squares of toilet paper, the therapist can separate the two-ply tissue into two squares for them so that they can double the chances to find good qualities in themselves.)

APPLICATIONS

This game works well with groups of children ADHD, ODD, and CD, different age groups, families, at home, school, or camp. It seems to cross ethnic boundaries in the United States, Canada, Ireland, and Hong Kong. Somehow a roll of toilet paper always seems able to emit a smile from all my players.

56

The Picnic in Space Game

Norma Y. Leben

INTRODUCTION

Annually, I return home to Hong Kong to conduct workshops, seminars, and case consultations for counselors and therapists. In 2000, I conducted the initial play therapy session for an interesting case when I used the Picnic in Space game.

The case was referred by Miss Wong, a caseworker with the Children & Youth Center. The case was about Lily, a 6-year-old Chinese girl, who behaved much younger than her age. Her peers nicknamed her Baby because she talked like a baby in a tiny voice. She was timid and did not know how to play with other children. When lining up to go from one activity to the next, she walked very slowly and usually trailed behind. Other children had to go back and guide her by the hand to keep pace with the group. In Miss Wong's social group for 3 to 4 year olds she still needed help. She still periodically sucked her thumb and even nibbled her food like a bunny.

Lily has an older brother who acted his age. Their devoted father Mr. Chan took both children to the C & Y Center four evenings a week for homework supervision, waiting until classes end. Lily handled her schoolwork adequately; however, both Miss Wong and Mr. Chan were very concerned about Lily's immaturity, thus the referral.

RATIONALE

Playing games with peers and adults is an excellent way to develop social skills. Through interactions with other players, children learn how to talk, listen, share, and express feelings and opinions.

DESCRIPTION

I selected my game, Picnic in Space, with the following objectives in mind:

- To teach Lily and her father to speak, play, and have fun together
- To help Lily discover the strength within her, build self-confidence, and self-esteem
- To encourage Lily's use of new social skills

Materials

- A 6 by 9-inch recycled, plastic cookie tray with intriguing ridges underneath. I renamed it my "space meal tray" (this tray makes the space concept more believable)
- Three plastic bowls for holding tokens, checker pieces, or poker chips for Lily, her father, and myself
- A handful of soy beans
- A jar of dry roasted peanuts and a small bag of "gummy bear" chewy candy for treats

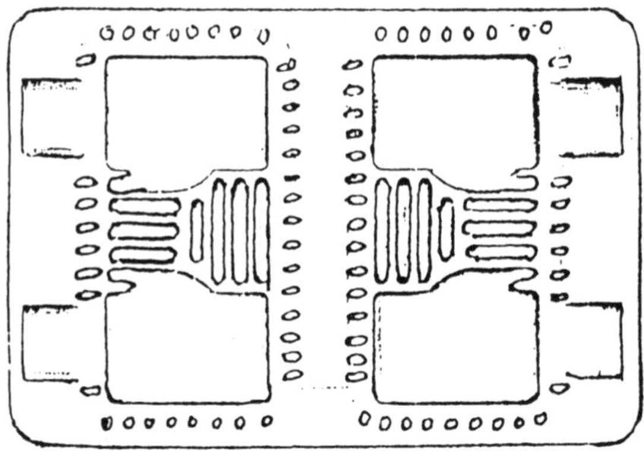

I included Mr. Chan, the father, in this session because I hoped he would learn some techniques to help Lily grow by watching me. Our play session lasted about 30 minutes. We spoke in Cantonese, but I have translated the dialogue into English so you may also learn how to play Picnic in Space.

Miss Wong escorted Mr. Chan and Lily into the playroom. First, I shook Mr. Chan's hand, then I extended my hand to Lily. I had to find her hand inside the extra long sleeve of a dark, blue sweater. I rolled up her sleeves a little and said, "Now, we can shake hands. This is what people do when they meet for the first time."

After we sat down around the play table, I took a good look at Lily. She was small enough to be easily mistaken for four rather than six. Her face was angelic, with gorgeous big, brown eyes, a cute little nose, ruby lips, and a fair, porcelain complexion. I immediately started using tokens in addition to positive, therapeutic statements.

Therapist: Lily, you have such kind, pretty eyes. I like the way you look at me. (I put a token into her bowl. Instantly, a smile came to her face.) I like that smile. That's happy. (I put another token into her bowl.)

Therapist: Lily, what is two plus three? (I wanted to estimate her academic level.)

Therapist: (I gave her a token.) That's correct. What a smart first grader! And, if you can say your answer in a louder voice I'll give you another token.

Child: (Louder) FIVE.

Therapist: (I gave her a token.) I like it. I'll give you a bonus token for saying that crisply with more confidence.

Child: (Big grin)

Therapist: Lily, do you know your ABCs?

Child: (Nodded her head)

Therapist: I want to hear you say them.

Child: (Said all the ABCs)

Therapist: That's wonderful for a first grader in Hong Kong. That is so smart of you. (Both Mr. Chan and I applauded and I put tokens in her bowl.)

Therapist:	(I handed several tokens to Mr. Chan.) Daddy, are you proud to see your little girl has grown to be a smart first grader? If you like what you see, you must let her know.
Father:	Lily, I'm so proud of you. You're a big girl now. This is a token for you.
Therapist:	Lily, I would like to play a game with you. Is that okay?
Child:	(Nodded her head yes)
Therapist:	(Pointed to her own ear)
Child:	(Spoke up) YES!
Therapist:	I just love your voice. Here is a token. The game we're going to play is called *Picnic in Space*. Lily, do you know about spaceships and astronauts?
Child:	(Matter-of-factly described a film she saw the previous week at school about space travel)
Therapist:	That's a good report with a clear voice. (Both father and I applauded and put tokens in her bowl)
Therapist:	Well, astronauts in space have to eat too. Because the spacecraft is so small, they can pack only freeze-dried food. The food is much smaller like this soybean. (Holds up a soybean.) Let's pretend the three of us are astronauts and we're planning for a picnic. What should we bring? You can say the item first then put a bean here in this space meal tray. OK, Lily would you like to go first?
Child:	(Nodded, then quickly said) Yes (received token). I want to bring some carrots. (Placed soybean on the tray.)
Father:	I want to bring some rice. (He placed soybean on the tray.)
Therapist:	I will bring some confidence because I'll have to rely on myself to do my part on this journey to space.
Father:	(Looked momentarily at therapist and nodded with acknowledgment)
Child:	I like Saltine crackers. (Puts another soybean on the tray with her thumb and index finger)

Father: (Picking up hint from therapist) I will bring courage because I've never been to space, and especially if I'm keeping my daughter company. I must have courage.

Therapist: I will bring joy and happiness so we can be in better spirit and make the trip more pleasant.

Child: Oh, I love to eat "cha-sui." (This is Cantonese style barbequed pork. She put another soybean firmly on the tray.)

Therapist: I just love your decisiveness and those capable fingers. Here are two tokens.

Father: I will bring intelligence because there are so many things in space to learn and understand.

Therapist: I will bring some juicy pears because we must nurture our throats. I heard the inside of the spaceship is very dry. We need our voices so that we can talk to each other.

Child: I want to bring some tea eggs. (Eggs marinated in tea, spice, and soy sauce.)

Father: (Interrupted her) How about bringing some candies? All children like candies.

Child: (Frowning) I don't like sweet things. I like salty things.

Therapist: Lily, I'm so happy to hear you say your preference. I'm giving you three tokens. Do you know why?

Child: (Big eyes and big grin) No-o-o.

Therapist: I'm giving you all these bonus tokens because you expressed your own opinion. Only big girls can do that. When you express your opinion, you are being honest. Daddy, what do you think?

Father: Yes, Lily. I'm so glad you can tell me that you prefer salty food. No wonder all the candies I bought you were kept in a jar. (He put two tokens in her bowl.)

Therapist: That completes the game. I wonder what have you learned from playing *Picnic in Space*?

Child: (Solemnly she spread all ten fingers on the edge of the table and admired them for a few seconds.) I have capable fingers. (She looked up at me directly in my eyes.) I can also tell Daddy what I like better.

Father: I learned today that my daughter is a big girl now. She can share her likes and dislikes. I'm very proud of her. (Put two tokens into her bowl.)

Therapist: Lily, do you want to know what we can do with the tokens you earned?

Child: Yes.

Therapist: For every token you earned, you can trade it for a gummy bear candy or a dry roasted peanut.

Child: (She happily counted out her 44 accumulated tokens with a big, big grin.) May I have 44 peanuts, please?

Therapist: (I handed the jar of peanuts to the father to count out 44 peanuts because I wanted Mr. Chan to learn about rewarding Lily. While Mr. Chan counted out peanuts, Lily held out her arms and asked me to roll up her sleeves.) "Lily, I just love those capable fingers," I said.

After this initial play therapy session, Lily was included as one of three children in Miss Wong's young children's play therapy group. Recently, Miss Wong sent me a videotape of Lily after six more sessions. There she was talking, running, smiling, and laughing just like any 6 year old, and it seemed to me she had made up the two years of lost developmental time.

APPLICATIONS

This technique applies to young children with ADHD, ODD, or low self-esteem. It is a very adaptable game and soybeans or any similar beans can be used to represent any theme of values or positive behavioral traits.

Reference

Leben, Norma, Y. (2000). *Directive Group Play Therapy: 60 Structured Games for the Treatment of ADHD, Low Self-Esteem and Traumatized Children.* Morning Glory Treatment Center for Children. Pflugerville, TX, (512-251-3298).

57

The Mood Board

Janice Jung

INTRODUCTION

In play therapy groups for children, the expression of feelings is often a primary goal. Although many children of course do express feelings in a variety of ways within group settings, however, they are often not able to verbalize them. Furthermore, children who have learned to shut off their feelings as a result of abuse or other types of trauma often do not know how to identify their own internal feeling state. Likewise, they often have not learned how to read the expressions of others or to empathize. The Mood Board is used with individuals and in groups of children to facilitate learning how to associate the facial expressions and general body language of others with particular feelings as well as to help children to identify and name their own feelings.

RATIONALE

The ability to express feelings congruently with internal states and feel safe in doing so is fundamental in healthy human relationships. Children who have experienced abuse or other kinds of trauma or who have learning disabilities or attention deficit hyperactivity disorder often miss out on the experience of learning this skill. If they can learn to identify and express their feelings in a safe environment that validates them unconditionally, an increase in self-esteem and healing can take place. Also, if they can be involved in creating materials to be used for the activity and the activity is a success, there is more opportunity for positively influencing self-esteem. If the activity is fun and nonthreatening, the skills that are taught within it may be easier to learn and integrate.

DESCRIPTION

The therapist begins by engaging the children in a discussion about feelings. This is done either by describing emotionally arousing situations ("How might you feel if . . .") or showing photographs or drawings of such situations and then inviting the children to show how their face and body might look if they felt that way, or, usually with older children, by creating a "brainstorm chart" listing as many feeling words as possible. Developmentally appropriate sizes and amounts of paper and markers or crayons (large and a few for young children, smaller and more numerous for older children) are made available to the children. The therapist and children then make simple face- and, if appropriate, body-language drawings depicting each feeling. The therapist attempts to facilitate the process so that only one picture is made for each feeling. Then, together, the group pastes or tapes the drawings, with feeling words on each, onto a large poster board (or more, depending upon how many drawings were made). This is the group's Mood Board. It is placed in a predominant area of the therapy room.

Next, everyone is given several small Post-It notes and asked to write their name on all of them. For practice, everyone in the group is asked to put their name-note on the feeling-illustration or illustrations that match what they think they are feeling at that moment. This is a good opportunity to reinforce the concept that humans can have more than one feeling at a time and that they can be having the same or different feelings as others in their immediate surroundings.

The Mood Board becomes an active element of the therapy room environment. The therapist, by model and description, invites the children, at any time, to move their name-note or notes to feelings that they realize they are having. Discussion or mere acknowledgment can occur whenever warranted regarding what a child has "shown" how they feel. It is important that those not wishing to engage in discussion are honored and allowed just to make this nonverbal show of expression of feelings. The therapist may or may not choose to share his or her own feelings on the Mood Board, but if this is done, it is important to keep these brief and generic in order to avoid interfering with the focus upon the children. It is my experience that over time the Mood Board facilitates more frequent, safer, and clearer sharing of feeling states and that this often generalizes into other environments once the children have had many positive and unconditional validations regarding their feelings within the group. Likewise, individuals having made a Mood Board for use during their play therapy time often show an increase in comfort in expressing feelings not only in session but also outside of the session.

APPLICATIONS

I began using the Mood Board in a therapeutic classroom for children aged 5 through 12 who had been labeled behaviorally disturbed/ psychiatrically impaired by a local school district. The technique has been used successfully in groups of latency-age children and teenagers who have experienced sexual abuse as well as in similar groups organized for the goal of raising self-esteem. More recently, this tool has been used with success in groups of adjudicated juvenile sex offenders for developing self-awareness, identification of and appropriate expression of feelings, and development of empathy. If an individual in nondirective play therapy could benefit by the Mood Board, I have simply made one with him or her and kept it in the playroom to be used by the child whenever he or she wishes.

Julia, aged 7, was referred to my office for symptoms of anxiety, perfectionism, oversensitivity, and obsessive-compulsive behavior. Her family had experienced a bitter divorce and both of her parents were planning to be remarried soon. After being an only child for her entire life, she was now going to have four stepsiblings, two in each home. In her first several sessions, she was slow to explore the playroom, always asking permission to hold the toys and insisting to clean up immaculately before she left. Her artwork consisted of drawings that were precisely copied from illustrations on the paint containers in the room. One day I invited Julia to assist me in making a Mood Board for the playroom. She appeared comfortable with her choice to trace the bottom of a paint jar to make perfectly round faces and then draw in eyes, noses, and various mouth shapes and differing eyebrows to depict the feelings of happy, sad, mad, surprised, excited, and nervous after discussing various scenarios.

She asked me to write the names of the feelings below each face, which I did. We then each wrote our names on several Post-It notes. Julia put one of hers on the "happy" face. After I said, "Oh, you are feeling happy right now," she said, "Yes. I am happy that I have a kitten at home!" I then put one of my name-notes on "surprised," sharing that I was surprised to hear that she had a kitten at home because I hadn't known that previously. To demonstrate use of more than one name-note at a time and also the expression of a more negative feeling, I also put another name-note on "nervous." I shared that I was nervous about a talk that I was going to give soon because I was not sure that I would remember everything I wanted to say.

At the next session, Julia initiated putting her name-note again on "happy." She did this for several weeks. This seemed to be a safe, easy, and probably socially "approved" feeling for her to express. After use of the Mood Board became routine, Julia entered one day and placed her name-note on "sad." This was acknowledged, but as she appeared particularly anxious that day, I chose not to pursue the reason. After a while, she somewhat vigorously punched her name-note on the "mad" picture. I responded with, "Julia feels mad." At that moment, Julia began to cry quietly and share that she had just moved into a new house and had to share a bedroom. Her new stepsister had picked up one of her toys and accidentally broken it. This outward expression of feelings was new and a milestone for Julia. Shortly thereafter, Julia's parents reported that her perfectionism had decreased dramatically, that she was beginning to use feeling words to talk about their family situation, and that she was more comfortable in general.

In summary, the therapeutic expression of feelings can be greatly enhanced with the use of the Mood Board. It is a simple and inexpensive technique that therapists can make in their own offices with the help and involvement of their child and adolescent clients.

58

The Pot of Gold at the End of the Rainbow

Karen L. Hutchison

INTRODUCTION

In October 1998, San Antonio and South Texas experienced flooding conditions that left many homeless or without necessities such as electricity and water. At that time, I was the counselor at a rural primary school in an area hit hard by the flooding conditions. As the sole school counselor, I was responsible for close to six hundred children, ranging from ages 3 to 11.

Primarily a child-centered play therapist, I modified my approach to become more directive for group work in order to deal with the multiple realities of flooding these small children had encountered. With this in mind, I came across a relaxation activity called Rainbow Wear (Allen and Klein, 1996). The activity gave me the dialogue foundation, but I adapted the activity to include a range of techniques in an effort to give the children a safe and accepting climate to deal with things that were out of their control. This activity allows children the opportunity to begin dealing with reality on their own terms, initiated by aspects that are most troublesome to them.

RATIONALE

The foundational relaxation activity was expanded to include guided imagery, music, relaxation, sensory input, symbolism, and art to help the children express negative thoughts and apprehensive feelings and turn them into positive thoughts and feelings of security. The children used imagery to view the harsh reality of the flooding and face losses within a framework that was manageable for them yet bridge to a more constructive aspect of self-support, self-healing, strength, and desensitization. The bridge is a holistic approach of the self-regulating system—the interaction between brain and body. The spirit, mind, and body interact as a unit for self-healing.

To soothe the spirit, mind, and body, I find that background music selectively and strategically utilized is a powerful facilitation to enhance the degree of inward reflection. Mounting research demonstrates that music allows the body to calm itself, conceding to the 60 beats per minute of the heart rate, lowers blood pressure, and relaxes muscles (Armstrong, 1997). Thus, the relaxation exercise becomes more effective and enhances the outcome.

Throughout this exercise, sensory input and symbolism merge in helping the children adapt to environmental disturbances in a safe, controlled way so that they are able to assimilate the experience. The emotions and cognitive processing that results help children manipulate and use the information. They are able to act out traumatic experiences, such as the flooding, repeating it over and over until they move toward an inner resolution and can better cope with the problem.

The symbolism is continued through art, which releases the repressed emotions and communicates nonverbally, bringing the painful issues to the surface. The children can better accept the reality, yet maneuver the disturbing inner conflicts. The outcome is resolution and the gain of needed coping strategies.

DESCRIPTION

The group consists of four to six children, sitting in a circle with the therapist. The children chatter about their day's events, sharing escapades of recess time. This time gives them an opportunity to adjust to one another and the therapeutic setting. To get the children engaged in the directed activity, the therapist tells the children to get comfortable and close their eyes. Soft, soothing music is played in the background. My favorite music is "Bluefields" by Marshall Styler. Because of the flooding issue, I carefully select music that does not include water sounds.

The therapist instructs the children to take three long, deep breaths, modeling and establishing the pace of the activity. The children are guided through each phase of the exercise with pauses purposefully placed to encourage inner reflection and visualization.

Therapist: Let the music soothe you. Feel the music within you. Listen for your heartbeat and hear your breathing.

Take very slow, deep breaths. You are sitting by your favorite window. Keep your eyes closed. Look on the ground. It has just rained because there are puddles everywhere. The skies are gray with heavy clouds. No one is outside playing. Now open your eyes.

We are going to look through our pretend window.

(A window is prepared ahead of time using tag board as the frame and Saran wrap as the glass. Along the top and side, there is a simple valance and curtains to make it as realistic as possible.)

Therapist: Remember when your eyes were closed, you looked at the ground, and you could tell it was still raining. How could you tell the rain was coming down? (Pause) Look through your pretend window and see if it is still raining. You may need to close your eyes again to hear the rain. When you are ready, draw a picture of what you see.

(Placed on the floor in front of each child are white butcher paper and crayons and colored chalks. Pace the lesson to fit the children's needs.)

In this particular group, all the children drew images of the flood. Some of the drawings reflected the dark stormy skies; others depicted rushing streams with debris from houses; others drew families huddled together on the top of one roof with the dog sitting nearby; and still others showed the terrifying experience of having their car submerged by rushing water.

As the drawings are completed, there is time for sharing. Some children choose not to talk at this time, while others begin telling of terrifying experiences they have been through during the week of floods.

As the sharing subsides, take the children through the exercise again but begin to incorporate more positive images.

Therapist: Close your eyes. As it rains, everything around you is taking a bath. Smell the flowers. (Under each child's nose, place fresh, aromatic carnations.)

Smell the leaves. (Place a bowl of crushed leaves under their noses.)

Smell the dirt. (The children smell dirt that is arranged in a vial.)

At this point, change the music to soft rain.

Therapist: The thirsty ground has so much to drink that puddles form around you. Open your eyes. (Pause to allow for transition in the activity.) We have puddles to tromp through. Let's go!

The group gets up and acts out stomping through puddles, trying to splash one another.

Therapist: Oh, look! There is a rainbow filled with colors—red, orange, yellow, green, and blue. Let's make our own rainbows. (Have a bottle of bubbles for each child to blow. The children blow bubbles, looking for the prism of color and chasing them. After a few minutes, guide the children back to the circle.)

Therapist: Let's look through our window again. (Just as before, each child looks through the make-believe window.)

What do you see? (Pause to allow for conversation.) Draw what you see.

Almost every child draws a rainbow that fills the page; some draw puddles with happy faces, some draw the bubbles with a prism of color, and some even draw the sun with smiling families clapping. After the drawings, share with one another.

Therapist: I am wondering if anyone has heard the story about what might be at the end of the rainbow. (Pause. This is a good time to include a story if time permits.)

Some say there is a pot of gold at the end of the rainbow. Is it really gold? (Even for small children, the answers vary from real gold to pennies and from dreams to fairies.)

Therapist: Let's pretend the rain has gone away, and there are rainbows everywhere. At the end of the rainbow, there is a pot of gold. When you find this pot of gold, it means the rain has gone away, and the ground will drink up the water. It means that rain can bring rainbows. (To end the lesson, give each child a gold-covered chocolate coin to eat. For the other hand, give them a "gold doubloon.")

Therapist: When you are feeling afraid because of the rain, reach into your pocket and feel the gold from the end of your rainbow. Then look for a rainbow in the sky. (With all the children in a circle, begin the relaxation phase to close the activity. The music is a bubbling brook with birds singing.)

Therapist: (Slow paced to allow individual processing) Close your eyes and look into the sky and see your rainbow. The rainbow is beautiful! Look at all the bright colors! Now, take a deep breath and decide to keep this rainbow with you always. Reach in your pocket and feel your gold that is your good luck piece. Listen for your heartbeat and hear your breathing. Let your mind relax and open up to happy thoughts. See your rainbow. Take a deep breath and when you are ready, open your eyes.

APPLICATIONS

I found this activity to work regardless of the issue by simply changing the focus. It is a means of relaxing and calming the body with music and guided imagery so that positive thoughts can emerge. It lowers the anxiety level to allow for redirection. The activity gives many outlets for emotional catharsis and encourages sharing so that children learn they are not alone in their experiences and thinking.

References

Allen, J. S. and Klein, R. J. (1996). *Ready . . . Set . . . R.E.L.A.X.* Watertown, WI: Inner Coaching.

Armstrong, T. (1997). *The Myth of the A.D.D. Child.* New York: Plume.

59

My Special Space

Mary T. Foret

INTRODUCTION

Therapeutic play can provide a means to incorporate educational and therapeutic techniques into therapy sessions. Clinicians can utilize play therapy techniques with individuals, groups, and families to explore difficult life experiences; interpersonal or intrapersonal experiences, to enhance self-esteem, promote creativity, and assist with learning appropriate social behaviors. Through the medium of play, individuals can develop the capacity to understand and integrate difficult concepts and to function effectively and appropriately in daily life situations.

A task that many clinicians have in therapeutic sessions is integrating the concepts of appropriate personal boundaries and limits. Many children, particularly those who have experienced emotional, physical, or sexual trauma, may have difficulty with expressing feelings and demonstrating appropriate assertive behaviors concerning physical and personal boundaries. Play can assist the clinician with facilitating the integration of the concepts of appropriate personal boundaries and limits.

RATIONALE

Children can assimilate difficult concepts such as appropriate personal boundaries and limits when utilizing the techniques of therapeutic play. The following technique can be utilized with individuals, groups, and families. This play therapy technique does not require specific artistic or mechanical skills and can facilitate verbal or nonverbal communication between the facilitator and the participants. Facilitators as well as peers can assist with the integration process of difficult concepts during the following therapeutic game.

DESCRIPTION

Materials

- Primary-colored rectangular placemats
- Primary-colored poster board cut in 20 by 14-inch rectangles (laminate the rectangles for permanent use)
- Musical toy (e.g., musical hot potato or any toy that plays music with a beginning and an end)

The clinician and children sit on the floor forming a circle. The children are encouraged to choose a colored mat, sit on the colored mat, and then maintain an arm's-length distance from each other. Next, the safety issues, limits, and general rules of the therapy session are reviewed and discussed. The general instructions to the game include the following:

First, the therapist may say, "We are going to play a game called Hot Potato. I want you to notice that everyone has a colored mat. This is your own personal space." The therapist provides a definition of personal space, stating, "Your personal space has boundaries and you will decide who and what will be allowed in your space during this game." The therapist then demonstrates appropriate responses, stating, "Can I touch your blue mat?" "May I hand you the hot potato?" "I touched your mat; please excuse me."

"First, we are going to go around our circle and I want you to say your name, age, and the color of your mat (include this question when appropriate: Why are you here?) We are going to stay on our colored mats during this game. Before we start the game, I want you to notice your own colored mats, the colored mats of other people in the group, your arms, hands, and legs, and so on. I am going to start the music and we are going to pass the hot potato around our circle. I am going to give my good listeners directions; pass the hot potato slow, slower, fast, faster, low, lowers, high, higher, and so on."

When the music stops, the one with the hot potato passes the hot potato quickly or slowly to any child in the circle. One of the objects of this game is to play within the boundaries of the established personal space of "self" and others. The therapist leads the discussion concerning the participants' experiences during the game. The therapist repeats the game as time allows. An attempt is made to allow enough time for every child to start the game with the musical toy.

APPLICATIONS

This therapeutic play technique has many applications and is useful with individuals, groups, and families. However, this game is particularly useful with children who have experienced emotional, physical, or sexual trauma. Utilizing this nonevasive game, therapists can assist individuals with developing constructive communication skills, setting appropriate personal and physical boundaries, and integrating difficult life experiences. In addition, this technique can assist with the development of listening skills, the ability to follow directions, and the individual's socialization process.

Section Five

Toys

60

Bubbles, Feathers, and Breathing

Teresa A. Glatthorn

INTRODUCTION

Many young children come to therapy with anxiety-related difficulties. Sometimes the anxiety is focused on a particular fear and responds well to systematic desensitization. Other children have more generalized anxiety. In both circumstances, the children will benefit from learning anxiety reduction techniques as part of their therapy (Eisen and Kearney, 1995; Hawton, et. al., 1998; and Wolpe, 1973).

RATIONALE

Anxious adults are generally taught progressive relaxation, which children can learn as well (Eisen and Kearney, 1953; Wolpe, 1973). Some children, however, respond better to visualization (O'Connor, 1997), which can be combined with deep breathing training. Much of children's anxiety is related to a sense of powerlessness in an environment they cannot change. Active relaxation techniques empower children to control their reaction to aspects of the world over which they have no control.

My Bubbles and Feathers technique uses visualization and deep breathing in activities that do not involve closed eyes, letting go, or long journeys of the mind, any of which can be difficult for anxious children. They are active and fun, using simple imagery and storytelling to teach relaxation skills in ways children enjoy. The humor, relaxation, and empowerment are all incompatible with anxiety (Wolpe, 1973), and thus extinguish it.

DESCRIPTION

The therapist first talks with the child about where he or she carries problems/worries in his or her body. Children may need coaching and examples, using their words (i.e., they might feel "icky" in the "tummy").

Bubble Version

The therapist and child talk about bubbles and the child's experiences with them. These prior positive experiences and the phrasing of them can be incorporated into the visualization. The therapist eventually models the effect of short, fast blowing of bubbles (lots of small bubbles) versus long, slow blowing (one large bubble). Each then practices making both large and small bubbles.

The therapist explains that bubbles can be used to help us relax. One starts by imagining the worries and what they look like in our bodies. Then he or she takes a slow, deep breath all the way into the bottom of his or her "tummy," making the stomach, abdomen, and chest fill up with clean fresh air. Then the child imagines sending the fresh air to collect the worries from those special worry centers in the body. Finally, the child exhales the air—full of worries—very slowly into the bubble wand, trapping the worries in a large bubble, and watches the worries drift away with the bubble. The process is repeated until the child feels the worries are gone (at least five to seven times).

Just as we know that only deep breathing or slow cleansing breaths create a relaxation response, only large bubbles are "strong enough to carry the worries away." In addition, the effectiveness of the activity is demonstrated dramatically if the child does a pre- and post-test of his or her level of anxiety using a mood ring or other item that responds to changes in skin temperature.

Actual bubbles and wands are not always necessary. Some children do just as well (or better) when doing imaginary bubble blowing. In fact, both bubble and feather props can and should eventually be phased out for practical reasons, and replaced with imaginary ones.

Feather Version

Some children don't care for bubbles or find them frustrating, sticky, or childish. The feather version thus offers an alternative activity, using the same concepts and methods, except the child is asked to imagine a rather large (12 to 18-inch) "magic feather" (or one can be provided). Everything is the same except that this time the worries are blown onto the edges of the feather. Feathers can only "grab the worries out of the breath" if the air is blown slowly onto the edges of the feather, starting at the bottom and progressing slowly up one side to the top of the feather and down the other side to the bottom. The blower needs to watch the wiggling of the wisps of the feather to make sure the worries are slowly and evenly dispersed.

APPLICATIONS

The use of the feather version is demonstrated in the case of a 6-year-old girl who was terrified of dental and orthodontic procedures and needed to have significant work performed in her mouth. In her therapy, this young girl used her favorite peacock feather as a transitional object and as a tool for her relaxation exercises during the desensitization training, as well as during the procedure once she was ready to undertake it. She learned to create a relaxation response using her feather, which was then paired with 1) in vivo discussion of the process in the play therapy room, then with her dentist and staff, 2) imagining of the steps of the procedure, 3) in vivo manipulation of the tools to be used, 4) waiting outside the dentist's office, 5) waiting inside the dentist's waiting room, 6) sitting in the dental chair, and 7) during the procedure itself.

Similar success is seen with the bubbles version.

References

Eisen, A. R. and Kearney, C. A. (1995). *Practitioners Guide to Treating Fear and Anxiety in Children and Adolescents: A Cognitive Behavioral Approach*. Northvale, NJ: Jason Aronson.

Hawton, K., Salkovskis, P. N., Kirk, J. and Clark, D. M. (Eds.) (1998). *Cognitive Behavior Therapy for Psychiatric Problems*. New York: Oxford University Press.

O'Connor, K. (1997). Using guided imagery to augment the play therapy process. In Kaduson, H. and Schaefer, C. (Eds.) *101 Favorite Play Therapy Techniques*. Northvale, NJ: Jason Aronson.

Wolpe, J. (1973). *The Practice of Behavior Therapy*. New York: Pergamon Press.

61

Let Me See Your Strong Muscles: An Engaging, Interactive Play Technique

Sandra L. Lindaman

INTRODUCTION

The Newspaper Punch, Toss, and Free-for-all technique described in this chapter is an activity familiar to therapists trained in Theraplay®. Although Theraplay therapists have specific reasons for using this technique related to the goals of the model, other types of therapy sessions may benefit from the structuring, engaging, nurturing, and challenging aspects of the interaction.

Theraplay® is a structured play therapy for children and their parents. Its goal is to resolve behavioral problems while enhancing attachment, self-esteem, trust in others, and joyful engagement. This treatment is used for a wide variety of problems including withdrawn or depressed behavior, overactive-aggressive behavior, temper tantrums, phobias, and difficulty socializing and making friends. Children also are referred for various behavioral and interpersonal problems resulting from learning disabilities, developmental delays, and pervasive developmental disorders. Because of its focus on attachment and relationship development, Theraplay has been used successfully for many years with foster and adoptive families. Theraplay also can function as a preventive program to strengthen the parent-child relationship in the presence of risk factors or the stresses of everyday life (Jernberg and Booth, 1999).

RATIONALE

Theraplay is modeled on four essential aspects of the interaction of parents and children in a healthy relationship: structure, engagement, nurture, and challenge. The newspaper activity is quite versatile because it incorporates all four aspects:

- Structure—to reassure the child of order, to model control, and to allow the child a positive experience of following another's lead
- Engagement—to make a connection with the child in an intensive and personal way
- Nurture—to appreciate the child's strength and skill and to soothe the child at the end of the exciting play
- Challenge—to set up a partnership activity that promotes feelings of competence and confidence

For therapists working in other methods, this activity can be beneficial to engage withdrawn children; structure overactive, inattentive, or oppositional children; provide a cathartic experience for children; assist parents to interact with their children in a desired way; and schedule a playful interlude within a treatment session.

DESCRIPTION

The Newspaper Punch, Toss, and Free-for-all is a sequence of three steps that requires only five or six full sheets of newspaper. First, the therapist holds a sheet of newspaper taut and the child punches through the sheet on a signal from the therapist. Second, after a number of punches the two crumple the sheets into balls that the child tosses into a hoop made by the therapist's arms. Finally, the two toss the balls at each other in an attempt to get rid of all of the balls on one's side within a specific time limit. Here's how the activity looks and sounds:

Therapist: I'll bet you have a strong arm muscle there, let me see.

(Therapist flexes own arm in demonstration, encourages child to do same, checks and admires child's muscle by touching or looking at it closely.)

I'm going to hold this newspaper tight in front of you and I want you to punch it right through the middle when I give you the signal. The signal will be "Go" . . . 1-2-3-Go!

(Therapist holds paper to her right or left side to avoid getting hit.)

Child: (Punches through paper with a satisfying rip.)

Therapist: Wow, that was great, now, get ready for the next one, when I say "banana" . . . apple, orange, strawberry, banana.

(Therapist matches complexity of signal and waiting time to child's capabilities.)

Child: (Waits for signal and punches)

Therapist: Great! Here's a tricky signal, when I wiggle my nose.

(Therapist winks eye, nods head, and uses various facial expressions and head movements requiring eye contact and child's attention to his or her face. The activity can be repeated with variations, for example, alternate arms, two or three sheets of newspaper, in relation to child's attention and ability.)

Now, take a piece of newspaper and make a ball like this.

(Both make balls out of the torn sheets. The therapist must help the child make the transition from energetic throwing to the quieter activity of making the balls by maintaining a high level of enthusiasm for the task.)

When I signal (as above), toss one ball into my hoop.

(Therapist holds out arms in a circle in front of her, child repeats several tosses on signal. Therapist may back up slightly on each toss to increase the difficulty. Therapist may instruct child to form a hoop and give signals for the therapist to toss the ball.)

You're a good thrower too. . . . Now, you take five balls on your side and I'll take five on mine. . . . We're going to throw them at each other until I say "Stop." Keep picking them up and throwing, try to get rid of all of your balls, Go!

(Therapist sets a timer, watches the clock, or counts to ten. If parents are present, they are teamed with the child and the contest is between the "Family Team" and the "Therapist Team.")

Child: (Usually laughing and excited at this point)

Therapist: Wow that was fun. . . . You really played hard . . . sit back and I'll fan you.

(Therapist fans with a remaining sheet of newspaper to calm and nurture the child or parent and child. In a future session, the parent assumes the active role of giving directions and signals as the therapist did in this example.)

The punch and toss activities can be used with most children aged 3 to early adolescence. The Free-for-all portion is not indicated for very active or aggressive children who can be overstimulated by the excitement and looseness of the game. On the other hand, the Free-for-all is an excellent choice for anxious, inhibited, or withdrawn children as it prescribes playful movement and discharges tension. Children who are afraid to punch can be helped by a third party or assisted and encouraged by the therapist until they are successful. The therapist will learn about the child's strength and coordination in this activity. It is up to the therapist to keep the activity successful and positive, so the therapist should be prepared to modify or assist if the child has difficulty. This task is not recommended for children younger than a developmental age of approximately 3 years because the fun of the activity is not as appealing to them as simpler forms of interaction. Because children with problems of sensory processing may be overstimulated by the task, it should be used carefully and modified as necessary for them.

APPLICATIONS

This activity is a common first session, get-to-know-you task in Theraplay treatment. It is an easy, appealing task to try if you wish to use a directly interactive game. This writer and other therapists have experienced success with this task in the following ways:

- To more directly engage a withdrawn child, perhaps one who won't talk or play on his or her own; these children are often relieved to have the therapist take the lead and involve them in an activity, particularly one that does not require talking. Also, accomplishment of these activities leads to a feeling of competence and confidence.
- To structure an inattentive, unfocused child and prolong the amount of time he or she can successfully participate; Myrow uses these activities with children with ADHD to "promote

self-control and the internalization of rules and structure, so that the child learns to modulate his own behavior" (1999/2000, p. 6).

- To help an oppositional child have a positive experience following an adult's lead; the challenge and the invitation to punch capture the interest of these children. The therapist's signals for the punch or toss build the child's ability to delay and add to the experience of following directions.
- To provide a cathartic experience; there is a great satisfaction in producing an explosive punch in a context that is safe and acceptable.
- To involve older, resistant children who do not want to participate in treatment at all; the use of playful, interactive group sessions for emotionally disturbed teens has resulted in improved staff-student rapport and mutual understanding, as well as improved student acceptance of traditional mental health interventions (Weber, 1998).
- To change the focus of a child's play from isolated video watching or computer play to social, interactive play; when children are "tuned out to people," they benefit from play that is people-centered rather than oriented to projects or objects (Morin, 1999).
- To help a child with Asperger's Disorder or a higher functioning child with autism become more comfortable engaging with others; interactive play has been used to improve awareness of and interest in others, eye contact, and toleration of transitions and unpredictability in the environment (Fuller, 1995).
- To create a partnership experience in play rather than competition; interactive play groups in educational and treatment settings have used similar activities to practice cooperation and empathy for others (Rubin and Tregay, 1989).
- To allow the child and family to experience the pleasure and release of play; periods of active play during focused trauma treatment help clients who have lost the ability to play or feel that play is inappropriate; play also helps the therapist and child tolerate the intensity and pain of the hard work (James, 1989).

References

Fuller, W. S. (1995). Theraplay as a treatment for autism in a school-based day treatment setting.*Continuum, the Journal of the American Association for Partial Hospitalization, 1995,* 2(2), 89–93.

James, B. (1989). *Treating Traumatized Children.* Lexington, MA: Lexington Books.

Jernberg, A. M. and Booth, P. B. (1999). *Theraplay: Helping Parents and Children Build Better Relationships Through Attachment Based Play,* 2d Edition. San Francisco: Jossey-Bass.

Morin, V. (1999). *Fun to Grow On: Engaging Play Activities for Kids with Teachers, Parents, and Grandparents.* Chicago: Magnolia Street Publishers.

Myrow, D. (1999/2000). Theraplay for children with ADHD. *Newsletter of The Theraplay Institute* 11 (Winter), 6–7.

Rubin, P. and Tregay, J. (1989). *Play with Them: Theraplay Groups in the Classroom.* Springfield, IL: Charles C. Thomas.

Weber, Peggy (1998). Theraplay groups for adolescents with emotional problems. *Newsletter of The Theraplay Institute* 10 (Summer), 1–5.

(Note: Thanks to my Theraplay colleagues for their excellent ideas about this activity description.)

62

Interaction Balls

Kyla Chambers

INTRODUCTION

A therapeutic device called the Interaction Ball™ has been developed by a marriage and family therapist for play therapists and other mental health professionals seeking to initiate communication and the sharing of feelings among their clients. The Interaction Ball™ is a brightly colored, pillowlike ball printed with a variety of bilingual (English/Spanish) emotions with corresponding facial expressions. For instance, "Happy" has a smiling face and is bright yellow. The Interaction Ball can be used with individuals and groups of all ages and abilities either in a therapeutic setting or as a parlor game. Hospitals, schools, universities, private therapy offices, domestic violence centers, and rehabilitation centers are utilizing this fun, nonthreatening, and valuable therapeutic tool.

RATIONALE

Questions often posed in the therapeutic process are "How does that make you feel?" as well as "And then what did you do?" Unfortunately most children, adolescents, and adults have difficulty answering these questions, perhaps they have trouble recognizing and verbalizing their feelings, behaviors, and consequences. Such disconnecting from painful feelings, traumatic experiences, and consequences might be due to built-up emotional walls so they won't or cannot feel in order to survive. For some, being too cognitive and not allowing emotions to flow is a survival tactic. Overthinking is an obstacle to identifying their feelings. "Nothing disturbs feeling so much as thinking" (Jung, 1921). Perhaps Dr. Jung had some cognitive clients. For others, not being able to identify how they feel is a result of believing there is a right or wrong answer and that feelings are good or bad. For instance, a child searches for the "right" answer to an adult's question. If the child is not "right" or "good" then they are "wrong" or "bad" and will be punished for their feelings. For people who have difficulty answering questions and identifying feelings, the Interaction Ball can be a nonthreatening tool with which to provide the feeling then pose the question. The Interaction Ball identifies the feeling for you—therefore, everyone is on the same footing without having to think of a feeling and believing they have to have the "right" answer. The Interaction Ball aids in the discovery, expression, and connection of feelings, behaviors, and consequences in a fun way.

DESCRIPTION

The Interaction Ball is a soft, cuddly, colorful ball. Inscribed are 20 feeling words and 12 "Your Choice" words in Spanish and English, with corresponding facial expressions and colors. For instance, Happy has a smiling face and is yellow, Angry has a frown and is red, and so on. The Interaction Ball promotes hand-eye coordination, learning left from right, increased reading skills, and acquiring new languages. The Interaction Ball is a proven therapeutic toy for therapists and lay persons. This simple interactive toy can be used by people of all ages and abilities, individually or in groups, professionally or personally, and has been well accepted by children, adolescents, and adults. The Interaction Ball is a fun, effective educational device that gives the feeling word to the participant then asks, "I feel ________ when ________." Thus, allowing for the feeling to be stated, then the event, behaviors, and consequences. This aids in the ability of a person to verbalize feelings and to express them more comfortably with others, promoting camaraderie of feelings of "You are not alone." The Interaction Ball is a nonthreatening, nongender, nonracial, nonpolitical, and nondenominational, simple-to-use toy. Metaphorically, the Interaction Ball allows for the intangible to be tangible and the unconscious to be conscious, as if one can hold emotions in the palm of his or her hand and see that is what is inside all of us. Moreover, if the person wishes to not discuss the feeling aloud he or she can catch, hug, or throw the ball allowing everyone to participate in the group process.

How to Use the Interaction Ball

1. Simply toss the ball from one person to another or toss it to yourself. When the Interaction Ball is caught, the particular emotion/feeling landed on by the right thumb of the participant is the feeling to be discussed.

2. The person who catches the Interaction Ball acts out the emotion/feeling (as in the game of charades), while the other participants guess what feeling is reflected (psychodrama). The Interaction Ball is then tossed to the person who guessed correctly, and the game continues.

3. The person who catches the Interaction Ball states what makes him or her feel that feeling: "I feel ________ when ________" or states the last time he or she felt that way. It is then optional for the facilitator to discuss the circumstances of what brought about the feeling or situation and perhaps explore the alternative behaviors and consequences of the feeling and situations. The person then tosses the Interaction Ball to another person and the process is repeated.

4. The person who catches the Interaction Ball states what makes him or her *not* feel that emotion: "I do *not* feel ________ when ________." It is then optional for the facilitator to discuss the circumstances of what brought about the feeling or situation, to *not* feel that way and perhaps explore the alternative behaviors and consequences of the feeling and situations. The person then tosses the Interaction Ball to another person and the process is repeated.

5. The person who catches the Interaction Ball uses the feeling word correctly in a sentence.

6. When the person who catches the Interaction Ball receives "Your Choice," they then can either retoss the Interaction Ball to themselves until their right thumb indicates a feeling, or the

person can choose a feeling that is or is not on the Interaction Ball.

7. The facilitator or a participant will state a topic such as recess at school. Each feeling word indicated by the right thumb must be referred to the given topic, recess at school, such as, Happy, "I feel happy at recess when someone picks me to play on their team." An adult topic might be the workplace. I feel happy at work when I am recognized by my supervisor for a job well done. A teen topic might be parents. I feel frustrated with my parents when they won't let me go to a party.

8. The person who catches the Interaction Ball states how his or her body feels when he or she experiences that particular feeling and how he or she acts/behaves: "My body feels ______ when I feel ________, then I act ________." It is then optional for the facilitator to discuss the circumstances of what brought about the feeling or situation and perhaps explore the alternative behaviors and consequences of the feeling and situations. The person then tosses the Interaction Ball to another person and the process is repeated.

9. The person who catches the Interaction Ball begins a story. "Once upon a time, a dragon was feeling ________" (the feeling indicated by the person's right thumb), then the person tosses the ball to another participant and the story continues with the new feeling he or she received, and so on. This can be used with a group, individual, or one on one between facilitator and client.

10. Word association can be used with the Interaction Ball. Simply toss the ball to a person. When the ball is caught have him or her state the feeling indicated by his or her right thumb then have him or her say the first word that pops into his or her head. Then toss the ball to another participant. This may be done quickly.

11. The person who catches the Interaction Ball, the feeling indicated by the right thumb, is the feeling that the participant writes about in a journal or draws a picture of.

12. The person who catches the Interaction Ball then acts out the feeling indicated in sandtray.

13. The Interaction Ball can also be used as an ice breaker game. A topic can be given and the person who catches the Interaction Ball has to relate an experience to the mood reflected by the right thumb. The person then tosses the Interaction Ball to another participant and the process is repeated.

14. The person who catches the Interaction Ball walks around the room displaying the mood reflected by his or her right thumb. The Interaction Ball is then tossed to the person who guessed correctly and the process is repeated.

The **steps** can be used individually or in any combination. The uses of the Interaction Ball are limited only to your imagination—so explore the possibilities.

APPLICATIONS

The Interaction Ball is helpful for all children, adolescents, and adults to verbalize feelings in a nonthreatening, fun atmosphere. It can be used to promote awareness of a relationship among feelings, behaviors, and consequences. The therapist can provide feedback as to the topics discussed also, allowing for alternative feelings, behaviors, and consequences to be explored. The Interaction Ball can be applied with individuals who either have or do not have a diagnosis. The potential for people and families who can use the Interaction Ball is but is not limited to those with the following conditions: posttraumatic stress disorder; eating disorders; chemical dependency; the sexually, emotionally, or physically abused survivors and their families; learning disabled; attention deficit hyperactivity disorder; anxiety disorder; conduct problems; developmental disorders; dependent personality disorder; depression, and Tourette's Syndrome.

Some group applications include parent education, employer/employee relations, grief and anger management. Other applications include physical therapists, occupational therapists, and recreational therapists. The Interaction Ball can be used with many different therapy techniques such as marriage and family therapy, premarital therapy, and play therapy. The Interaction Ball is being used in, but not limited to, such places as private therapy offices, hospitals, domestic violence centers, treatment facilities, private families, school districts, universities, 12-step programs, and churches across the country and internationally. Some of the institutions include the Betty Ford Center in Palm Springs, CA; the Los Angeles Unified School District in Los Angeles, CA; the Jefferson County Mental Health in Littleton, CO; and the Deirdre O'Brien Child Advocacy Center of Morris County, Inc. in Morristown, NJ.

Reference

Campbell, J. (1976). *The Portable Jung*, p. 209. New York: The Penguin Group.

63

Play Cabinet

Nancy Kuntz

INTRODUCTION

Children who undergo long-term hospitalization are subjected to various medical procedures, isolation, and interruption of their daily order and routines. The exposure of external stresses may lead to displaced anger and aggression. At times the child may withdraw and not engage in responses. One method used to decrease aggression and anger is to use play therapy (Kuntz et al, 1996). However, play therapy is not a priority when the child is undergoing intensive medical care. This technique describes a method of establishing a play cabinet for children. The play cabinet has been created at two hospitals in Orange County, CA.

RATIONALE

Play cabinets encourage play with hospitalized children to promote normal life experiences and support the child's cognitive, social, and emotional health. In addition, the opportunity to play facilitates hardiness and resiliency for children and allows them to master critical experiences.

DESCRIPTION

The use of a play cabinet on any nursing unit enables the hospitalized child to receive constructive, therapeutic play incorporated into his or her daily care. The cabinet can be stocked with both sterile and unsterile toys. Books, blankets, pillowcases, and age-appropriate toys can turn a hospital room into the child's safe haven for the time he or she is hospitalized. If the cabinet is in close proximity to the ward, there is access to toys, without taking nurses off the unit to find objects to encourage play.

Play incorporated into daily care allows a child of any age to engage in play and communicate his or her emotional state. Nurses develop care plans; however, play is usually delegated to child life specialists, occupational therapists, physical therapists, or volunteers. The use of play can help nurses understand the child's level of development, expression of fears, control of environment, as well as assess the child's response to hospitalization. If play is part of nursing care, the interdisciplinary team can share valuable objective data on how the child is progressing emotionally, developmentally, and physically. Toys, which are readily available, encourage play and enable the child to develop relationships with the nurses.

The nurses can develop a wish list of toys to be stocked in the cabinets based on four age groups:

Infants

Infants can benefit from soft, homemade blankets and pillowcases, which are gentle against their skin. Mats can be in their rooms to promote crawling and playing with balls, toys, and puppets. Hard, fat, chubby books are great to read short stories and allow the infant to carry around the room. Music provides comfort and distraction; a favorite lullaby can be played before nap or at bedtime to induce sleep. If the toy cabinet has books, some can be alternated and categorized. The tapes can be shared and a library of tapes can be established. The television should not be encouraged in the infants crib as a play alternative. Infant stimulation could be encouraged with mobiles, rattles, and colorful toys. The test can be used as a screening test to establish baseline growth and development. Toys for infants could encourage motor development and develop neuromuscular control. Research has revealed that variation of stimulation in the physical environment is important.

Toddler and Preschool Children

Toddler and preschool children could also benefit from soft pillows, blankets, and stuffed animals. Some children may bring these from home. Other suggestions for toys are blocks, cars, carts, dress-up clothes, cups, dishes, dolls and sets, push-and-pull toys, puzzles, rocking horses, tool benches, and water-play items. Providing age-appropriate books and music will set the tone for interaction and play. Simple art play can be encouraged with crayons, markers, stamps, and inks. Toddlers need to be able to engage in pretend play. Props such as hats, clothes, and dishes can be used.

School-age Children

School-age children often want to watch television and play video games. This is great for their alone time, but if items from the cabinet were available, play would be encouraged. Examples of toys would be action-play figures, board games, puzzles, soft balls, and craft kits. Books could be offered, and the child could read as well as be read to. Music could be played using headphones or out loud. The children could make a simple journal to tell their story. Crafting is fun and allows creative expression. Children can also paint, draw, stamp, weave, knit, and write letters. School-age children need to interact and play.

Adolescents

Adolescents could also use age-appropriate games, books, music, and videos, which could be included in the cabinet. Other ideas include crafts, models, mosaics, journals, jewelry kits, stamps, inks and cards to make, and handheld video games. They also enjoy having their walls decorated with cards, pictures, and posters to make them feel more comfortable. Adolescents may be challenged to play with more complex, interactive games, crafts, reading, and physical activity.

APPLICATIONS

My favorite accomplishment as a nurse was to develop and keep up the play cabinet developed first at Children's Hospital of Los Angeles. Nurses on the bone marrow transplant unit helped develop and maintain the cabinet. The toys were sterilized and could go into the laminar flow rooms easily. Parents felt at ease to leave because their child would play while the nurses were in the room. If they had issues with play we could bring them to the team discussions and come up with goals and recommendations. If the child was not playing often, it was due to pain or other physical problems. The child could have his pain assessed, treated, and return to play. Play needs to be a priority in pediatric nursing units. Hopefully, these suggestions will encourage children to have hospital rooms conducive to play.

Infants have benefited from care plans with interventions incorporated into care. The following interventions could be utilized in an infant's nursing care plan:

1. Incorporated play into care procedures (i.e., play peek-a-boo during vital signs; use stuff animals during assessment; encourage play with toys during bath time).
2. Provide a block of time when infant is disconnected from IV medications and fluids to be heplocked. Take large balls and toys to mat and encourage mobility, ball play, and so on.
3. Use books to imitate words and actions.
4. Teach parents new play techniques.
5. Provide rattles, mobiles, stuffed, textured toys, books, and telephones. Alternate toys.
6. Consult with psychologist for help with issues blocking play and advice for special infant needs (i.e., drug-abused infants and the like).

References

Caldwell, B. M. and Bradley, R. (1984). *Home Observation for Measurement of Environment*. Little Rock, AR: University of Arkansas at Little Rock.

Kuntz, N., Adams, J. A., Zahr, L., Killen, R., Cameron, K. and Wasson, H. (1996). *Therapeutic Play and Bone Marrow Transplantation Journal of Pediatric Nursing* (11) 6 (December), 1996.

64

Rubber Darts

Sylvia Fisher

INTRODUCTION

The use of plastic toy guns in play therapy has been a controversial topic for years. The therapist is not promoting violence, yet violence is in our world. Children come to us with the problems in their world; the therapist did not create them. This technique is particularly effective for children who have been abused, oppressed, picked on, victimized, or otherwise unjustly treated. The conditions for its use must be highly structured and safe.

RATIONALE

Children often feel they have no power in this adult-oriented society. They are always being told what to do, where to go, and when and how to do it. When children have been traumatized by an act(s) against their person at the hands of others or have been victimized by the attitudes of others, they feel even more powerless than the ordinary child. By allowing children to shoot toy guns at a drawn object on a wipe-off board, their sense of self-esteem can be restored and they can feel more empowered.

DESCRIPTION

My clients are introduced to the guns along with all the other toys in my playroom during our first session. I take them on a tour of the room, showing them where materials are kept and letting them know they can choose any activity/play they wish.

I constantly remind the children and reinforce for them that there is no right or wrong in my room and that I will protect their confidentiality. When a child expresses a curiosity about the guns, I allow the child to explore. When the child shows a higher level of interest in using the guns, I set up the parameters of gun-play.

Gender has not played a role in the desire to use the guns when aggression has been directed toward the client, however more boys than girls choose to play with the guns to shoot at a target like the traditional bulls-eye and keep score.

I have a number of plastic toy guns in a drawer that is open and accessible. The guns are bright colors of red, blue, orange, and green. Most of them are silent. Only the red and blue guns accommodate the rubber suction darts (orange and blue). I establish a ritual of safety before this play can begin: "There is only one safe place to shoot these guns. We lean the wipe-off board against the door and that is where you shoot. I will pull back the white knobs (which cock the gun) for you, if you like. You can put the dart in the gun only after the knobs have been pulled back and you are facing the door."

When children have been abused, for example, I encourage them to draw the situation or the perpetrator on the 2 by 3-foot board. They make the size of the drawing according to their need. I ask if they would like to shoot darts at their target and explain the safety rituals. I reassure them that I will keep them safe and nothing can happen to them or to anyone else in the playroom. I also tell them they can stand as close to the board as they want. When the gun is discharged, it makes a loud sound. When the darts hit the board, another sound is heard, and a different sound is made if the suction dart is pulled off the board. This activity involves five senses: visual, auditory, kinesthetic, olfactory (the markers smell), and taste (I show children that if they moisten the dart with their finger from their tongue, the darts stick better to the board.)

I have seen the size of their drawings change after shooting at their target for more than one occasion. The object of their fears can become smaller, look sillier and more distorted while the child becomes larger and more powerful. This visual representation is validating to the child and reinforces his or her newfound experience. The children then feel a sense of mastery and control—their fears reduced. They feel empowered by using toy weapons. The ultimate triumph is when they erase the board and make it all disappear.

APPLICATIONS

The technique of allowing the child to be the aggressor is extremely empowering. The therapist sets clear boundaries, keeps the child feeling safe, and is the witness validating the child's experience. Clear distinctions are made to separate play from reality. The child's coping skills improve after this type of release and often begin more verbal expression in therapy and at home. The issues that may be helped range from "mean" parents, a hated teacher, bad dreams, bullies, and cruel friends to more severe abuse.

The child is now in charge and is the victor.

65

Sand-and-Water Play or Sensopathic Play

Joop Hellendoorn

INTRODUCTION

Sand and water are play materials that most play therapists consider necessary for their therapy room. At the same time, sand-and-water play is a sadly neglected topic. This may sound strange, because "sand play" is well known, especially in Jungian play therapy (Allan and Berry, 1993; Kalff, 1966). Here, however, the sand tray serves as a basis for the construction of a personal play world, with the aid of many miniature toys. Not the sand itself is used for therapeutic purposes, but the world that is constructed in the sand. On water play, I know of only one study in English, that of Hartley, Frank, and Goldenson (1952), parts of which were reprinted in Hartley, Frank, and Goldenson (1993). Their work, however, focuses not on water in play therapy, but in the teaching of young children. They suggest water induces a feeling of mastery, relaxation, and liberation, and provides satisfaction for immature children and an outlet for aggression. In this sense, water may also be an important tool in therapy. On the combination of sand and water in play, I found only one publication in English (Woltmann, 1993). The Gloop technique described by Cabe, N. (1997) highlights the basic nature of kinesthetics in therapy, but its use for treating sensory deprivation is rather narrow.

In this contribution, I will briefly outline the theoretical foundation and the practical use of sand and water in play therapy.

RATIONALE

The Dutch play therapist Vermeer (1955, 1969, 1973) developed a specific theory on the use of sand and water in play. She worked from a phenomenological point of view, searching for the existential meaning of sand-and-water play in the development of children. She in turn was inspired by the French philosopher Bachelard who wrote a beautiful series of books (1942, 1943, 1948, 1949) on the significance of the four elements earth, water, air, and fire for human existence.

According to Vermeer (1955), sand and water[1] are basic, unformed materials that appeal directly to the most basic sense, the tactile sense. Playing with sand and water means, primarily, touching and surrendering to the affect this touching evokes. Thence evolved Vermeer's term *sensopathic play*. *Senso* refers to the sensory, kinesthetic experience elicited by touching and manipulating the unformed material. *Pathic* refers to the surrendering, giving yourself over to the experience, when you let yourself be touched by the material and what it evokes.

Sand can be touched and felt in many ways. You can move your whole hand or just one fingertip through it, rummaging it, fingers spread or closed. You can let it flow through your fingers, shift it from one hand to another, then let it drop on the back or on the palm of your hand. You can smooth it, rough it, heap it, press it, put a finger in, or bury your hand or even your whole body in it. Sand is formless in itself, but relatively stable. It will hold a rough imprint, and it is suitable to make a mountain or a hole. All these actions involve different ways of touching, which evoke different feelings and different images.

Water is formless and unstable. Indeed, its main property is its fluidity. It always adapts to the form of its container. According to Hartley, Frank, and Goldenson (1993), water may induce a feeling of mastery, of relaxation and liberation, or it may afford satisfaction of immature drives

---

1. Apart from sand and water, clay and sometimes paint may have the same properties, when they are used, not so much to create something, as to touch and be felt. In an article on clay (Young, 1998) I found an implicit reference to the tactile qualities of this play material. This, however, was not elaborated on. The article's content was about playful creation with clay.

and an outlet for aggression. Water is clear and clean. It can be used to clean or cleanse, to satisfy an existential thirst, or to play baby and symbolically start your life all over again. But beware, the water may be poisoned, or you can drown in it. You can move your hands through it slowly and almost dreamily, or aggressively; you can stir it softly or make violent waves or a heavy flood. Again, different actions evoke different feelings and different images.

Often, children use sand and water combined. There, the relative amount of water determines the specific properties of the mixture. With just a little water, the sand becomes rougher and crumbly. Add a little more, and it becomes more solid and stable, holds its form, and will be excellent for "making sand pies," for using little sand molds, and for making sand balls or mountains. If one keeps on adding small amounts of water, the texture will change all the time, at first solidifying, gradually becoming more muddy and soft. The softness of mud, however, is very different from that of dry sand. To some persons, mud feels smooth and pleasant. To others, it may feel sticky, cold, unpleasant, or even dangerous, like quicksand.

Woltmann (1993), as a psychoanalytic child psychotherapist, points to the anal connotations of sand, water, and clay. Water can be equated with urine, mud and clay with feces. Developmentally, urine and feces are the first plastic materials children play with. Later, sand and water take their place, as socially more acceptable sources of gratification. In his view, children often use sand-and-water play to regress to earlier developmental stages, and to express primitive sexual feelings as well as conflicts from later stages of sexual development.

Because of these regressive properties, psychoanalytic therapists sometimes advise against sand-and-water play. Vermeer (1973), from her phenomenological standpoint, takes a more multifaceted view. To her, regression may have a progressive quality, because it helps children reach toward the foundations of their existence and to rebuild from there. Sensopathic play, she contends, affords an opportunity to linger, to dwell on the tactile, kinesthetic experience, and on the feelings this evokes. Its strength is that it does not demand form or fantasy. For children in conflict, sensopathic play often provides the emotional relaxation they need to help overcome their resistance to express their problems in a tangible form. In that way, sensopathic play can be a precursor, and is sometimes even a prerequisite, to thematic fantasy play. However, Vermeer acknowledges that in some children sensopathic play, because of its inherent unstableness, can be destabilizing or anxiety provoking. This is especially true for children with ADHD or a deficient sense of reality, as in borderline or psychotic disorders.

DESCRIPTION

Encouraging sensopathic play cannot be described as a single technique. Rather, it requires a therapeutic attitude that is aware of the opportunities and the dangers posed by sand-and-water play. Here, I will give some suggestions for its use.

First, sand and water need to be easily accessible in the playroom. In addition, there should be different-sized containers and other materials for sensopathic play, such as a sand tray, buckets, sieve, sandmolds, watering can, siphon, and so on. Preferably, there are different containers for dry and for wet sand. Children should be able to start with dry sand and mix in water to their heart's content.

Although tools such as a sand mold, spade, or spoon are gladly used by many children, one should keep in mind that just using your hands is more basic, keeps closer to the tactile sense,and thus might be therapeutically preferable. When a child starts by using a tool, I might say, "That works well, but it may be even more fun with your hands," and suit the action to these words by using my hands when I assist the child.

Because of the resistance of many children against sensopathic play, which may be termed as *dirty*, the therapist often needs to serve as a model. That is, the therapist shows that touching sand or rummaging mud is a natural play action. One frequently occurring example: At the start of a session, I usually take some time to talk with my client about what happened during the week. I sit down on a low stool next to the sandbox, and while we are talking I let my hand go slowly through the sand, knead it, let it slip through my fingers, and so on. Often, the child will follow my example. This not only relaxes but also facilitates the transition from talking to playing. The same position could be helpful when a child does not know what to play. While verbally reflecting on the child's difficulty to choose, I sit down and relax, slowly touching the sand with my hand. Next, I may reflect on how pleasant the sand feels to the touch. A little later, I might invite the child to try it.

When serving as a model, the therapist will specifically mention the positive feelings sensopathic play may evoke. When the child tries it out, however, it is essential to observe the child's facial expressions and body language, and to verbalize what the child feels. Feelings of disgust, dirtiness, menace, or fear are quite common and should be understood and reflected before suggesting that these negative feelings may also have a positive side, like forbidden fruits: excitement, smoothness, or thrill.

Often, sensopathic play will be not the whole, but part of the play scene. As stated before, sensopathic play may be a precursor to fantasy play. It is also my experience that meaningful imaginative play often evolves on a sensopathic foundation (Harinck and Hellendoorn, 1987). During fantasy play or when the child is busy selecting what he or she will play with, there are countless opportunities to encourage the use of sand and water. When a child is selecting toy animals, or playing with them on the floor, the therapist could suggest the animals might like to have their feet in the sand, or they might like something to drink, or to swim in. When play is about a family, they might like to get into the sand, go for a swim, or whatever. When a child selects (or seems attracted by) a boat, water animals like ducks or hippos, or mud-loving animals like pigs, offering sand and water to go with them is quite natural. Indeed, *not* offering them would be, in my view, a definite omission on the side of the therapist. When the child tries to make a hill or a hole in the sand, a little water makes this much easier. Any toy that is put into the sand leaves an imprint. I always verbalize this.

Sensopathic play may take many forms. It can be more or less pure, as in making waves, a waterfall, or a flood that turns the earth to mud. However, more often than not it is mixed with fantasy elements. Quicksand, for instance, becomes dangerous because people could sink into it. A stormy sea gains in significance because of the ships that threaten to wreck. Mud can be used to make bombs against an enemy. On the constructive side, a wall can be made to keep out the floods, and animals or people can use the mud to make a mountain or build a city. Mud can serve as food or as a magic potion. Water may cleanse. Sometimes, when children threaten to be overwhelmed by the danger or dirtiness they evoked, the therapist needs to introduce such a legitimizing element.

APPLICATIONS

Encouraging sensopathic play is especially suitable in the working-through phase of therapy with neurotic children. Usually, these children are inhibited and have difficulty getting involved in play. Frequently, their play remains superficial, just touching on the outside. Many of them have low self-esteem and constantly feel they are judged (negatively, of course) by peers as well as by adults, and thus also by the therapist. Joint sensopathic play can help them get involved, decrease their resistance toward the therapist, get to the core of their experiences, and deepen the content of their play.

Sensopathic play should not be encouraged in therapy with ADHD children, for whom it would be too disinhibiting. Neither should it be stimulated in children with psychotic disorders, for whom it would be too anxiety provoking. In fact, it might be advisable not to have water and sand available in therapy rooms for these children.

References

Allan, J. and Berry, P. (1993). Sandplay. Schaefer, C. E. and Cangelosi, D. M. (Eds.). *Play Therapy Techniques*, pp. 117–123. Northvale, NJ: Jason Aronson.

Bachelard, G. (1942). *L'eau et les Rêves* [Water and dreams]. Paris, France: Librairie José Corti.

———. (1943). *L'air et les Songes* [Air and Daydreams]. Paris, France: Librairie José Corti.

———. (1948). *La Terre et les Rêveries du Repos* [Earth and dreams of repose]. Paris, France: Librairie José Corti.

———. (1949). *La Psychanalyse du Feu* [The psychoanalysis of fire]. Paris, France: Gallimard.

Cabe, N. (1997). Gloop. Kaduson, H. G. and Schaefer, C. E. (Eds.). *101 Favorite Play Therapy Techniques*, pp. 83–86. Northvale, NJ: Jason Aronson.

Harinck, F. J. H. and Hellendoorn, J. (1987). *Therapeutisch Spel: Proces en Interactie* [Therapeutic play: process and interaction]. Lisse, Netherlands: Swets & Zeitlinger.

Hartley, R. E., Frank, L. K. and Goldenson, R. M. (1952). *Understanding Children's Play*. New York: Columbia University Press.

———. (1993). Water play. Schaefer, C. E. and Cangelosi, D. M. (Eds.), *Play Therapy Techniques*, pp. 125–130. Northvale, NJ: Jason Aronson.

Kalff, D. (1966). *Sandspiel* [Sandplay]. Zürich: Rascher Verlag.

Vermeer, E. A. A. (1955). *Spel en Spelpedagogische Problemen.* [Play and play pedagogical problems]. Utrecht, Netherlands: Bijleveld.

———. (1969). *Het Spel van Het Kind.* [Child's play]. Groningen: Wolters-Noordhoff.

———. (1973). Projectieve methoden bij pedagogische advies- en hulpverlening [Projective methods in child counseling and child treatment]. Th. Bolleman (Ed.). *Pedagogiek in Ontwikkeling* [Pedagogics in development], pp. 149–170. Tilburg, Netherlands: Zwijsen.

Woltmann, A. (1993). Mud and clay. Schaefer, C. E. and Cangelosi, D. M. (Eds.). *Play Therapy Techniques*, pp. 141–157. Northvale, NJ: Jason Aronson.

Young, M. D. (1998). Synthetic clay in play therapy. Kaduson, H. G. and Schaefer, C. E. (Eds.). *101 Favorite Play Therapy Techniques*, pp. 133–134. Northvale, NJ: Jason Aronson.

66

Heartlines and Lifelines: Narrative Reconstruction to Aid Dollhouse Play

Suzanne Getz Gregg

INTRODUCTION

Dollhouse play remains a prominent feature in contemporary playrooms and a crucial element in theoretical formulations of play therapy. Traditional props offer a wide range of options for symbolic representation (Slade and Wolf, 1994) of the various formats of the modern family and for the myriad experiences of life both in and out of families of origin. Each child has a story to tell, whether or not he or she has recognized a personal need to actually tell it. As therapists, we are wise to stay attuned to the accuracy with which each child tells his or her personal story as well as to his or her available coping resources in the pursuit of emotional well-being.

RATIONALE

The principles of constructivist theories (Noam, 1988; White and Epston, 1990; Stern, 1990) support and guide us in our interactions with young children around issues of early family life. Young children show in action what older children and adults are able to tell about their personal histories. One portion of memory is an accurate rendition of the facts (recall) of early incidents. Another portion of memory is constructive in nature, weaving elements of wish and fantasy into a mix that is strongly skewed by the intense emotions associated with the incidents. In effect, there are multiple realities of the same set of events: the factual reality, the experiential reality, and the narrative reality. A desired outcome of narrative reconstruction is a portrayal marked by both accuracy and resilience (Bloomfield, 2000). In other words, children (and adults) can face the difficult and painful truths of their early personal histories, then move beyond them to lives that are "decent and responsible and caring" (Kopp, 1972). In our universal search for meaning, we aim to make sense of our past as well as to create a future full of hope, dignity, and integrity.

DESCRIPTION

The first part of a child's story is told in the stance the child takes to the dollhouse itself, which is typically a dominant structure in clinical playrooms. A child might readily approach, hesitantly approach, or actively avoid the house by blocking it out of sight or even turning his or her back on it. The time lag between entry into the playroom and a child's overture to the dollhouse may indicate whether family issues are prominent in the child's life. A 7-year-old boy, whose family was attacked in their house one night when he was 3 and had already been diagnosed with autistic disorder, spent months with his back to the house. Once he turned toward it, he spent the next few months sequentially replaying every visual and auditory feature of the attack.

The second part of the story is manifested by the props children choose to fill the house. Can an actual doll family live in the house, or does the child need to create emotional distance by bringing in an animal family? A 5-year-old girl whose black father married a white wife after the death of her black mother spent weeks putting black families on one floor and white families on another. The girl's maternal grandparents had conveyed to her that she would be disloyal to her mother's memory if she allowed this intruder into her inner life. Over time, the doll families visited with each other, until they finally coexisted on the same floor. In reality, emotion followed cognition as the child began to develop a true affection for her attentive new stepmother. Interpretation must always be tempered by an accurate assessment of the child in terms of age and temperament and circumstance.

Children's realities these days are as complex as our world. They are witness to every perturbation of human experience. They are subjected to every form of assault against the formation of a sufficient attachment (Hughes, 1998). The greatest disorganization of the human psyche arises when early experiences are ambiguous, arbitrary, confusing, and unpredictable (Ainsworth et al., 1978). In play, the house may be under attack from wild animals or other violent, frightening forces. A 3-year-old girl whose house play was always stormy and unsettled finally revealed to her mother the incest being perpetrated by her father. The greater the portrayal of disorganization, the greater the original disconnection between accurate cognition and authentic emotion. A 5-year-old boy who was with his mother in a motel room on the night she died, alone with her body until the maid arrived in the morning, could not readily hold both fact and emotion in mind without fright and decompensation. He initially stepped on me to reach furniture for the house, as if I were as inanimate as his recently deceased mother.

When reenactment through dollhouse play, however, remains posttraumatic in nature, we are cautioned by Gil (1991) to respond in ways that disrupt the traumatic replay. It is advisable to provide other methods to facilitate growth when play alone is insufficient. We can assist, for example, by providing facts appropriate to the child's age and stage of development, which can be received without emotional collapse. Heartlines and Lifelines are two techniques that can serve as concrete representations of personal life histories, framing reality in words simple enough for a child to comprehend while still preserving emotional integration.

APPLICATIONS

Heartlines

Invite the child to draw a large red heart, and then a dashed line down the center of the heart. Begin to teach by saying, "It takes a mom and a dad for a baby to be born. When a baby is born, half his heart belongs to his mom and half belongs to . . ." As the child typically responds, "his dad," invite him to write *mom* and *dad* on each side, or do this directly for a child who is too young. Continue teaching by saying, "This is his first family—mom, dad, and baby." Invite the child to draw a box around the heart and write *family*.

When the therapeutic issue is separation or divorce of the parents, add an arrow out of the box for the parent who moved away. Ask, "What happens to the child's heart when the parents split up?" Perhaps the child says, "It's broken." Actively listen. "Ah, it hurts." Then ask, "What would make it better?" Typically a child says, "If they get back together." Offer an alternative. "Your heart stays inside you and it's always yours. It's just your first family that breaks up. Part of the love in your heart stays with your mom and part with your dad." Therapeutically, we strive for this ideal.

Then bid for multiple attachments, staying true to developmental models of early relationships (Fraiberg, 1980). "Who else is in your heart?" Add caring relatives to the side of the heart that follows family lines. Add nonfamilial others outside of the family box. When appropriate, add the new spouse if mom or dad has married. Clarify by saying, "This was your first family and you had love in that family. Now you have two families and they both love you." This extensive chart of loving others serves as contrast to the perception of a shrinking world at the time of separation. Every heart is unique, such that one's life can be known by reading the tracks on one's heart.

Lifelines

Narrating the actual events of a child's early life is one more step in the process toward health. Along a horizontal line, make entries to mark the child's birth, birthdays, moves, and significant family events. We provide facts and review events in ways that children can comprehend, even when their developmental trajectories have been compromised. One young girl with multiple physical deformities had endured 37 surgeries by the age of 5. Laying out the Lifeline of her hospitalizations brought her difficult truth into our shared experience. As we anchor events along a child's personal Lifeline, we convey that he or she is growing to be exactly who he or she is meant to be.

From Piaget's (1955) classic studies of causality, we learn that young children construct answers to complex and difficult questions from limited experience and with primitive conceptual formulations. It is hard enough for adults to understand the dynamics of their own behavior, harder still to convey these realities to children without disheartening them. As we help clarify thorny relationship issues fraught with moral and ethical dilemmas, children reach better-formulated conclusions. A 9-year-old girl, relinquished by both birth mother and adoptive mother, transformed in play an evil witch mother who devoured her daughters to a struggling mother who sent them to jail so the judge could teach them how to behave. Lesson learned, he sent them home.

Through Heartlines and Lifelines, we assist children in naming the truths of their personal lives. At any age, only the truth is the truth, and it can set us free, even if it is harsh. We help children examine how to live a just life in an unjust world. We teach them our belief that every sad story can have a happy ending by incorporating basic trust, cognitive rigor, and a healthy optimism. Our view of our place in the world can be reconstructed at any age and circumstance in the presence of a caring other.

References

Ainsworth, M. D. S., Blehar, M. C., Waters, E., and Wall, S. (1978). *Patterns of Attachment: A Psychological Study of the Strange Situation*. Hillsdale, NJ: Lawrence Erlbaum.

Bloomfield, H. (2000). *Making Peace with Your Past: The Six Essential Steps to Enjoying a Great Future*. New York: HarperCollins.

Fraiberg, S. (1980). *Clinical Studies in Infant Mental Health*. New York: Basic Books.

Gil, E. (1991). *The Healing Power of Play*. New York: Guilford Press.

Hughes, D. (1998). *Building the Bonds of Attachment: Awakening Love in Deeply Troubled Children*. Northvale, NJ: Jason Aronson.

Kopp, S. B. (1972). *If You Meet the Buddha on the Road, Kill Him! The Pilgrimage of Psychotherapy Patients*. New York: Bantam Books.

Noam, G. G. (1988). A constructivist approach to developmental psychopathology. E. D. Nannis and P. A. Cowan (Eds.), *New Directions for Child Development*, 39, 91.

Piaget, J. (1955). *The Language and Thought of the Child*. Cleveland, OH: Meridian.

Slade, A. and Wolf, D. P. (1994). *Children at Play: Clinical and Developmental Approaches to Meaning and Representation*. New York: Oxford University Press.

Stern, D. N. (1990). *Diary of a Baby*. New York: Basic Books.

White, M. and Epston, D. (1990). *Narrative Means to Therapeutic Ends*. New York: Norton.

67

Shaving Cream

Corinne H. Greenberg

INTRODUCTION

Professionals who study and work with children know the importance of play for children; they also know that often a disturbed child will shut down and not let anyone reach his or her inner being. Child therapists know that letting the child express him- or herself through play and art will often unlock the barriers of deep distress and trauma.

Professionals who work with children know that many young children are developmentally unable to verbalize their feelings, fears, and problems. Physically and sexually abused children and youth often do not wish to disclose events concerning the abuse they experienced. Children and youth who have difficulties expressing themselves verbally due to their developmental stage, disability, or emotional shutdown will often communicate thoughts and feelings through play techniques.

I am seeing an increasing number of younger children referred by social services or attorneys due to abuse and foster care. The referral source is often seeking a play therapist and some of these children are as young as 2 or 3 years of age.

I feel it is important for professionals to be aware of the developmental stage of the child and to provide age appropriate activities. Children in

Erickson's (Erickson, 1950, 1982) stage of autonomy and Piaget's (Singer & Revenson, 1996) sensorimotor and preoperational stages enjoy gross motor activities and respond positively to playing with shaving cream. Many older children who have shut down emotionally in these early developmental stages due to abuse or trauma also enjoy playing with shaving cream and benefit from this tactile experience.

RATIONALE

Smearing and piling up shaving cream are primitive activities. This involves the sensorimotor stage as the child uses his or her fingers, hands, and arms. Children feel, smell, see, and hear the shaving cream come out of the can. They enjoy the funny sounds as the shaving cream gets low in the can, and they are in a safe place to have fun with this. In many social settings such as home and school they are not allowed to carry on over the strange and funny sounds.

DESCRIPTION

The therapist places cans of shaving cream on the shelves with other creative media such as paints, clay, crayons, scissors, and paper. The children are informed that they are allowed to choose what they want to do during the session. Children might spend the entire session with the shaving cream for several sessions and then return to it when it meets their needs as they often do with other play materials.

Shaving cream can be sprayed on the playroom table, and then the child can dig in and smear the shaving cream or build with it and make all sorts of objects. Some clients have made snow, snowmen, people, cars, homes, the beach, and many other objects that they want to experience.

Children of all ages like to mix the shaving cream with water in a dishpan. Some use an egg beater from the kitchen center to make bubbles and some want to wash all of the dishes in the play area as well as the dolls with the shaving cream and water. The children like the way the water and shaving cream feel on their hands and arms, and some play like they are shaving their arms and face. Children enjoy splashing the white foam and seeing the bubbles expand as they splash.

Children may like to carry the dishpan down the hall to the sink and empty it. They have an increased sense of pride as they are carrying their pan of soap and bubbles only to watch them go down the drain. The lingering clean scent of shaving cream on their hands is also fun for many children.

APPLICATIONS

Children with encopresis seem to gravitate to shaving cream frequently.

I have also found that many of my clients who experience incidents of encopresis due to trauma such as abuse or living in foster care, decrease or eliminate all incidents of encopresis after several sessions of playing with shaving cream. These children seem to want to add paint to the shaving cream and smear it on their hands and the table; some children have the desire to smear it on the wall or chalkboard as well.

This activity works well in clinic settings, the child's home, hospitals, guidance counselor offices, shelters, and outside settings. This is also a fun activity for groups participating in a summer or after school therapeutic program. When using the shaving cream outside, the clean-up is easy, just wash it off tables and outside play equipment with a hose.

Other Uses

I use the shaving cream activity in my child development classes and play therapy workshops. Most children and adults love the feeling of the shaving cream between their fingers and on their hands. This activity encourages individuals of all ages to talk and laugh, and it even brings back childhood memories for adults in play therapy.

An extra fun thing to do is put some of the shaving cream in a ziplock bag, add one or two different colors of paint or food coloring, and see the colors blend and make different colors. This can be used when you don't want to clean up a mess such as with the hospitalized child or a homebound ill child.

I have noticed that parents, too, like to play with a package of color and foam to help with their stress during the intake or family session!

You can find many uses for shaving cream; it travels in a tote bag or purse very well, and you can take it almost anywhere!

Figure 67.1

References

Erikson, E. H. (1950). *Childhood and Society*. New York: W. W. Norton & Company.

———. (1982). *The Life Cycle Completed*. New York: W. W. Norton & Company.

Singer, D. G. and Revenson, T. A. (1996). *A Piaget Primer: How a Child Thinks* (Rev. ed.). New York: Plum/Penguin Group.

68

Talking Cards

Peter Mortola

INTRODUCTION

I was inspired to create a large collection of Talking Cards based on the work of Dr. Violet Oaklander (Oaklander, 1996). During the process of doing my dissertation research on her methods of training adults to do therapy with children (Mortola, 1999), I was impressed by how powerful the use of images was in her work with both children and adults. For example, I often saw Dr. Oaklander use a deck of Medicine Cards (Sams and Carson, 1988) with adults in her trainings and with children in her therapeutic work. Based on the Native American way of viewing animals as having special healing powers, the Medicine Cards are a collection of colorful drawings of animals and descriptions of those animals (e.g., regarding the mouse card, the text of the accompanying book states: "It is good medicine to pay attention to detail, but it is bad medicine to chew every little thing to pieces").

In the therapeutic context, Dr. Oaklander might ask a child to pick one of the many animal cards (e.g., a porcupine, a dolphin, an ant) to represent how he or she was feeling that day. By using the card, the child has a "conversation piece" that he or she can look at and talk about while at the same time revealing something authentic about him- or herself.

Additionally, the comments in the text accompanying the Medicine Cards can be reviewed to see if they "fit" for the child or not, thereby allowing the child to make additional statements about themselves in an assertive way.

Based on Dr. Oaklander's methods with the Medicine Cards, I started collecting pictures from every magazine, calendar, catalogue, and old book that I could find to create well over one hundred Talking Cards that I have been using ever since. It is the power of working with images to foster conversation and involvement in the therapeutic process that I believe is at the heart of my success with them.

RATIONALE

In a discussion regarding the role of imagery and detail in conversation, Tannen (1989) quotes a line that was spoken to her by a friend during a long-distance phone call: "I wish you were here," stated the friend, "to see the sweet peas coming up." In reference to this conversational fragment, Tannen asks:

> Why is this more moving than the simple, "I wish you were here"? . . . it is because of the sweet peas—small and ordinary and particular. The sweet peas coming up provide a detail of everyday life that brings everyday life to life. The sweet peas create an image—a picture of something, whereas "Wish you were here" suggests only an abstract idea of absence. (p. 134)

Tannen states that the use of details in conversation to create images acts to facilitate "involvement" between those in conversation. Both the speaker and the listener are involved in the process of imagining and trying to make sense of a scene through the details provided:

> Details create images, images create scenes, and scenes spark emotions, making possible both understanding and involvement . . . it is in large part through the creation of a shared world of images that ideas are communicated and understanding is achieved. (p. 135)

In my experience, use of the Talking Cards has certainly aided in the creation of a "shared world of images" between myself and the child or adult with whom I am working.

DESCRIPTION

A number of steps is required to create the Talking Cards. First, cut out random pictures and images from all sorts of magazines, calendars, catalogues, and books. Then glue the most interesting and compelling images of this bunch to 6 by 9-inch pieces of heavy construction paper. The relatively large size of these cards and images makes it easier for individuals to share their chosen card with others (e.g., across a circle in a group setting).

In choosing the images, look for interesting pictures that carry some emotional weight (e.g., a butterfly, a tin man, a moody sky), but also choose some that are ambiguous and open to interpretation (e.g., beads of dew on a spider's web, an advertisement showing a man from the waist up as an astronaut and from the waist down wearing shorts and swimming fins).

Sort these images into categories (e.g., people, places, and animals) and label them on the back of the cards accordingly. Occasionally the therapist can direct a child to use only the people cards, for example, to pick images that represent her family. Care should be used in the selection of the people cards in order to represent as much diversity as possible (e.g., gender, age, ethnicity, race, action, fun, seriousness, adventurousness), but also try to represent diverse animals and places as well. The last step is to laminate the cards so they will not be easily bent or damaged.

Keep the cards in an old metal box or some other interesting container that looks like it could be holding treasure. This heightens the child's or adult's interest and engagement with the cards. Because of the lovely slick surface of the cards created by the lamination, the therapist can toss a stack of them across the floor and they will spread out like a deck of playing cards. This dramatic touch also seems to enhance their appeal. When the cards are all spread out across the floor in a colorful and chaotic collage, it's difficult for both children and adults to resist rooting through them. Once they start the search for the card that best fits them at that moment, they become deeply involved in the process of projecting their own experience onto the cards. Paradoxically, this process helps them to be aware of and in touch with their own emotions, thoughts, and experiences as they shuffle through a random pile of images.

APPLICATIONS

I have used these cards with both individuals and groups. As a kind of "check in" at the beginning of a session I might say, "Pick a card or two to represent how you are feeling today." I have found that clients will often ask me if they can pick more than one card after finding two or three that they can't seem to let go of. In this way, I have often seen clients use more than one card as a way to articulate and work through their conflicting emotions or experiences.

I have also used the Talking Cards as a way to find out how a particular session went for an individual or a whole group. In that case, I might say, "I'd like you to pick a card or two to represent something you have learned, something you have felt, or something you have experienced while we worked together today."

To move toward closure in the terminating session for an individual or a group, I might say, "I would like you to pick three cards: One that represents who you were or how you felt when this group started, one that represents who you are now, and one that represents who you would like to become in the future."

I have used the Talking Cards like a hybrid of a projective test and a tarot deck. In this way, they facilitate rich descriptions of personal experience in a fun and nonthreatening way. As Tannen described, the use of the images seems to help develop "understanding and involvement," not only between myself and the client, but also between the client and their own experiences and feelings.

References

Mortola, P. (1999). Narrative formation and gestalt closure: helping clients make sense of "disequilibrium" through stories in the therapeutic setting. *Gestalt Review* 3(4): 308–320. Hillsdale, NJ: The Analytic Press.

Oaklander, V. (1996). Gestalt play therapy. *Handbook of Play Therapy, Volume Two: Advances and Innovations*. O'Conner, K. J. and Schaefer, C. E. (Eds.). New York: John Wiley and Sons, Inc.

Sams, J. and Carson, D. (1988). *Medicine Cards: The Discovery of Power Through the Ways of Animals*. Santa Fe, NM: Bear & Co.

Tannen, D. (1989). *Talking Voices: Repetition, Dialogue, and Imagery in Conversational Discourse*. Cambridge, NY: Cambridge University Press.

69

The Fluster-ometer

Lawrence C. Rubin

INTRODUCTION

In the course of performing psychological evaluations, play therapy, and counseling with anxious, ruminative children and teens, particularly those with poor self-image and academic/play inhibition, a consistent pattern has become evident. These clients, often lacking a means of monitoring and (positively) evaluating their performance, tend to easily lose concentration as task demand, difficulty, or ambiguity increases, to the point of what one insightful young client called "brain freeze" or "brain block." Such clients are not aware of a steady and increasing stream of negative self-verbalizations until they are frozen on a particular question, blocked from choice or expression in the playroom, or distracted from a specific thought. This process of escalating self-distraction to the point of immobility has been labeled "flusteration" (from flustered and frustration).

These clients need a simple, nonthreatening way to develop awareness of, monitor, and modify this behavior. Once they have developed working insight into and control over this negative pattern, they can take the tool into other settings, most notably school. The "fluster-ometer" is a simple, gamelike, cognitive/behavioral technique that allows for self-monitoring and deflecting of this pattern in order to keep the client focused and productive.

RATIONALE

This technique can be therapeutic for several reasons. First, because the device is created in the therapist's presence and with his or her assistance, relationship building occurs while the client builds skill in self-monitoring and correction. Second, it utilizes a simple visual measuring device (a gauge) that the client is likely to be familiar with from other contexts, such as the car, kitchen, and board games. Third, it is relatively nonthreatening, because it is both gamelike in design and capitalizes upon play rather than serious cognitive deliberation. Fourth, the client may feel more empowered by using a self-created as opposed to manufactured tool. Last, it is very portable, assuring its use in other settings.

DESCRIPTION

The fluster-ometer is a dial made out of cardboard to resemble a temperature gauge with three zones: green (cruising zone), yellow (fluster zone), red (brain block). The dial has several bubble spaces so the child can personalize the self-verbalizations he or she makes in each one. Examples for the green zone would be: "Hey, I know this," "This is pretty easy," and "What I need to do here is . . .". Examples for the yellow zone are: "I should know this," "I feel stupid," and "Why can't I get it?" Examples for the red zone are: "I am stupid," "I'll never know this," and "My parents will be so upset." The therapist and client tailor the verbalization to the child's personal experience in the testing, therapy, school, or social situation. The needle, or fluster arrow, is made of cardboard and held in place with a push-pin or thumbtack so it can be moved in both directions.

Once the process of "flusteration" is identified and discussed with the client, time is spent cutting out, coloring, and labeling the various zones on the fluster-ometer using real experiences or situations from the client's life. When the client is observed engaging in flusteration, or volunteers the information from his or her life experience, the game begins. The client and therapist position the dial to whatever zone the child is or was experiencing, that is, cruising, flustered, or brain-blocked. The goal is to clearly identify the thought or thought process that occurred or is occurring and to reposition the dial using a combination of positive self-statement and whatever relaxation techniques the therapist typically relies on. Monitoring the downward movement on the dial while using these anxiety reduction techniques is the immediate goal, while implementing them outside of the therapy room is the long-term challenge.

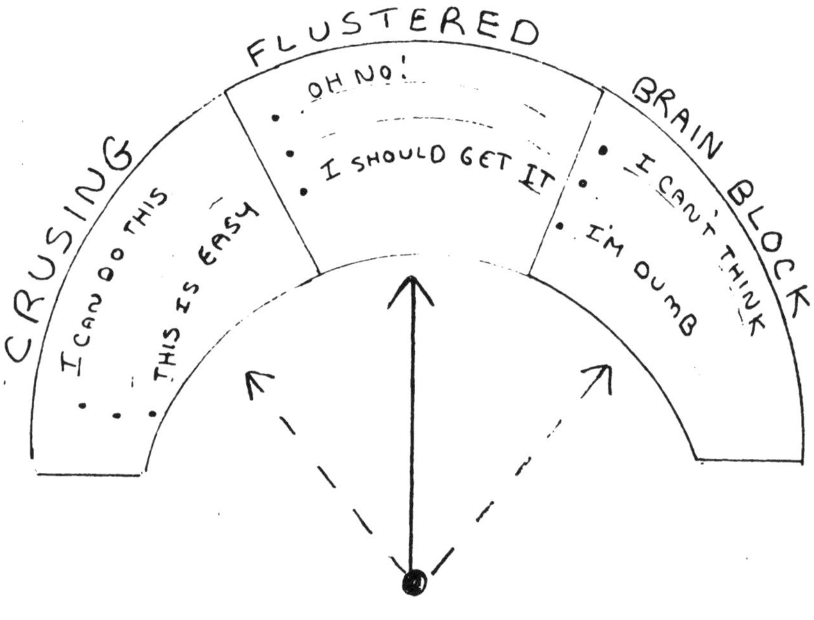

Figure 69.1

APPLICATIONS

This technique is designed for use with overanxious, ruminative, and inhibited children and teens who manifest performance anxiety during test-taking, or unstructured/free-play situations. Depressed clients who offer or even subvocalize negative self-talk could benefit from this technique. Further, clients with attention problems who distract themselves with irrelevancies could be redirected with the fluster-ometer. With each of these clients, and in each of these contexts, choice, focus, and positive self-statements are necessary; however, when these processes are derailed by negative self-verbalization, a deflecting technique is needed. Even if negative self-talk is not immediately apparent, the therapist can elicit possible self-statements that the client may be subvocalizing. Replacement of those statements with positive ones, in the context of relaxation, serves as a preventive in future situations.

This technique has been successfully used in testing situations by guiding older children and young teen clients who derail themselves back on track and into a more productive mode. It has also been used with younger children in the playroom who have difficulty choosing activities, making decisions during play, and have difficulty adhering to limits. In the latter case, these oppositional clients are shown how the stream of negative self-verbalization results in a roadblock between them and the therapist. Parents have reported the use of this technique at home during homework time as well as in school.

70

Let's Play Ball

Mary Lou Sherry

INTRODUCTION

I am a school counselor who may travel to several elementary schools during the course of the week. Transporting tote bags filled with toys, board games, and various play objects can be a challenging task.

One toy item I always include in my bag is some type of ball. It can be made of plastic, sponge, rubber, vinyl, or whatever synthetic material that is used in today's market in the manufacture of a ball. I have found this toy to be extremely valuable working with children in the primary, intermediate, and junior high grades. I believe any therapist or counselor who works with children in any environment, be it school or other health facility, will find ball playing a useful and productive strategy.

RATIONALE

Children from infancy stages, to early childhood, adolescence, and adulthood have been utilizing some type of ball playing over a long period of time. It is a simple, natural way of communication that many children enjoy either by themselves or with others. Almost all children see it as a fun activity and nonthreatening. In this light, playing ball can provide challenges and competition to youngsters who might otherwise be fearful of failure and rejection.

Playing ball can be viewed as therapeutic because any activities can offer the therapist the opportunity to connect, establish, and build rapport, while securing information needed for assessment and treatment of the individual. It is therapeutic for the child because it provides the child with little restraints and a nonstructured atmosphere. Playing ball is looked upon as a fun activity by almost all children and consequently can lower their initial anxieties in meeting with the therapist. The child is then motivated to work with the therapist to find a solution to the presenting problem.

DESCRIPTION

Materials

- Rubber ball, ball, or soccer ball
- Plastic basket hoop and sponge ball ($1.00 in dollar stores), or a wastepaper basket can be used as a substitute for a hoop
- Plastic baseball bat

Depending on the amount of space and time the therapist can expand or limit the ball playing activities. As soon as the child enters the room, the therapist throws the ball to the client and greets him or her with a Hi and a warm smile. The therapist continues talking and providing information about his or her job in the school. This allows opportunities for the child to share some facts, feelings, likes and dislikes about him- or herself, and some family background.

Often the child will bring up issues like parents' separation, divorce, and family losses through illness or death, or problems within the school environment. Depending on the time element and child's interest, the therapist might move on to playing basketball, soccer, or whiffle ball (space availability) using identified materials. The therapist plays with the child and a scoring system is maintained. For example for a basketball game, mount hoop on wall or door, identify shooting distance, 3 points for long shot, 1 point for short one, or whatever child and therapist agree on. Depending on observed needs for the child, therapist may win or lose in ongoing matches. In many instances, older children are quite good, like the challenge, and enjoy beating the therapist, and the activity helps lower the child's resistance to invasive questions.

APPLICATION

"Let's Play Ball" can be used with all ages of children. I have found it to be very useful with children with the following characteristics:

ADHD—provides this youngster with freedom of mobility in throwing and catching the ball; it can increase gross motor skills through bodily movements.

Low self-esteem—builds on self-confidence and competence level as child is allowed to grow in abilities without the threat of rejection.

Aggressive/angry—allows the child physical movements/exercises in competitive games while allowing freedom to express feelings connected with the child's issues.

Shy withdrawn/traumatized—activities offer no threat to the child and provide a safe place to play by him- or herself, with the therapist, or within a small group.

CASE EXAMPLE

It was early in the school year when a seventh-grade boy was referred for disruptive and aggressive behavior. I learned from the principal that the boy had a history of fighting with peers and was suspected of school vandalism prior to enrolling at the present school. My initial meeting with this boy was typical of other initial contacts with students. I identified my role in the school, confidentiality rights, and the reason for the referral. At this time I was not yet utilizing the Playing Ball technique described herein. At this first meeting, he presented himself as having little concern, some anger, and much disinterest in connecting with me now or in the future. Reluctantly, he gave minimal responses to my inquiries regarding school and family background. It appeared he was being raised by his maternal grandparents. He had little contact with his father. His mother and younger sister were living in another town. He did have periodic visits with them, which he seemed to enjoy. He spoke on occasion with his father, but expressed his anger at his father's lack of communication and unkept promises to him. At this meeting, I did learn of his great love and interest in basketball.

I used that piece of information and my periodic visits to the dollar store to purchase the plastic hoop and sponge ball, which opened the doors for this young boy and therapist to work together in finding healthier ways to cope with his life situations, constructive behaviors for expressing anger. As we approached the end of the school year, he came in one day and said, "I didn't lose my temper" or give an "attitude face" in this situation. He proceeded to describe an event that occurred on the playground with another classmate. Prior to our sessions, he most likely would have gotten into a fight, but not this time. He managed to avoid this behavior by counting to ten, walking away, and focusing on something else other than his feelings of anger. In the second instance, he is tuning in more to the negative messages he may be giving by his body language and working on more positive ones. He expressed feelings of pride when some of his teachers noted changes in his attitude and behavior. I believe the many sessions we shared playing basketball provided groundwork for this youngster to become involved in counseling and relate to the profession in a positive and affirmative manner now and in his future.

71

Creating a New Story with the Sandtray

Daniel S. Sweeney

INTRODUCTION

For children, adolescents, and adults who have experienced emotional turmoil and trauma, it is crucial that the therapeutic process impart hope. A blending of theoretical concepts can be very helpful in this regard. One of the benefits of the narrative approaches to therapy is the focus upon giving clients the opportunity to tell their story and to create new ones. One of the benefits of solution-focused approaches is the focus on envisioning a future without the problem. The use of the solution-focused *miracle question* does this, by helping clients consider a possible future without the presence of the current challenge. These are techniques that can be drawn into the world of play therapy.

Projective and expressive interventions such as sandtray therapy can provide clients with a meaningful and effective means of benefitting from these techniques. Adaptation of these techniques through the use of nonverbal and expressive mediums can assist clients to process intrapsychic issues in a different, and frequently safer, manner.

RATIONALE

It is easy for some to tell one's story and envision the future, but it may be considerably challenging for others. For children, who lack the verbal, cognitive, and abstract-thinking skills of adulthood, verbalizing these things is often an unrealistic goal. For the client of any age who has experienced trauma, verbalizing these things may be equally unrealistic. The advantages of employing an expressive approach for these clients are considerable. The sandtray technique is an effective means in this regard.

Schaefer (1994) suggested several properties which provide the sense of distance and safety that clients gain in a medium such as Sandtray therapy: (1) Symbolization—clients can use a predatory miniature to represent an abuser; (2) "As if" quality—clients can use the pretend quality of Sandtray therapy to act out events as if they were not real life; (3) Projection—clients can project intense emotions onto the miniatures, who can then safely act out these feelings; and (4) Displacement—clients can displace negative feelings onto the miniatures rather than expressing them toward family members. Sandtray therapy provides not only the opportunity for abreaction to occur, but facilitates the process through the setting and media.

There are many advantages in the use of Sandtray; Homeyer and Sweeney (1998) list several, including the unique kinesthetic quality of Sandtray; the unique setting for the emergence of therapeutic metaphors; the potential for overcoming client resistance, providing an effective communication medium for the client with poor verbal skills; and the potential to cut through verbalization when used as a defense.

Telling one's story in the sandtray not only provides the opportunity for abreaction but also brings clarification and objectification to the client's presenting problem. It may not be possible to make complete sense of a traumatic event, but giving expression to the complex intrapsychic issues is a key step in the healing process. This is often best facilitated in an expressive mode.

Imaging and envisioning a changed future, one without the problem or with an adaptation to the problem, is a powerful treatment mechanism. When clients imagine positives and possibilities, it creates hope and generates emotion that can work against the problem. Particularly when the presenting issues seem overwhelming and insurmountable, picturing a different scenario can begin a process of healing or provide momentum to move beyond a therapeutic impasse. In the treatment process, it may be more important for clients to tell their story and realize that there is potential for color in a current life of darkened shades.

DESCRIPTION

With the use of Sandtray, it is important to utilize appropriate materials. The sandtray is more than just a container of the sand. It is a container of the psyche as well. The selection of the tray and miniatures should be deliberate and intentional. The "standard" size tray, which is approximately 30 by 20 by 3 inches, with the inside painted blue (to represent water and sky), is recommended. A tray that is smaller may be too confining, and a tray that is much larger may be too expansive and thus overwhelming for the client and the psyche. The rectangular shape facilitates dividing the sandtray scene into sections, noting that clients often need to separate and compartmentalize issues.

Miniatures are the words, symbols, and metaphors of the clients' nonverbal communication. It is through the use of the miniatures that clients are able to express feelings, thoughts, beliefs, and desires that may be too overwhelming for words, or that may be more typical for clients using sandtray, providing an expression for that which is still beyond words.

Several categories of miniatures are necessary, including but not limited to: people, buildings, vehicles, animals, vegetation, deities, mythical creatures/objects, structures, and natural objects. Miniature selection should be sensitive to race, culture, gender, and other demographics. They should be grouped together by category and preferably displayed on open shelves. A modest yet broad collection is more than adequate.

This particular sandtray intervention is essentially an adaptation of Mills's (Mills and Crowley, 1986) Pain Getting Better technique. Mills instructed her clients to draw three pictures: (1) draw the pain; (2) draw the pain "all better"; and (3) draw what would help the first picture change into the second. The sandtray provides a wonderful and three-dimensional palette within which to create such pictures. Mills writes about the use of this technique with children coping with physical pain. It clearly has applications beyond this.

Clients are asked to create three trays. The first tray is a scene or world that is a depiction of the client's presenting problem. The instructions can be as general or specific as the therapist deems appropriate. This may involve a request that clients re-create a traumatic situation or that clients create a tray that depicts their emotional state. Recognizing the challenge for some clients to approach painful issues, it may be helpful to use a graduated or developmental approach and get more specific as clients are ready to address deeper intrapsychic issues.

The second tray involves a scene or world that is a depiction of what life would be like with the trauma-response resolved, the conflict worked through, the negative emotion gone, and so forth. The client is free to express self in any way whether or not the tray has the order and organization that may be hoped for in the client's life. This is not a time to interpret the client's creation, but a time for the client to consider possibilities through metaphor and symbols without intrusion.

The third tray involves a scene or world that depicts how to get from tray one to tray two. It is most important not to force the client with a prescriptive agenda in this stage. The client can use passive or aggressive themes, natural or supernatural methods, and as few or as many materials as desired. To emphasize this in another way, it is not important that this process or creation make sense or be logical. It is not important that the therapist understand the client; it is important that the client feel understood.

The therapist can choose to verbally interact with the client at any level, with the encouragement to gauge interaction by the client's own affective and verbal level. Clients can be asked to describe what they have created, make a story about the scene(s), describe and/or create dialogues for miniatures, and so on—or clients can be free to not say anything at all. If this truly is an expressive medium, clients can fully express self without words. It is not necessary to interpret the client's creation. It is important that the client give the meaning to the scenes.

APPLICATIONS

This technique can be used with children, adolescents, adults, couples, and families. Children dealing with externalizing or internalizing disorders are frequently met with interventions that are so prescriptive as to limit their opportunities to express underlying emotional issues. Clients dealing with relational conflict, physiological challenges, abuse and trauma, grief, and so on are often met with this same difficulty. Although the need for multidimensional interventions must be considered, the need for clients to tell their stories and consider the possibility of a future with hope is crucial. The sand and miniatures create this opportunity.

References

Homeyer, L. and Sweeney, D. (1998). *Sandtray Therapy: A Practical Manual*. San Marcos, TX: Lindan Press.

Mills, J. and Crowley, R. (1986). *Therapeutic Metaphors for Children and the Child Within*. New York: Brunner/Mazel.

Schaefer, C. (1994). Play therapy for psychic trauma in children. K. O'Connor and C. Schaefer (Eds.), *Handbook of Play Therapy, Vol. 2*. New York: John Wiley & Sons.

72

The Magic Wand

Virginia B. Allen

INTRODUCTION

Child therapists, through training and experience, understand the therapeutic language of children. The child therapist appreciates and utilizes the child's work of play toward attaining the goals of therapy. A child therapist understands the value of verbal and nonverbal activities in the playroom.

One notable characteristic of child therapists is the understanding that children often live in two worlds: their real world and their fantasy world. Often the boundaries between these worlds are not clear for the child in therapy, however understanding and clarifying the fantasy world as compared to reality enhances the therapeutic environment. To better understand how the child would change all or part of his or her life assists the therapist in "stepping into" the child's world. It also assists the therapist in setting appropriate therapeutic goals.

A child therapist uses a theoretical base for his or her therapeutic intervention along with a variety of techniques. The Magic Wand technique is one way that facilitates the child in verbalizing about his or her fantasy world. This technique provides information to the therapist about how the child would change his or her life if only he or she had the power of the wand.

RATIONALE

Working with a child in therapy can often be significantly different than working with adults. Often children are nonverbal or verbally nonresponsive to the therapist's reflections or questions.

Children are sometimes unwilling or unable to answer direct questions or queries asked by the therapist. Additionally, the child therapist knows that children are more likely to share information about themselves and their feelings if they can place themselves in a different role or attribute their answer to someone or something else.

The Magic Wand technique is a way to provide the child with the safety net he or she needs to share verbally thoughts and feelings about his or her fantasy world and him- or herself in that world. With the magic wand, the child can tell about how he or she wishes life were different. Holding the magic wand provides a safe environment for the child to share his or her fantasy world with the therapist.

DESCRIPTION

The magic wand itself can be anything from a purchased wand decorated with bright colors and shapes on the outside, glitter and shapes that move in liquid on the inside, or a uniquely shaped stick. Avoid wands with streamers attached as they tend to be too distracting and not as easily accepted by boys. Instead of one wand, different types of wands could be made available for the child to choose whichever one he or she would want to use.

The wand is left in a prominent place in the playroom for the child to find. Alternately, the therapist can keep the wand in a drawer or box. The therapist can ask the child if he or she would like to see the wand, and then produce it with some degree of fanfare.

While the child is holding the wand, the therapist (depending on the age of the child and the creativity of the therapist) tells a story or explains about the magic of the wand. Basically, the child is told that when the child holds the wand he or she has the power or ability to clearly see how he or she would like life (or a specific part of life as set up by the therapist) to change. The therapist can assist the child in visualizing the changes in his or her mind by suggesting the child think about specific people, events, or environments.

After the child can visualize the changes, the therapist tells the child the wand gives him or her the power to describe with words, outloud, these changes. If the verbal descriptions are brief and without much detail, the therapist can reflect suggestions (that is, feelings, environmental changes, and so on). The child can either answer or wave the wand to indicate acceptance or rejection of these suggestions.

This technique can be modified in a variety of ways to gain understanding of how a child wishes (fantasizes) things could be different from what they are in his or her life. For example, this technique could be used to explore how a child would like to change him- or herself, change others' behaviors or feelings, change the environment he or she lives in, or how he or she would like to see him- or herself differently in relationships with others or in the family.

APPLICATIONS

This technique is applicable to all children but works especially well with younger children (ages 4 to 8). It works very well with children involved in a divorce situation, especially a high-conflict divorce. It is also an excellent technique for working with children in abuse situations.

The magic wand allows the child to verbalize fantasies about how he or she wishes life would be different from a safe position. Younger children accept the notion that the wand can help clarify and verbalize his or her fantasies. The child knows from the therapist's description that the wand can't actually change his or her life, but verbalizing his or her wishes about changes can clarify goals and desires.

The Magic Wand technique provides the therapist with the opportunity to understand the child's reality by understanding the fantasy or the mirror image of his or her reality. It can provide the therapist with a better understanding of how the child would like to see him- or herself behave or be accepted differently in relationships with others.

The Magic Wand technique is another way to provide the therapist with an opportunity to understand a child's life. It is a technique that provides the opportunity for the therapist to understand the child's perceptions of his or her world by understanding the child's fantasies of what he or she believes would be a better life. It is a technique that provides the therapist with the opportunity to understand the child's present situation by understanding the child's desires for changes in his or her life.

73

Emotional Tone Game

Heidi Gerard Kaduson

INTRODUCTION

Children who are deficient in social skills or have anger management problems often do not know how they sound when they are saying a certain statement. Many times their tone is nasty or hostile, when they are really feeling insecure or afraid. It is necessary when working with children like this to assess whether they are able to understand what emotional feelings sound like, and what different emotions look like when they are trying to read other people's affect. Cox and Gunn (1980) have pointed out three reasons why children may fail to respond appropriately in social situations: (1) the child may not know what the appropriate behavior is; (2) the child might have the knowledge, but lack the practice; or (3) the child's emotional responses may inhibit the performance of the desirable behavior. The child with insufficient knowledge of the desirable behavior may not have attended to the correct use of the prosocial behavior by others, or such appropriate models may not have been available in the child's environment. Therapists have tried many different ways to get through to children regarding social cues. Often children without the ability to read social cues are having trouble with friends, authority figures, and other instances where it is important.

In fact, without social awareness many children end up either isolated and withdrawn or aggressive and identified as having a behavior disorder. This technique was developed as both an assessment tool and a teaching tool for children with social skills deficits.

RATIONALE

When children are in play therapy, they are more open to learn something new because of the intrinsic value of play and its communicative value to children. If children do not feel threatened by a play technique, they are usually willing and able to learn new material. The fun of play makes them less anxious and more open. With the Emotional Tone Game, children role play different sounds and facial expressions in order to get a chip. The repetition of the game over time allows the children to learn how to read other people and how to sound more effective in their own communication.

DESCRIPTION

In order to play the Emotional Tone Game, the therapist needs the following:

1. A set of cards with a feeling listed and drawn on each card, such as mad, sad, frustrated, happy, afraid, and so on.
2. A piece of paper with the "sample sentence" typed on it in large print.
3. A bag of bingo chips.

The sentence created for this technique is *"I have a dog, and I have to take her for a walk."* This sentence can be changed to fit the therapeutic situation.

After the game is set up by putting the paper with the sentence on the table and the stack of cards next to it, the therapist tells the child that they are going to play a game called the Tone Game. The person with the most chips wins. The therapist models how to play by taking a card and reading the emotional word aloud (for example, *mad*) to illustrate how the game is played. Then the therapist tells the child that s/he will have to say this sentence in a "mad" way so that the child would guess the emotion that the therapist is trying to show. The therapist illustrates the technique by saying "I have a dog, and I have to take her for a walk" with a very mad tone and facial expression. Once the child understands the rules, and that s/he will get a chip for each correct answer, the game begins.

The therapist goes first, and mixes the cards. The therapist picks a feeling card and does not show it to the child. Then the therapist acts out the sentence with exaggerated tone and facial expression. If the child is correct on the emotion that is being displayed, s/he gets a chip. The child then picks a feeling card and reads the same sentence with her/his emotional tone and facial expression. The therapist would get a chip if s/he guesses the emotion illustrated by the child.

The therapist can then assess if the child is able to produce socially appropriate tones and expressions or not, and teach the child how to do them better by modeling the emotion when the therapist comes across the same emotion. In many cases, it is beneficial to stack the deck so that the more subtle feelings are placed toward the end of the game.

APPLICATIONS

This technique has been useful with all children who are having social skills problems. It has also helped in the assessment of whether a child can read social cues of others. Teaching through this technique is easily done and fun for the child. It is most helpful if the therapist guesses wrong on some of the feelings so that the child will win by having more chips. The more fun that is used in the game, the more the child will play it over and over and learn by doing.

Use of the more expressive emotions first gives the child the edge and illustrates the easily understood emotions like "mad," "sad," "happy," and "scared."

Reference

Cox, R. D., and Gunn, W. B. (1980). Interpersonal skills in the schools: Assessment and curriculum development. D. P. Rathjen and J. P. Foreyt (Eds.), *Social Competence: Interventions for Children and Adults*. New York: Pergamon Press.

74

Bubbles and Boundaries

Teresa M. Christensen

INTRODUCTION

Children who have been sexually and physically abused struggle with many issues, including personal and interpersonal boundaries. Throughout my work with children affected by abuse, I was consumed with various recommendations about how to address such issues in play therapy. As I began to review various techniques and toys in my playroom, I found myself feeling a bit unsatisfied about their effectiveness at reaching issues specific to boundaries. While some techniques appeared to work at the onset of the relationship, as more complex issues arose, I realized that different interventions were needed. At these times, I provided stimulus directly related to boundaries, yet sessions seemed more like lessons full of content and lecture with little opportunity for expression of emotions and experiential play.

Therefore, I began to brainstorm ideas about how to address the issue of boundaries in a more experiential and concrete manner. It was then that I remembered a lesson I learned in grade school regarding "space bubbles." I remembered the activity being quick, simple, and fun as it began with a brief discussion about how everyone has an imaginary bubble that is their personal space. Each person makes choices about who, where, and when other people and things come into a person's space bubble. There was then an experiential element where children used their arms to indicate space bubbles as they interacted with one another.

This memory sparked my interest, which led to my decision to incorporate this Space Bubble activity and various other resources to design my own activity related to interpersonal boundary work in the context of the play therapy session, hence the emergence of Bubbles and Boundaries.

RATIONALE

According to various experts and my experience with children affected by abuse, problems related to personal and interpersonal boundaries often plague the lives of our young clients well into adulthood without some form of intervention (Gil, 1991; Schaefer, 1980; Terr, 1991; van der Kolk, 1987). Inappropriate sexualized behaviors, aggressive acts toward self and others, withdrawal from and interpersonal ambivalence toward others, confusion about appropriate and inappropriate touching, inability to perceive and act on the environment in pursuit of mastery, and impaired socialization skills with peers include examples of issues faced by children affected by sexual abuse (Gil, 1994; Terr, 1991). Therefore, the Bubbles and Boundaries activity was designed to address some of the goals related to helping children learn how to: 1) express emotions appropriately; 2) respect the personal space and bodies of self and others; 3) differentiate among good, bad, and secret touching (Hindman, 1992); 4) control certain aspects of their environments; and 5) communicate their personal boundary needs with others.

DESCRIPTION

The play therapist sits on the same level as the child, preferably on chairs or the floor in a circle. The play therapist introduces the concepts of good, bad, and confusing touch by telling a story, reading a book about bodies, touching, and interpersonal boundaries (such as Hindman, 1992), or through other unique means. Then the play therapist passes out bottles of bubbles and bubble blowers to both the child or children and him- or herself. After a few moments of allowing everyone to simply enjoy blowing the bubbles and watching them, the play therapist begins to reflect and comment on the ways that bubbles are forming, popping, floating, falling, and so forth, paying specific attention to how bubbles are touching each other (good, bad, or confusing).

Next the play therapist encourages the child to reflect on what his or her bubbles are doing. The play therapist begins to process issues related to personal space (boundaries) and touching (interpersonal interactions) by asking the following questions: 1) By watching your bubbles, what happens (actions, feelings, thoughts) to let you know what kind of touch is happening (good, bad, or confusing)? 2) What do you think those bubbles could do (words and actions) if they didn't feel good about the way they were being touched? 3) How about you, what could you do or say if you ever wanted someone to stop touching you in a certain way? 4) Then what would happen? As an illustration, here is a simulated *Bubbles and Boundaries* session.

Therapist: Did you see those two bubbles burst when they touched? I wonder why?

Child: (No response)

Therapist: I wonder if one of those bubbles didn't want that other bubble to touch it.

Child: Yeah, that one bubble didn't like being pushed like that, so it decided to blow.

Therapist: Oh, I wonder if that was a good, bad, or confusing touch?

Child: Bad, so bad that the bubble blew up and disappeared.

Therapist: I see, I wonder how that bubble felt when it decided to blow up?

Child: Really scared!

Therapist: You are saying that you knew it was a bad touch because the bubble felt scared and decided to blow up and disappear. (Pause) I wonder what else that bubble could have done besides blow up?

Child: I know, run away.

Therapist: I see. What about your bubbles, what kind of touching are they doing?

Child: Ooh look, these two bubbles are sitting together on my blower. I think that they like each other. They are holding hands.

Therapist: Wow, I wonder what it feels like to hold hands?

Child: Happy! Because they are friends and they both want to touch hands.

Therapist: Do you think that is a good, bad, or confusing touch?

Child: Good touch.

Therapist: I wonder if there have been any confusing touches that have happened between any of these bubbles today? (Pause) How would we know?

Child: I don't know. (Long pause) Unless one of the bubbles told us.

Therapist: Wow, that is a point! You are telling me that we wouldn't know if confusing touch was happening unless one of the bubbles told us. What do you think that bubble would feel?

Child: Very sad (long pause) . . . and scared.

Therapist: What might the bubble think?

Child: That they are dirty or a bad boy.

Therapist: Gosh, I am sort of confused, because the bubble didn't do anything wrong. It wasn't the one bubble's fault that the other bubble touched him that way. What could the bubble that felt sad and scared do?

Child: Pop!!! (pause) or tell the other bubble to stop and run away.

Therapist: Yes, that is something that the bubble could do and can do next time another bubble touches him in a bad or confusing way. What if the bubble were a child, what could he do then?

Child: Run away, hide, and get the police to come.

Therapist: Sounds like you have a lot of ideas about what to do if something like this were happening to a child. It also sounds like you are saying that a child could get away and then tell someone who could help. My, (pause) what a brave child that is!

The activity proceeds, allowing the child time and room to reflect, question, and explain interactions among bubbles with process comments from the play therapist for a designated amount of time (approximately 20 to 25 minutes). After removing the bubbles, the play therapist engaged the client in a discussion about the content and feelings that emerged in the session. Time permitting, the play therapist might ask the child to verbalize or draw a picture about what was learned about personal space and touching. The play therapist then tells the child that he or she may use the bubbles anytime he or she wants to talk about personal space (boundaries) and touching (interpersonal interactions).

APPLICATIONS

I have utilized this technique in individual, family, and group counseling with children presenting a variety of issues, not just those affected by abuse. In particular, I have incorporated *Bubbles and Boundaries* in all of my group play therapy encounters as this activity provides an ideal forum for addressing personal, interpersonal, and group-level boundaries. Although I have not attempted it, I am curious about the efficacy of this technique with couples who are struggling with boundary issues. Clearly, the emotional level and content processed is open to the play therapist or clinician based on his or her relationship with the client(s). Overall, I have been amazed at the strength of the mental and emotional responses often evoked by this activity.

References

Gil, E. (1991). *The Healing Power of Play: Working with Abused Children*. New York: Guilford Press.

Hindman, J. (1992). *A Very Touching Book . . . for Little People and for Big People*. Ontario, OR: AlexAndria Associates.

Schaefer, C. E. (1980). Play Therapy. G. P. Sholevar, R. M. Benson and B. J. Binder (Eds.). *Emotional Disorders in Children and Adolescents*. New York: Spectrum.

Terr, L. (1990). *Too Scared to Cry*. New York: Harper & Row.

van der Kolk, B. A. (1987). *Psychological Trauma*. Washington, D.C.: American Psychiatric Press.

75

The Message Balloon

Cindy A. Stear

INTRODUCTION

"I never had a chance to say good-bye." So often this is what a child's behavior tells us following the death of a parent or significant other. Children may express their sadness through somatic complaints, irritability, regression, school problems, or dramatic tantrums. This may easily be misunderstood by the remaining caregiver and may add to the surviving parent's difficulty working through his or her own grief. I have used the message balloon ritual with children in an outpatient setting, as well as with adolescents in a residential program. All have welcomed it and moved forward in their grief process. Many even experience it as fun! This is a variation of a grief therapy technique for adults.

RATIONALE

The ritual provides children with validation of their loss. It offers a tangible, comforting ritual through which they can physically and emotionally work through feelings of sadness, anger, guilt, and abandonment. It allows a nonthreatening venue for facing emotionally charged issues. It can serve as a turning point for children in arrested stages of grieving. The therapist is connected to the child in a state of active nurturance, which is essential in the early stages of grief when strong dependency and safety needs present and emotions are often raw and overwhelming. This relationship and the message balloon ritual allow the healing to begin. The ritual can also serve as a launching point for children who have been actively grieving a loss and are now ready to move forward by building new connections and involvement. It helps the child let go of the emotional weight of the death—thus freeing him or her to hold on to the positive memories, internalized values, and so on.

DESCRIPTION

This session requires a helium-filled balloon shaped like a butterfly, available at any store that sells helium balloons. The butterfly is a metaphor children generally readily understand—the caterpillar as the physical person, the cocoon as death, and the butterfly as the emergence of the ongoing spiritual being. If the child is too young to have been exposed to caterpillars and butterflies, a brief story can be told by the therapist to express this message.

At a preceding session, the child is told that in the next meeting they will be doing something special to express any messages he or she would like to his or her deceased parent. The child is asked if there is anyone else he or she would like to attend this special session. Depending on the age and placement status of the child, it can be very useful to have the surviving parent or a significant group home staff member attend. This provides additional support for the child during and after the session. The child may designate a particular role for this individual, such as reading a poem or playing a special song on a tape player. Alternately, the child may wish the person to stand quietly. The focus is on giving the child control, which he or she did not have regarding saying good-bye.

During the session, the therapist explains that the balloon will be used to release feelings that have been inside since the parent's death, and that are now safe to come out. The therapist helps the child to write a message or draw a picture expressing the feelings the child is struggling with. The therapist may write down the child's words if the child can verbalize them but does not know how to write. The child directs this, so the child may choose to simply draw a picture of a favorite activity he or she misses doing with the deceased parent. These messages/pictures are then taped to the balloon. The child is informed that the balloon will be released and that as it rises it can take with it the child's feelings of sadness, loss, anger, and so on. Sometimes the child will ask at this point if he or she can have a picture of the balloon to keep. It is useful to keep an automatic camera in one's office for purposes such as this. This allows the child to feel more control of the letting go/holding on process.

The therapist, child, and any support person then take a walk to a quiet area outside the office. The child chooses where to stand for the ceremony. The therapist asks if there is anything the child wishes to say. Additionally, the child may choose to read a poem or have a song played. Then the therapist expresses what he or she believes the deceased parent would have wanted to say to the child if given the opportunity. Typically, "I am proud of you and how you have grown. I miss you and wish I could be with you. I am happy you have loving people helping you in your life. You are a very special child." The weights are removed from the balloon and the child releases it. It is important to allow the child to watch the balloon's flight for as long as he or she needs to.

APPLICATIONS

This technique is useful with children experiencing normative bereavement as well as those with delayed or displaced grief reactions. It can also easily be used with grieving children and adolescents with developmental disabilities.

Section Six

Games

76

The Number Facts Game

Heidi G. Kaduson

INTRODUCTION

Children with learning disabilities and Attention Deficit Hyperactivity Disorder may have trouble memorizing math facts. Even with repetition of the number facts through factor trees or flash cards, these children still have times when they cannot retrieve the number or need to use their fingers to produce the answer. Some teachers are hesitant to allow the child to use fingers or a number line. Even when this is allowed, however, many children feel stupid and uncomfortable because they cannot produce the answer to the question in time or compare themselves to other children functioning at a higher speed. This type of problem is usually associated with some type of learning disability, but not always severe enough to require accommodation from the school.

No one knows for certain what causes a learning disability. We do know that learning disabilities run in families, so if a child has a learning disability, chances are someone else in the family does as well. In addition, we know that learning disabilities have nothing to do with intelligence. It means that the brain works differently from other people's brains. These children learn a different way, and it is the job of the teachers and adults in the child's life to learn how the child learns, and teach that way. In order to help these children struggling with a math disability, or the difficulty of memorizing information, the Number Facts Game was created.

RATIONALE

Because academic pressures are on children to perform at grade level, all of the teaching that is done in school might be enough to have children learn number facts. When they do not grasp it, however, there may be another way to have them learn it. With the use of the right side of the brain, and the body movements involved in the Number Facts Game, many children have found it easier to learn the number facts. This is a different way of learning that could prove successful to many children. It is fun and motivating, which is also helpful in keeping the children interested in the game and therefore learning.

DESCRIPTION

Before the child enters the playroom, the therapist will take 15 pieces of 8½ by 11-inch paper. Each paper contains one of the numbers from 1 to 15. The pages can be of different colors to enhance the fun and playfulness of the game. The therapist then tapes the papers onto the playroom floor in random order, but close enough to each other so that the child could jump to or touch each one. This would be similar to the distance between spaces in the game *Twister* (Milton Bradley).

When the child enters the playroom, the therapist would tell him or her that he or she was going to play a game called the Number Facts Game. Each participant stands on one of the numbers. For example, the therapist might stand on number 6, and the child might choose to stand on number 4. The child then calls out a number higher than 6 (i.e., 9) up to 15, and the therapist would have to jump to number 3, which would be the number used to equal the total the child called out. Then the therapist would take a turn and call out a number higher than the number the child is standing on (i.e., 6). The child could hop, jump, or touch the number that would equal the total (in this case because the child was on 4, she would jump to 2). The therapist would try to make the leaps for the child very small.

Following the addition play, the game changes to having each participant call out a number fact, and the other person has to jump to the total of the two number facts up to 15. Playing this in both ways gives the child more opportunities of learning the number facts with fun, rather than just rote, repetition.

After playing the game several times, the child can use lower numbers so that the therapist has to subtract, rather than add. When the child is confident in the addition area, the therapist will do the same. The child will show mastery of the numbers as he or she begins to call out numbers that would require the therapist to leap across the room, indicating that he or she knew the number fact and where it was located.

APPLICATIONS

This game is especially useful with children with math learning disabilities and children who have difficulty memorizing facts. It can be used with other facts that go together such as states and capitals, multiplication, division, and so forth. Using the game in groups is also helpful with supportive assistance from the leader because some children will be more successful than others.

77

The Pickle in the Middle Technique

Michelle Hodsdon

INTRODUCTION

Divorce often creates a situation in which parents are so involved in arguing about the best interest of their children that they ignore what is in the best interest of their children. In many antagonistic divorces, parents use the child's needs and dependence as power to hoard and keep from each other or as a weapon of blame to throw at each other.

In either case, the child's needs are being used, not met. The child is left in the middle of two battling parents, often feeling isolated and abandoned, to struggle with fears, loyalty conflicts, and emotional needs of his or her own. The therapist has the difficult task of helping the parents shift their focus back on the direct needs of the child and to meet their child's needs in the spirit of cooperation, not competition.

RATIONALE

I developed the Pickle in the Middle technique to help parents and children understand the family system created by divorce. The technique makes therapeutic use of the three-man keep-away game that we used to call Pickle in the Middle. In the game, two players stand apart throwing a ball back and forth while a third player stands in the middle, trying to intercept the ball as it is thrown between the other two players. If the player in the middle catches the ball, he becomes one of the players on the outside and the player who threw the ball goes into the middle.

The game provides a perfect metaphor for the family system created in divorce: the two parents stand apart throwing the child's life and needs like a ball with the child in the middle, struggling to regain control and attention.

The technique allows the family and the therapist to focus on the dynamics of the relationships and the divorce system without becoming distracted by specific issues and content. A game of catch reveals simple raw material about relationships without evoking the power struggle that often accompanies issues or content. In addition, most family members have had some experience with a ball and enter into the exercise comfortably and easily.

DESCRIPTION

The only piece of equipment necessary for this game is a ball. I use a large nerf ball to help prevent injury and office damage. You may choose to use a large rubber ball.

To begin the game, have parents stand about ten feet away from each other with the child in the middle. In families with more than one child, each child should take individual turns being the Pickle in the Middle. In this way they can experience the dynamics of the divorce separate from sibling dynamics.

Parents begin to toss the ball back and forth to each other with the intent of preventing the child in the middle from catching it. The goal of the Pickle in the Middle (the child) is to intercept the ball. Things can get wild so be sure to clear enough space in your office. Once the child grabs the ball, he or she moves to the outside position and the parent who threw the ball moves into the middle. Everyone should have a chance to experience each position (the child should experience each parent in the middle). If the natural flow of the game does not give each person a chance at all positions, the therapist may interrupt after a period of time and ask people to shift positions.

I repeat this procedure with each child in the family and make the necessary adjustments so that each person experiences each position for about three to five minutes.

After everyone has played the game, the therapist can process the game with the family. I start out by asking each family member:

How did it feel in each of the different positions? Why?

Which position was the most comfortable for you? Why?

Which position was the most uncomfortable for you? Why?

Which spot do you identify most with? Why?

I then explore the movement of the ball and the players.

Did one parent keep the ball for a period before tossing it?

Did the parents work as a team to keep the ball away from the child?

Did one parent try to dominate or try to team up with the child?

Did the child give up easily?

Did the child in the middle stay to one side more than the other?

After processing these questions and any others you might find useful, the therapist makes a quick, simple link between the relationship material revealed in the game and the divorce dynamic. The therapist can also identify for the family the feelings often experienced by children in the middle of divorcing parents. Parents can also be made aware of the power struggle and the fear dynamics that may cause them to be less receptive to their child's needs.

Don't process the game too much; the metaphors created in the game will speak for themselves. It is surprising how quickly even 5-year-old children can grasp the metaphor. The Pickle in the Middle technique can be used effectively with very young children so long as they are mobile.

Variation

As the family becomes more comfortable with the metaphor of the Pickle in the Middle game, the game can be modified from a diagnostic technique into a therapeutic one.

In one modification, the "pickle" comes out of the middle, the three players form a triangle, and the ball is randomly thrown among all three players. As the game progresses, the pattern of family communication and power becomes visible. The therapist can use this material to educate the family about their current patterns of relating and prescribe a different pattern of ball tossing to model a more effective pattern of relating (e.g., if the parents are each throwing the ball to the child and not to each other, the therapist points out the triangulation and tells the parents they must throw the ball to each other as well. If the child is throwing the ball to only one parent, he or she must start throwing the ball to the other parent).

Once the family has made the link between their ball tossing and family dynamics, the therapist can begin to attach content to the game by assigning a specific family issue to the ball. The therapist and the family member who has the greatest stake in the issue gets the ball. That person now has to decide how he or she is going to handle the issue using the ball. He or she can throw the ball to another person for a response or hold onto control of the ball. The therapist uses the ball as a marker to follow the flow of communication and power. This allows the therapist to point out and correct areas where there is a lack of proper communication or when someone is inappropriately included or excluded from the pattern of relating.

These games can be expanded to include stepparents and siblings. The technique is so simple that it can also be executed and processed in a group situation with several families.

APPLICATIONS

The Pickle in the Middle technique provides a simple, concrete model for some of the dynamics of divorce. The game can make the family more aware of their patterns of relating and gives the therapist a powerful metaphor as a tool to correct maladaptive patterns in the family system.

The nature of the game requires parent cooperation and can help the parents work together as a team to meet the needs of their children. The game also increases the child's assertiveness skills and helps the child regain focus on his or her needs as separate from those of the parents.

The Pickle in the Middle technique has offered my clients a fun and effective way out of the middle of the divorce "pickle."

78

Topics

Sylvia Fisher

INTRODUCTION

The focus of play therapy is using nonverbal approaches. Even children with well-developed language skills have difficulty expressing emotions with words, yet there are times when words are necessary and useful. It is often challenging for the children to initiate a discussion of feelings, but they may be willing to participate if they have a good rapport established with the therapist who can approach the topic of feelings. I use a clear plastic container with a lid, which I have labeled "Topics to Talk About." Inside are topics, each on a separate piece of paper, which the child selects.

RATIONALE

I keep this topics jar in plain view, but I wait until the child expresses an interest in it. Sometimes, I show the child the jar and explain what can be done with it. When a child chooses an arbitrarily written topic on a piece of paper, the child is more likely to speak freely without pressure or expectations. It may give the child permission to discuss an issue not previously conscious. In addition, the child can address an issue that is not directly about that child, but rather as a "topic." This technique has been most successful in counseling groups of children in a school setting. I seldom use it in private practice.

DESCRIPTION

In school-based group therapy, I allow a student to be the chooser of the game or activity for the session. Each week, in rotation, a different student becomes the chooser (which I track on a list). Sometimes the topics jar is chosen, and sometimes I present it at the beginning of the session. When the check-in time is used to report objective data too often (what the student did for the weekend), I bring the topics jar to the table. In some groups, the students have included me in the rotation of being a chooser. I then ask the students how old they want me to be in response to the topic, and I follow their request. When I have been asked to be 2 years old, however, I respond with a reality check and say that I can't play that age. They revise the age at that point.

Each piece of paper (about 2 by 5 inches) contains a different single word or thought: crying, getting lost, cheating, losing, friends, divorce, dreams, pets, lying, punishments, family dinners, holidays, anger, running away, and so on. The topic papers (all the same color so that students cannot memorize particular topics) are folded in half with the written part on the inside; the student reaches in to select a random piece of paper.

The student reads the word outloud or I read the word as necessary and the chooser is allowed to begin a response. The comments come from real experiences or may be made up (projections of the student). The student can talk about this word in relation to someone else or him- or herself. The issues raised by the topic itself may be speculated. In other words, it is not required that the student actually experienced an issue related to the word. For instance, the student may pull the word *death*, but not having experienced that kind of loss, the student might not know what to say. I might then ask if he or she has ever had a pet die, or what would he or she do if his or her pet died, of if he or she knew someone whose pet had died and how does he or she think that person might feel? The possibilities are endless.

Each student follows in turn responding to the same topic. There are no judgments made, no right or wrong answers (about which I keep reassuring the students especially in a school setting) and each student is allowed to respond freely. There is, however, often a spontaneous and interactive discussion among all the students on a topic. I ensure that each student has an opportunity to have a first turn before others take a second turn or the discussion begins. Sometimes, the chooser likes to select a second topic and continue the rounds.

APPLICATIONS

This technique is particularly helpful in groups of peers in a school setting. Children do not feel singled out to address certain issues, some of which may be emotionally charged. This is also useful when children are reluctant to share verbally or have difficulty initiating a verbal interaction. For the latter two situations, I have used the topics jar successfully with individual therapy as well.

In the school setting with groups, students tend to want to hear what the others have to say. Taking turns about the same topic allows them to identify with a common theme and shows them respect for others' feelings and experiences at the same time.

Through this playful approach, children have an opportunity to explore feelings and expressions for which they might not have another venue to give them voice. The responses can all be projections that the student does not have to claim as personal issues. This creates a safe environment for self-expression in a nonthreatening and supportive way.

79

Playing Possum

Jo Anne Mitchell

INTRODUCTION

In my counseling work, both in elementary school and in private practice, I saw many children who showed negative signs of stress. Children presented with somatic complaints, body rigidity, school phobia, nervous habits, fatigue, excessive dependency, difficulty with sleep, emotionality, lack of self-control, and various attention getting behaviors. In general, I also found that most children did not know how to manage stress effectively and most of the adults in their lives did not know stress reduction techniques either. They seemed to be in a vicious cycle of passing their distress from one person to another, compounding the situation. I developed a game, Playing Possum, to teach children how to relax and feel a sense of control, through prescribed breathing. We then would play the game with other significant people in their lives, so the behaviors could be reinforced. I have used this technique with individuals, families, in small-group counseling, and in classroom guidance. It is appropriate for children, aged 6 through preadolescence, depending on their developmental level. Children, parents, and teachers all enjoyed this game. As a school counselor, I would teach this as a classroom guidance lesson, starting in first grade. I would repeat the lesson as needed, in each grade level, especially in preparation for standardized testing. I knew this was a successful technique when the fifth grade students requested to Play Possum every year, which, of course, we did.

DESCRIPTION

Materials

- A possum puppet or picture of possum
- Large rubberband
- Balloon
- Tape of relaxing music

Procedure

1. Discuss stress and how your body reacts to it, in an age appropriate way. Have the child become very aware of how his or her body feels by asking him or her to focus on different parts of the body.
2. Mildly scare person with a quick "Boo." Then process, "How does your body feel? Where is your stress point?" (place where their muscles tightened up)
3. Demonstrate muscle tightness with a large rubberband. When his or her muscles are relaxed, the muscles feel like "jello" (wiggle the rubberband to show how loose it is). When the muscles are strong, they feel harder (twist the rubberband and show that it is stronger). Have person feel his or her upper arm and notice how it feels like "jello." Then have him or her tighten the muscle and feel the difference and then relax it again. Explain that he or she controlled the muscle, but sometimes, because of stress or worries the muscles become too tight and have a hard time relaxing (twist the rubberband until it is in knots—ouch!).
4. Introduce an expert in relaxation, either with a possum puppet or picture. My possum puppet is named Priscilla (yes, I name my puppets). She is an expert in relaxation because that is how she survives by playing dead or possum when danger is

around. Have the puppet demonstrate how she relaxes and turns her muscles into "jello."

5. Explain that the possum is able to relax by breathing in a special way. Discuss lungs and where they are located in the body and demonstrate with a balloon. Then teach "balloon breathing" (directions following). Have the child practice balloon breathing and relaxing. Do this lying down, standing, and sitting.

6. Now it's time to play Tiger and Possum. Have the child lay on the floor, balloon breathe, and play possum. Play a relaxing tape, and then the counselor (with puppet, if you have one) checks the child's body to see if he or she is really "dead." Help the child relax so the "tiger" (counselor) does not have him or her for dinner. Allow the child to relax for a minute and explain that this is the calm feeling. He or she can slowly sit up and process how he or she feels now as compared to how he or she felt during the game.

7. Discuss when and where he or she can use this technique, such as when he or she is angry, tense, scared, upset, nervous, trying to go to sleep, or in pain. The child can use this anytime and anywhere when he or she wants to calm down and get the knots out of his or her muscles.

Balloon Breathing

1. Instruct the person to put one hand on the chest and the other hand on the belly button.

2. Breathe in *slowly* through the nose, filling up lungs (balloons) all the way to the belly button. Hold it for two seconds. Exhale *very slowly* through the mouth (like blowing through a straw) until the balloons (lungs) are deflated. The child will see and feel the lungs expand and contract because of the hand placement.

3. Demonstrate with a balloon, air coming out slowly. Then demonstrate the air coming out of the balloon quickly. Explain that if a person were to exhale quickly, like a wild balloon, it would hurt the body and not allow the muscles to relax.

4. Repeat this breathing five times. Rest. Repeat again another five times if needed.

In our fast-paced, rapidly changing, and sometimes violent society, children are faced with increased stress and anxiety. Some children cope with this stress better than others, depending on their temperament and resiliency. For those children who need help developing healthy coping skills, this technique provides a way to give them a sense of control in a fun, nonthreatening, and concrete manner; it is also a lifelong skill, which can greatly increase their physical and mental health.

80

Make Your Own Feeling Game

Joop Hellendoorn

INTRODUCTION

Young children often have difficulty verbalizing their feelings. In their spontaneous conversation, feelings are seldom mentioned. When asked about them directly, children may not be able to find the right words, or they may show resistance to express and talk about negative or conflicting feelings. Kaduson (1997) developed the Feeling Word Game, aiming to enhance verbalization of feelings by using a storytelling format.

The technique introduced here is an elaboration of the Feeling Word Game. Apart from the storytelling, the game itself is constructed.

RATIONALE

Communication with children is often easiest through action and play. For many children, especially younger children, action and play are natural media for expression of thought and feeling, much more so than words. Moreover, playful action decreases possible defenses. Games are usually pleasurable. Making the kind of game proposed here provides an opportunity to enact and illustrate feelings that may be difficult to talk about in a nonthreatening way. This aspect is enhanced because of the work involved in cutting and pasting pictures that fit in with the feelings named.

DESCRIPTION

The therapist sits at a low table or on the floor, at the child's level. The therapist has a cardboard circle (about 3 inches radius) ready and a cardboard arrow (about 3 inches long). The arrow is to be loosely fixed to the middle of the circle by means of a pin, so that it can be whirled around. The circle is divided in eight (or more) segments. Colorful magazines with lots of pictures are also available.

Therapist and child start by putting the cardboard circle and arrow together, then proceed to name different feelings. These are written or printed on pieces of paper, each of which is pasted on a segment of the circle. The child is encouraged to actively name feelings, and then to find pictures that illustrate those feelings from the available magazines, to cut them out, and paste them in the relevant segment. These activities give a lot of opportunity to talk about the different feelings, what they can be caused by, how to express them, and so on. Trying out facial expressions pertinent to each different feeling can be very funny and gives rise to a lot of laughter.

Usually it takes some time to construct the game in this way. Next, it can be actually played. The first player whirls the arrow around; the other player is requested to tell a story about the feeling that is indicated. It is often a good idea that the child does the first whirling and the therapist makes the first story, thus serving as a model. Such a story may be about yourself or about a fantasy figure. The therapist should take care to keep the story simple but significant for the life circumstances of a particular child.

APPLICATIONS

This technique can be used with all children but is particularly helpful with those who are overly anxious or who have conduct problems. Constructing the game satisfies children who need instant gratification and find it difficult to wait for their turn. This is also true for children with Attention Deficit Hyperactivity Disorder. With these children, however, special care is required with the cutting—one needs a safe type of scissors! Anxious children often are relieved that the stories need not refer to their own feelings but may be about fantasy figures. In my experience, this elaboration of Kaduson's techniques enhances its efficacy, because it is even less threatening. It can also be used with a family or a small group of children.

Reference

Kaduson, H. G. (1997). The feeling word game. Kaduson, H. G. and Schaefer, C. E. (Eds.). *101 Favorite Play Therapy Techniques*, pp. 19–21. Northvale, NJ: Jason Aronson.

81

Angry Kleenex Game

Denise K. Filley

INTRODUCTION

Anger is one of the major emotions that often brings children to see me. Because I believe strongly in sensory play therapy, I looked and looked for a technique that provided both the sensory and physical aspects of anger release. I learned this technique years ago and it has been one of the most effective I have used and taught for anger release play therapy.

RATIONALE

Most of the children who come to me for treatment of anger have disconnected the lines of communication between their sensory and physical input/output and their emotions. They take in sensory input and then repress it, stuff it essentially, somewhere in their bodies. They don't let it near their emotional tanks for fear of feeling something too overwhelming or scary. Because anger is such a sensory and physical emotion, this stuffing of emotions builds up and often causes the anger to release in unsafe and unhealthy behaviors for both the child and others in his or her world. I have found the best release of this emotion is something moderately physical that also taps into the senses of the child.

Water and sand seem to be the best sensory media I have found that children respond to in a positive, nonthreatening way. This technique causes communication internally through: 1) the senses by using water, 2) physical release by using anger release, 3) muscle release, and 4) visual release by drawing.

DESCRIPTION

Materials

- White paper
- Crayons (no markers or other tools—only crayons)
- Kleenex
- Small cup of water
- Tape

The child is asked to think of a situation, person, and so on from the recent past that made him or her angry. When the child has had a few moments to get in touch with this situation, I ask him or her to draw a picture of it on white paper with the crayons. He or she can draw the situation, the person, or an abstract picture/symbol that has meaning. Some of the anger release occurs through this drawing. When the child has finished the picture, I ask him or her to tape it to a wall or door at eye level. Then the child takes a Kleenex, soaks it in the cup of water, and squeezes out some of the excess water from the Kleenex (it should still be pretty wet). The child should stand about 3 to 4 feet away and hurl the Kleenex at the picture. The object of the game is to have the Kleenex be just wet enough that it sticks to the picture when it hits it. The child can continue to hurl wet Kleenex at the picture until he or she feels he or she has released the anger. Sometimes after doing this for a few minutes, I encourage the child to verbalize at the picture when throwing the Kleenex. Many children do this spontaneously. When they finish, I process with them about the picture and how it felt to let the anger out physically. We discuss the physical feelings in their muscles as well as the sensory release of the Kleenex and water, and lastly their emotional release.

(Note: It is imperative not to use markers or other drawing media other than crayons because when the markers get wet from the Kleenex, the colors run down the wall and stain the walls!)

APPLICATIONS

This technique is applicable to any child who has anger issues to work through. It is excellent for children who have suffered trauma or abuse to release the anger and assist them in reconnecting with the sensory part of their bodies and emotions. There are no real age limitations; I have had adults use this technique at home. It can be done virtually anywhere, even outdoors, so it is a flexible technique available for use to therapists in most any setting, including in-home therapists. I have also taught this to parents to use in directing their child to the technique when angry behaviors at home begin to appear.

The drawing and visual aspect of the picture are excellent for visual learners or communicators. The physical throwing and the contact with the Kleenex and water are excellent for tactile learners. And the verbal expression at the picture is helpful for the release of emotions by the auditory learner.

82

The Time Travel Game

Brenda Lawrence

INTRODUCTION

Most children who enter my office are captivated by the enticing array of miniatures, the sandbox, and the multifarious world of mythic beasts, animals, and human creatures in the puppet area. Clay, paint, and drawing for many children also become vehicles for self-expression. I have worked with a number of children, however, who come to play therapy with little interest in toys or curiosity for investigating creative possibilities with art materials.

Play is children's work, a natural means for self-expression, communication, and learning. Through the metaphor of play, the child can project feelings and process painful experiences, while keeping a healthy distance from material that could be overwhelming and impossible to work with in a more direct or verbal fashion. The Time Travel Game has been a bridge to creative play for those children difficult to engage as well as for those who just love to play.

RATIONALE

Determining what interests the child, what in his or her experiences holds a special fascination, is a vital part of having the child feel understood and unconditionally accepted. The event that has sparked the young person's imagination, be it a book, a movie, or whatever, can become a springboard for engaging the child, building trust, and launching a playful journey toward healing and growth. The story from the child's repertoire of imaginings reveals symbolic images full of innate potential for the development of the child.

DESCRIPTION

Once a theme or story that has captured the child's imagination has been identified, have the child share that tale in as much detail and description as possible. The therapist can then suggest using the "time travel machine" to go to the setting of the story, become the characters, and act out the narrative. Encourage the child to be the director and to cast each of you in the roles he or she deems appropriate. The child will choose roles with which he or she has become identified. These roles will become the vehicles for projecting feelings and acting out issues.

A fold-out puppet theater or even a cardboard box easily becomes the device for transporting the therapist and child to any place or time, past, present, or future. If the child wishes, simple theatrical props culled from among the play materials in the therapy room (costumes, swords, etc.) can add detail and drama.

As the story evolves, it becomes the metaphor for play. Improvisation naturally becomes the mode of operation. Over time the story can metamorphose into a form in which the child gains mastery of the feelings or behaviors that were, at the beginning of this process, problematic.

APPLICATIONS

Children with diverse issues and problems are drawn to this expressive modality. The device of traveling in time becomes the entrance into the child's psyche and emotional structure. This approach is acceptable and nonthreatening to the child because it is a "game," something fun to play. Paralyzing fears, separation anxiety, selective mutism, and phobias are a sampling of childhood difficulties that have been responsive to this play technique. Indeed, it was created in my office by a child.

CASE EXAMPLES

Excessive fears and feelings of extreme vulnerability were presenting problems for a physically challenged child. His extreme medical condition had allowed few childhood experiences that resembled everyday play. His postnatal world was fraught with multiple, lifesaving but incredibly intrusive medical interventions. He was not drawn to things that required manual dexterity particularly at the time when he entered therapy. A fall that broke his arm suddenly made his frailty seem overwhelming. He fiercely wanted his hands free to support himself with his walking canes. He was disdainful of "children's toys," and art materials conjured negative associations of school. The world of the mind through books and film was his field of play. The Time Travel Game became the vessel to enter scenes from the movie *Titanic*, which held both fascination and horror for him. He identified with the young hero, Jack, who DeCaprio played and was infatuated with Rose, the young and beautiful heroine. Cal, the villain, became the hated object. I was usually assigned the part of Rose, Cal, Rose's mother, Ruth, or the captain. The office became the ship. At times, in the first weeks of treatment, when the ship was sinking, the office became "toxic" for a few intense moments, and the child would say, "We have to go outside!" and of course we did. In the grounding reality of the outdoors, he would calm down, sometimes ending the play at this point and sometimes choosing to return to the ship and continue the narrative. For weeks he played and replayed this story, gradually weaving his personal issues into the changing tapestry of the tale. In his real life, he learned to overcome his fears as he manipulated the "Titanic" story.

The story of another child follows:

I keep no animals in my office, but at times incorporate the fauna of the natural world (frogs, turtles, snakes, etc.) and our domestic pets—dog, cats, and chickens—into the child's therapy experience. One child's passion and involvement with animals was worked into his therapeutic milieu. We developed a ritual, wherein he and I spent ten minutes together at the end of his session with my little poodle. The unexpected death of my dog triggered deep feelings of loss and grief in him. These genuine feelings became an opportunity and opening to work with another layer of a prior, unresolved personal loss in his life. As children do, he projected old feelings onto his new situation. The Time Travel Game became the vehicle for mourning. He would have us play out many different scenarios; traveling back in time prior to the dog's death, changing events, making opportunities to say good-bye, and so on.

Through the play of this drama, there was catharsis and resolution, a passing through the stages of loss and mourning to continuance.

83

The Feelings Card Game

Maryanne Bongiovani

INTRODUCTION

Knowing what feelings you have and being able to talk about your feelings is very important in therapy. As I began working with children, I realized that children were not always able to talk about feelings and that even when they could, not every child was at the same level. Some children talked easily about their feelings and other children could not even describe or identify certain feelings.

RATIONALE

The Feeling Card Game is a game that I use during my first or second session with each child I see. It helps me to assess what each child knows about feelings and how well each child can discuss his or her own feelings.

DESCRIPTION

Commercially bought cards showing various feelings can be used for this game, or cards can be made up with the name of a feeling on the card as well as a face that depicts that feeling. The face can be cartoonlike or a photograph of a real person. There is a feelings chart that is commercially available that has many different faces showing various emotions. The chart could be cut up and each face could be put on an index card. Between six and 12 cards is a good number to use. Eight cards is a good number to use when working with young children because more than eight makes the game too long to keep a young child's interest. Ten to 12 cards are a good number to use with older children because it allows for the discussion of a greater variety of emotions.

The cards are spread facedown in a random pile in the center of the table. The child is asked if he or she wants to go first. Whoever goes first picks a card, turns it over, and reads the feeling listed on the card. He or she then describes a time that he or she experienced that feeling. The game continues with the next person or the therapist picking a card and describing a time that the feeling was experienced. The game continues with each person taking a turn until all the cards are finished.

If a child cannot describe a time when he or she felt a particular feeling, the therapist can ask for a description of what could occur that would cause a person to have the feeling listed on the card.

APPLICATIONS

This game has been used with children between the ages of 4 and 14. It is very helpful at the beginning of therapy as an assessment tool. By playing the game during one of the first sessions, the therapist can determine if the child can identify his or her own feelings, and the therapist can also determine how comfortable the child is with talking about feelings.

When working with 4-, 5-, and 6-year-old children, the feelings named on the card often have to be read to the child. After the feeling is read and discussed, the child could be asked to show the therapist a face that would show the feeling being discussed. If the child is shy, the therapist could demonstrate the facial expression that feeling might produce and have the child copy the therapist's expression. With this age child, it is sometimes helpful for the therapist to go first or help the child with the first card. The young child often has to begin by generally describing a situation that could cause a feeling. Once the child has described a situation, the therapist can help with an example from the child's own life that could produce the feeling and after this instruction, many young children can come up with examples from his or her own life for the rest of the cards.

When the game is finished, the therapist knows whether or not the child is ready to talk about his or her own feelings or whether more basic work first needs to be done with naming and talking about feelings in general. Some young children may only be able to repeat the name of the feeling after the therapist says it. The therapist can still give a description of what might cause someone to have that feeling. Even if the child still cannot talk about what experiences might bring about cértain feelings, this gives the therapist some good information, and the therapist can work with the child to enhance what he or she does know. Further work with feelings can be done by using picture books or puppets to act out various feelings. There are now books on the market that name feelings and talk about them. Story books are also helpful because children's books make use of so many pictures as they tell a story. After several sessions of working on feelings with the young child, the Feelings Card Game can again be played with the child to see what progress has been made.

With children of all ages, after the game has been played, the therapist will have a good idea of whether the child is ready to discuss important issues or whether work will have to begin at a more basic and unthreatening level.

The Feelings Card Game is also useful in measuring the progress of therapy. It can be used again and again at various stages in therapy to determine what gains the child has made. It can be useful as a measure of the child's ability to talk about his or her own feelings, and it can also be a useful tool to look at what situations the child discusses in relation to the various feelings.

84

The Gestalt Imagery Game for Grief

Dora C. Finamore

INTRODUCTION

Gestalt therapy grew out of the theoretical constructs of Gestalt psychology. It is a dynamic and existential method of therapy. Gestalt play therapy can be most effective to help a grieving child. It allows the child an opportunity for self-expression at whatever stage of the grief process the child is experiencing. Many children have their first experience with death as a result of losing a parent, grandparent, sibling, friend, or animal companion. All too often, the child is left feeling confused, hurt, shocked, angry, and sad without an outlet for safe and appropriate release beyond the funeral ritual. The child perceives many messages, spoken and unspoken. When the child is not supported and actively encouraged to grieve the loss as a natural part of life, the healthy development of the child, as well as his or her spirit, is amputated. Gestalt therapy allows a child to express emotions fully in the here and now. It is theorized that only in the moment of experience does one completely make full contact with emotions. Many times, the anxiety or tension that arises from a painful memory is squashed and not allowed full expression. When one becomes fully aware of all sensory and motor activity as a result of tension, and then gives expression or discharge to that tension, does the person become free of the past. The focus of Gestalt therapy is on the present and on the phenomenological experience itself. It is an effective therapy for anyone who is experiencing grief.

RATIONALE

The Gestalt therapy experience helps create a permissive and safe atmosphere. The child is invited to accept all feelings and increase awareness of the self and his or her relationships with others in the here and now of the experience. The grieving child is invited to express those feelings that are tolerable at the moment. Thus, it is humanistic and respectful of the child as a child and does not rush the process.

Fritz Perls, founder of Gestalt therapy, created a method for greater expression of authentic feelings by having patients transfer between fantasy thought and the here and now. This imagery game is derived and modified from Perls's method and is applied to work with grieving children. The therapist is the facilitating agent who creates a safe arena for the Gestalt game, or experiment, as Perls referred to the work. The child confronts the problem by reenacting the experience and presenting feelings completely and fully. Unfinished business is thus transformed and integrated, outwardly demonstrated, and inwardly felt. The therapist does not ask "why" questions or for the child to explain him- or herself. For a child who does not have the cognitive capacity for abstract thinking, it is a very effective tool toward self-expression.

DESCRIPTION

A relaxing piece of music serves as a background to prepare the environment. The child is invited to participate in a fantasy experience akin to a pleasant dream. The child finds a comfortable position, using pillows to enhance physical support. The therapist suggests that the child close his or her eyes if he or she desires. The therapist sits on the floor with the child modeling a relaxed and open posture. The child is invited to take a few deep and slow breaths, concentrating on the experience. The therapist suggests that the child then imagine in his or her mind's eye, a place that is safe and happy, guiding her to vividly sense details of the "special" place to make it come alive. When the image is vivid with great clarity, the child is asked to return to the here and now of the room. The therapist encourages the child to compare the experience of the fantasy place with her present feelings. The process is then repeated highlighting any changes that are perceived. The experiment is repeated several times until the child perceives a level of comfort in the here-and-now feeling of the grief-related issue or problem. Often, fears, anxieties, maladaptive fantasies, and deep feelings of sadness and sorrow become apparent. The therapist then processes the experience with the child to help him or her understand how this technique can be used when he or she feels tense, sad, angry, confused, and fearful to empower him or her by getting in touch with his or her authentic grief feelings.

APPLICATIONS

This technique has been used effectively with children who are grieving. It is nonthreatening, respectful, supportive, and has the power to heal. It has been helpful for children ages 6 to 11. It allows the child to relax, play in fantasy (a natural state for children), express authentic feelings of sorrow, and gain a greater awareness of all grief feelings as normal and healthy. Many times, the child will return to the therapy session and eagerly suggest that they play the fantasy game.

This holistic approach of therapy helps the child integrate all "parts" that have been rejected or disowned, thus affirming the child's complete Gestalten.

85

The Crown Game: On Being Kings and Queens

Dennis C. Gold

INTRODUCTION

Probably the most important aspect of engaging in therapy with children is the ability to obtain entry into their personal/private world. Play therapists have used many different ways of trying to enter into the private world of a child. Projective techniques have long been utilized as an effective method of getting a child to open up. The King/Queen Game is one way of obtaining a brief entry into a child's thoughts and feelings.

RATIONALE

The technique is one that is both transparent and yet disguised, which is common among projective techniques. When the child plays this game, we are afforded a brief glimpse into what's important to him or her and how he or she sees his or her own world. Many times children will divulge information that they would not divulge without the use of this game

DESCRIPTION

On a table near the child I have placed a crown that is of the dime store variety and can be bought in costume and discount stores. It is made of gold-covered plastic and has what appear to be "jewels" embedded in it. It also has a small piece of Styrofoam that allows it the flexibility to fit different-sized heads.

Before I hand the crown to the child, I explain to the child that this is now the year 1701 and we are in Paris, France. We are assembled before the Royal Court in the great drawing room. We are in the process of crowning the next queen/king. There are maidens in fine gowns everywhere, and all the knights are wearing their armor. I then hand the child the crown and ask him or her to place it on his or her head. I then state to the child, "You are King/Queen for this moment. What would please you the most, your highness?"

At that point the child is given the space to provide a response to being king or queen.

This technique can reveal a great deal of information about a child. One child might talk about an abusive parent and request that the abuse be stopped. Other children will wish for valuables or material things like toys. Information could be revealed about deceased family members who are sorely missed. Another child might volunteer information about a sibling or his or her parents.

In this way the play therapist gains a brief entry into the child's value system and beliefs. The added element of an actual crown and the feeling of being regal can sometimes unlock information that might not otherwise have been offered.

This technique also reveals something about power and control. How does the child deal with being a royal figure? How does he or she look at the power he or she now has and what does he or she do with it? Role plays can be engaged in this way where one can further develop the information the child has revealed and use it in a therapeutic manner to offer the child a chance to resolve his or her difficulty.

APPLICATIONS

The technique is helpful with all children. It allows a brief, private entry to the child's world through its projective nature. It allows a bit of role playing and creativity. There is an opportunity for the child to express him- or herself and at the same time to reveal him- or herself. It can provide a lot of material that can be further developed throughout the play therapy process.

CASE EXAMPLES

When the crown was placed upon his head, one child became somewhat tearful and said that if he were king he would bring back his brother from the dead so they could still play together.

Another young girl stated that she would stop her stepfather from coming into her bedroom at night. A third child stated that "I would stop all parents from ever hitting their children." It is easy to surmise from these examples that much clinical material can be brought out in the open with this technique.

It appears that the actual crown and the introduction of the technique are all very important and help influence the utility of The King/Queen Game.

86

The Feedback Game

Chari Campbell

INTRODUCTION

The Feedback Game is generally used when working with children in small group counseling. One of the many advantages to counseling children in a group setting is that, with the help of a counselor, children can learn from each other. When children are taught how to give feedback to another child in a manner that does not engender defensiveness, this feedback can serve as a powerful incentive for a child with maladaptive behavior to develop more effective coping and interpersonal skills.

RATIONALE

Feedback provides information to the child about him- or herself that he or she did not previously have. More specifically, the child learns how his or her behavior impacts others either positively or negatively. Although this new knowledge does not ensure that he or she will choose to change his or her negative behavior, he or she now has a genuine choice. Harnessing the positive peer influence in a small group setting can have a therapeutic effect on a child who has difficulty making friends. Thus a child who has a history of being ostracized or picked on by his peers has the opportunity to learn what it is that he or she is doing to alienate others and, within the safe context of a group counseling setting, to try some new behaviors that are likely to receive a positive response from others.

Without intervention from a counselor, most children do not know how to give feedback gracefully. A typical response given to a bothersome peer is some form of name-calling, such as: "Shut up, Weirdo," "You are a jerk," and so on. Obviously this type of harsh and nonspecific feedback is not effective in helping children with behavioral problems to learn prosocial skills. Therefore, in the Feedback Game children are taught a three-step feedback model that will help them communicate feelings of annoyance more effectively. Of course, children are also taught that feedback can be used to communicate positive feelings in the form of compliments, and they are encouraged to use positive feedback often.

The steps of the feedback model are written on a large poster board attached to the wall. They are:

1. Describe the behavior. Be as specific as you can.
2. Tell how the behavior makes you feel.
3. Explain what the behavior makes you want to do, or what you wish the person would do instead. Be as specific as you can.

As the counselor describes each step in the model, he or she may provide several examples to the children to help them better understand. In addition, the children may take turns practicing giving feedback, both positive and negative, to someone who is outside of the group, without using the outsider's name. This is done with the use of the Empty Chair technique. Children are asked to pretend that they are talking to someone outside of the group. They are reminded not to use the person's name. In a go-around, each child first practices giving positive feedback. Coaching and modeling, by the counselor, are needed to help children to remember to use all three steps and to learn how to be specific about the behavior. For example, instead of: "I like it when you are nice to me and it makes me want to be nice to you," children learn to say: "I like it when you let me play with your toys and it makes me want to share mine with you."

Next, they practice giving negative feedback and discuss how it feels to give it. Most children discover that it is more challenging to give negative feedback in a helpful way. A child may start by saying: "When you butt in line, I hate you and it makes me want to knock your block off." The counselor and group members may help the children select words that are more likely to be heard by the person they want to have listen. For example, children learn to say, "When you butt in line, it makes me mad, and it makes me want to tell on you or not be your friend." Also, the counselor encourages children to monitor their tone of voice while giving negative feedback. A message delivered with a calm voice can be accepted more easily.

DESCRIPTION

The counselor tells the children: "Today we are going to play a game called the Feedback Game. Close your eyes for a minute and think of three words your teacher might use to describe your strengths if she were talking to me about you. Nod your head when you have thought of your three words but do not say them outloud." The counselor passes out three cards to each child if they have writing skills. The children can write one word on each of three cards or whisper the word to the counselor to write. Children need to be assured that they may spell words any way they want. Correct spelling does not matter in this game. Next, pass out three more cards and ask the children for three words the teacher might use to describe her concerns about your behavior. The counselor provides examples of positive and negative descriptive adjectives as needed.

This process may be repeated using six more cards to write words each child thinks his or her mother would use to describe his or her strengths and problem behaviors to someone; and again, using six more cards for each child to write words he or she thinks friends or classmates would use to describe him or her. Next, the counselor collects all the cards, shuffles them, and places them in a stack in the middle of the circle. The children are told: "We are *not* going to try to guess who wrote each adjective. Instead, when we read one of the cards, each of you will get a chance to tell us which group members you think that adjective describes and why."

Important processing questions for the counselor to ask when the feedback is being given are: 1) "What does (group member's name) *do* that leads you to describe him or her this way?" 2) "If this word were used to describe you, how would you *feel*?" and 3) "What *might you do* if people described you this way?" These questions allow the child who is receiving feedback to learn not only how he or she is viewed by others, but at the same time, to receive empathy and perhaps useful advice. The child is not asked to comment on what is said about him or her, however he or she may speak if he or she wishes.

Additional processing questions that may be helpful are: "Does anyone else see (member's name) this way, and why?" And, "Who else in our group might this adjective fit?" It is important that the counselor completes the processing using the first three questions each time an individual child receives feedback. At the close of the game, the counselor helps the children summarize what he or she learned by asking questions such as: "What did you learn about yourself today?" "What did you learn about someone else in our group?" "How might you use what you learned back in the classroom?" "At home?" "With your friends?" Other helpful processing questions are: "Was anyone surprised about the feedback you received?" "Was anyone surprised that a word you wrote to describe yourself was not selected by our group members to describe you?" "Which feedback made you feel proud?"

APPLICATIONS

As previously noted, this technique is used when working with children in small group counseling. It is particularly effective in a school setting where the group members know each other outside of the group. For example, children from the same classroom are able to describe problematic behaviors of their peers very accurately. After the Feedback Game is played, the counselor can coach children through the steps as opportunities for spontaneous and meaningful feedback arise within the group. The Feedback Game is introduced during the working stages of the group, when the children know each other and the counselor well and a high degree of trust and comfort has been developed. Feedback should be given only on behaviors that are under the child's voluntary control. Children ages 6 and older can learn to give feedback effectively. Over many years of counseling with young children in the school setting, I have found this technique to be useful in helping children to self-monitor and modify problematic behavior as they develop more effective prosocial skills.

87

The Rock-Feather Game

Melissa F. Kalodner

INTRODUCTION

It can be quite a daunting task to teach relaxation techniques to young children. Most children would find progressive relaxation, diaphragmatic breathing, and visual imagery far too challenging to complete with any degree of success. The following game enables children to learn the basic skills of relaxation training through a means well suited for their developmental and cognitive abilities: play.

RATIONALE

Play is the natural form of communication for children. Children can discover things about themselves and their environment by engaging in play, while developing creative solutions to current stressors. They *want* to engage in play. The actual act of play is intrinsically motivating in and of itself, with no need for external rewards. Although children often have difficulty verbalizing thoughts and feelings, play gives children the medium needed for safe expression. Also, the sillier the play activity, the better the chances are of captivating the child's attention and imagination.

DESCRIPTION

The therapist needs to bring to the session a colored feather (which can be found at any craft store) and a medium-sized rock. These props will be used to play the game. There should be approximately four feet of space between the therapist and the child, with the feather and rock placed in the middle. The introduction to the client and the game itself proceeds as follows:

Therapist: We are going to play a fun game called the Rock-Feather Game. See this rock? What words can you use to describe how it feels? (Hand rock to client.)

Child: It feels hard. The rock is kind of heavy, too!

Therapist: Yes, the rock *is* hard and heavy. (Gently take rock from client.) Can you pretend to be a rock? All you have to do is curl your body into a tight, tight ball and squeeze *all* your muscles real tight so you become hard and heavy, like this. (Therapist "becomes" a rock and holds for three seconds.) You try!

Child: (Laughs, then "becomes" a rock)

Therapist: (Encourages child by making sounds like "grrrrrrrrrrrr") Good job! You looked just like a rock! (Hands child a feather) Now, how does this feather feel to you?

Child: This feather doesn't weigh anything. It's so soft. Not at all like a rock.

Therapist: Light as a feather and soft, too! (Gently take the feather from the client and put aside.) Now let's pretend to be a soft feather that weighs nothing, like this. (Lie on floor and relax your body, with arms and legs stretched out.) Can you be a feather?

Child: (Places body on floor and relaxes)

Therapist: Ahhhhhhhh. Nice and relaxed. Light and soft, just like a feather. Okay. When I say *rock,* you have to stop whatever you are doing and become a rock. But when I say *feather,* you relax and become the softest, lightest feather you can be.

Throughout the session, call out *rock* and *feather*. When these words are said, the therapist and child become that object. Encourage the client to practice the Rock-Feather Game at home and play it with family and friends.

APPLICATIONS

This technique is helpful with all children, but especially with children who have difficulties related to anxiety, hyperactivity, or anger management. The therapist is teaching a relaxation technique in a playful manner that children will easily engage in. Future sessions can then build upon the game; adding specific instances when becoming a rock or a feather may be useful to calm the child down, or reduce anxiety or anger.

88

Cottonball Fight and Cottonball Soothe Game

Evangeline Munns

INTRODUCTION

Children and parents often have feelings of anger or resentment toward each other when their relationships are troubled. Finding ways of appropriately expressing negative feelings for either the child or parent can be a difficult task. There are, however, ways that can be acceptable to both, especially if anger is expressed in a playful manner involving fun and laughter for all members where no one gets hurt. In addition, being part of an activity where everyone can "let go" and laugh about it helps to create a healthy connection among all members.

RATIONALE

It is difficult to express negative feelings toward those you love and are dependent on. Repressing such anger can result in conscious or subconscious rejection of the person one is angry with. Expressing anger directly can serve as a release of tension but there can be consequences bringing guilt, anxiety, and fear of losing the love of someone who is important in one's life. The key is to be able to express feelings of hostility without harming or hurting anyone. If it is expressed in a game and with humor, then it can be more readily accepted and serve as a healthy release for everyone concerned.

DESCRIPTION

Cottonball Fight

Therapist and child and parent(s) (plus siblings if one is doing family play therapy with all family members) sit in a circle facing each other, with a pile of cottonballs (about 12 balls) in front of each person. The activity starts in a controlled fashion where each person takes a turn calling out the name of the person he or she is throwing the ball at. The therapist may give a direction like this: "Take one cottonball at a time and throw it at someone. Start out by calling out the name of the person to whom you are throwing. You can throw as hard as you like because the balls will not hurt anyone" (the leader can then demonstrate this).

The activity gradually speeds up until the therapist calls out: "Anybody can throw as many cotton balls as they want at anybody without calling out a name first."

The leader then demonstrates by throwing a series of fast-paced balls to whomever and at times grabs a handful of balls and throws it at someone. This modeling from the leader helps to disinhibit the less-confident members of the group.

Usually everyone joins in gleefully, but if there is a member who doesn't seem fully involved (i.e., throwing balls but with head down and not looking at to whom he or she is throwing) the leader can playfully encourage him or her by calling out that person's name and with a smile say something like, "Hey Johnny look up—here it comes" while throwing a ball at him. In the vast majority of cases, the person will throw a ball back at the leader while giving eye contact and returning the smile.

The leader allows the free-for-all throwing of the ball for a few minutes and then calls out: "Let's see how fast we can get the cottonballs back in the bag, except save one ball for yourself."

Cottonball Soothe

The leader then asks everyone to turn to their neighbor and gently touch his or her face saying something like this: "We've worked so hard we now need to wipe the sweat off your brow."

The leader then proceeds to demonstrate, using the cottonball to wipe the forehead, nose, cheeks, chin, and so on of the person beside him or her. Thus the whole exercise ends up in a caring, positive manner.

APPLICATIONS

This activity is an excellent one for relationships where there is conflict, whether it is between parent and child, siblings, or marital partners. It has been used during family play therapy treatment methods such as Theraplay (Jernberg and Booth, 1999; Munns, 2000) in working with parent/child relationships that are dysfunctional, distant, rejecting, or nontrusting. It is a playful way where participants can connect with one another in spite of their differences and can serve as a breakthrough in their relationship with each other. Letting go of some negative feelings and being able to laugh together can be very healing.

This activity is also a good one between therapist and child, especially when a child is withdrawn and is afraid of any kind of expression, verbal or physical. It is a playful way of drawing the child out. It is also useful for aggressive children as a way of releasing inner tension in a way that is not hurtful to others. The cottonball soothe part of the activity is very important for such children, because it allows for some form of restitution--taking care of a person as his or her final act.

Marital Partners

The cottonball soothe part of this activity can be extended so that as a partner soothes the other's face by gently but firmly stroking the other person's forehead, eyelids, cheekbones, mouth, chin, ears, and so on, he or she says: "You just relax; just sit there. I'm going to take good care of you and you don't have to do anything."

The leader may demonstrate this first if partners seem a little frozen in their manner. Another extension of this activity is to give a compliment as you wipe the person's face or hands such as, "I hope this feels good and I think you have beautiful high cheekbones" (or nice chin, or a lovely dimple, etc. as the person touches the body part).

Large Group

Both cottonball fight and soothe can be used in small or large groups. If the group is small, then everyone sits in a circle. However, for a large group it is more effective to have the group split into two straight rows with people facing each other, on their knees, with about three feet of distance between rows. The leader drops a bunch of cottonballs (at least 15 balls) in front of each participant. The leader gives instructions ahead of time about throwing the balls, one at a time, calling out the name of the person to whom he or she is throwing. When the leader calls out free-for-all, participants pelt the balls at whomever they want without calling out names first. After a few minutes of throwing, the leader asks everyone to put the balls back in the bags, saving one ball for him or herself in order to do cottonball soothe with the person in front of and facing them in the opposite row.

This activity can serve as a tremendous release of tension and a way for people to connect with each other through fun and laughter.

References

Jernberg, A. and Booth, P. (1999). *Theraplay: Helping Parents and Children Build Better Relationships Through Attachment-based Play*, 2nd ed. San Francisco: Jossey-Bass.

Munns, E. (2000). *Theraplay: Innovations in Attachment-enhancing Play Therapy*. New Jersey: Jason Aronson.

89

Target Practice

Inés Schroeder

INTRODUCTION

Many latency-aged children struggle in the initial sessions of therapy to find a way to connect to an adult—the therapist. Often, the child is brought to sessions without his or her consultation or understanding of the purpose of treatment. This can have dramatic results when a therapist then tries to engage with the child in order to build rapport and eventually assist the child in the treatment process. Target Practice is a game I often play with children in order to begin the process of sharing in a way that feels less threatening. The great thing about this game is that the therapist is in control of the depth of the issues discussed each time the game is played.

RATIONALE

Children ages 8 to 13 are in a developmental stage where rules and limits are very important to them. Often, games become an important avenue in their play to interact with peers. At times, it is best to interact with children through the play medium in order to facilitate children's understanding of several important issues. First, allowing children to engage in the play medium establishes the importance of their comfort in the process within the therapeutic sessions. Second, children tend to interact in sessions because it is structured as part of a "game." This allows them to feel more comfortable engaging because it is an activity with which they are familiar. Third, it provides for added distraction when the topics addressed in the play seem overwhelming for the child. The therapist is then given an opportunity to note the discomfort of the children and return to the topic in the future.

Many children also have difficulty discussing problems with adults, especially adults with whom they are unfamiliar. It is much easier for them to share general information or unimportant facts when first engaging. For this reason, the Target Practice Game offers the child an opportunity to see the therapist as someone different than other adults, someone willing to engage with them in activities that are fun and provide for a great level of intensity in the topics addressed.

DESCRIPTION

Prior to the child coming to session, the therapist can create a series of statements that will elicit information about the child. These statements may be generated on the computer and can be printed out on paper that is perforated for business cards (found in most business supply stores). By having the statements computer generated, it gives the impression of a structured, prefabricated game even if you explain that you created them. Even if a computer is not available, the statements can be written on papers of equal size (or on the same perforated business card paper mentioned previously). Twenty to 25 cards per game are optimal. The game can be played for a certain amount of time or until all the cards are answered.

The game is played by having the child and therapist take turns in choosing one statement card placed face down in a disordered manner. Once the card is read (by the child or by the therapist for the child), the statement is discussed by the person who drew the card. Following the first person's statements, the other person is able to ask questions or add a comment. When the person is finished with the card drawn, the person then proceeds to the second phase of the game. Here, the therapist can set up either a velcro dartboard game, a ring toss game, or a small basketball hoop and basketball. When none of these options are available, the therapist can even use a trashcan and toss paper "balls" as the activity.

Score is kept for each player. The person with the most points following the period of play wins. No actual prize is necessary. Most children enjoy the satisfaction of winning.

The therapist must be prepared to answer questions when it is his or her turn. When the questions begin to focus on particulars to the client, the answers the therapist offers should provide thought for the client and assistance in developing strategies. For example, a child coming for services for aggressive tendencies will have cards focusing on these issues once rapport has been established. A therapist could share an experience of a fight in grade school that he or she was able to resolve by using words when the statement card says, "Tell about a time you were proud of yourself."

In each stage of the therapeutic process, this game can be modified to match the level of rapport between the child and the therapist. In the early stages, questions may be general and light with a focus regarding the likes and dislikes of the child or his or her future goals and fantasies. The questions can be general and easy. Topics that are nonthreatening will allow for rapport to build and maximize the child's comfort. Examples of some possible statements follow:

"Tell what your favorite color is and why."

"Tell about a place that you would like to visit."

"Explain what activities would you do to make a day perfect."

"Tell about a funny moment in your life."

"Tell about your best friend."

"Share three things about yourself that you feel are important."

"Share one thing about yourself that you would change. Why?"

In the intermediate stages of the therapeutic process, statements could focus on the specific issue for which the child is coming for therapy. The statements can lead to greater self-exploration as well as development of strategies for change. Examples follow:

Child coming in for services due to disruptive behaviors in school:

"Tell about a fight you had recently."

"Talk about a way you can handle a disagreement without fighting."

"Share two ways that you can tell someone that you don't agree with him or her without being disrespectful."

Child coming for services due to a death of someone close to them:

"Tell about one feeling you have when you think about death. Explain."

"Share your thoughts about what happens to people when they die."

"Tell about one thing that you would have liked to have said to ________ (the name of the person/relative/friend) before the person died."

Child coming for services due to anxiety:

"Tell about one thing that makes you worry."

"Talk about two ways that you can make yourself feel better when you worry."

"Share one person you feel comfortable going to for help."

In the final stages of the therapeutic process, this game can resurface as a way to bring closure to the work accomplished. The statements created can focus on the things learned, the feelings discussed, and the feelings regarding the termination of services. Used several times throughout the course of treatment, this game allows the child to have familiarity with the technique, structure in the sessions, and time to play. This game provides the child with something comfortable and will also provide familiarity to ease through the transition of termination. In addition, the child can be encouraged to create statements in sessions with the therapist to bring up issues he or she has and as a way of sharing any final concerns.

APPLICATIONS

This technique is useful for children at a variety of age levels and problem issues. Children who cannot read can have the cards read to them. The activity can be modified for a variety of skill levels. It can also be modified to a group setting to assist the children in sharing their information in a structured way. The group can play individually, in teams, or as one team to see how many points the team can achieve together.

90

Meeting Mr. Tricky

Saralea E. Chazan

INTRODUCTION

Many times latency age children come to psychotherapy because of problems with following rules. They may present with behavior problems of various kinds such as hitting or talking out of turn. Alternatively, other children are quiet and try to hide their lack of compliance and favor lying or stealing. For each of these children, their wishes have overcome efforts by others to socialize them. Children who are impulsive and hyperactive tend toward externalization and are overtly recognizable. The quieter children may be more difficult to detect. Lack of compliance with rules may indicate confusion over right and wrong. Following rules is a necessary developmental acquisition. Without this capacity to comply when necessary, the child is seriously hampered in interactions with both adults and peers.

RATIONALE

Play is a safe sphere for self-expression. Children of all ages share freely in play activity because of the pleasure of playing. Indeed, when it is no longer pleasurable, play stops, for example, the child loses control and tries to hit the therapist or break a toy. At these moments the boundaries of play have been breached. Therapist and child must tend to mending the fences by setting firm limits, and then play can proceed. Because the main avenue for communication with the child is through play, we need to transform noncompliance into the language of play. Certainly any direct questioning of the child about his or her behavior would result in either disavowal ("I don't know") or complete denial ("What are you talking about? It never happened"). A common defense is to turn the adult's attention elsewhere ("Joey is the one who gets in trouble all the time") or bring forth a barrage of tears. Noncompliance can be safely recognized in the unacceptable behaviors of others. Play therapy exploits this tendency of the child to attribute blame to others by bringing the "culprits" into the sphere of playing.

DESCRIPTION

In play therapy with school-age children, playing games is one of the major activities. Most board games have rules and present us with a microcosm, a set-up in miniature, of the challenges the child faces in the everyday world. Our assumption is that in playing the game the child will demonstrate the behaviors that get him into trouble at home and in school. In order to win, the child will deviate from the agreed upon rules and try to hide what he or she is doing from the therapist. The therapist can call attention to what the child is doing and the confrontation may end in anger, tears, withdrawal, or denial. The child has once more been caught, yet he or she feels it is not "fair." Alternatively, the therapist may decide not to confront the child (particularly a very young child) and play out the game on his or her terms. Alternatively, a strategy can be used that recognizes what is happening and lets the play proceed. The rules remain recognized, the child changes the rules, and the child and therapist play with their awareness of this change. Using this technique, the playful interaction is focused playfully around the noncompliance.

The therapist and child are playing a storytelling game. The child is sorting out the cards and begins to laugh mischievously. He tells his story.

Child: (Challenging) Don't I get a chip? (Child stands on his head)

Therapist: What does this mean?

Child: (Swoops down and grabs several chips) I win. Nine to ten. I tricked you. (Laughs)

Therapist:	There's Mr. Tricky. (Child laughs.) Mr. Tricky is so rich. (Therapist looks away.)
Child:	(Steals chips)
Therapist:	Where are the chips? Where did they go?
Child:	I ate them. (Giggles)
Therapist:	You ate my chips!
Child:	(Laughs, falls forward on the floor, raises himself on his haunches and points) There's a tree behind you!
Therapist:	(Turns to look)
Child:	(Laughs and takes more chips)
Therapist:	Who could have taken my chips?
Child:	(Jubilantly) It wasn't me!
Therapist:	It wasn't you. It must have been Mr. Tricky! Mr. Tricky comes and gets the chips. What can we say to this Mr. Tricky?
Child:	I didn't take anything, it was Mr. Tricky! (Giggles, steals)
Therapist:	What did you do?
Child:	I tricked you again! See all of my chips! (Child gives chips to therapist.) Let's count them and play again.

APPLICATIONS

This technique can be used with children of all ages who enjoy playing games. By making the externalization of blame part of the interaction, the noncompliance (Mr. Tricky) can become part of the game. Once the child plays out these intense feelings of needing to win by any means without experiencing shame, he is more receptive to cooperative play with the therapist. Mr. Tricky then is a welcome guest.

91

The Black-Eye Peas Group Game

Adeyinka M. Akinsulure-Smith

INTRODUCTION

I developed this technique while I was working with children in a foster care agency. In this setting, I quickly learned that children placed in foster care have experienced many losses and trauma resulting in difficulty trusting others. Additionally, many of these children find it hard to express their thoughts and feelings. Needless to say, these factors often made it difficult to engage these children in the therapeutic process. It became clear to me that in the initial stages of play therapy providing children in foster care with opportunities to use their cognitive, emotional, and creative skills to express themselves while building trust with them is paramount.

This technique was originally created to engage a group of four sisters who were placed in separate foster homes in play therapy. The children were seen for play therapy together in a group format. Due to their past experiences with their biological family, their separate foster families, and with the foster care agency, these four siblings had come to mistrust each other and were reluctant to speak to each other or anyone else about anything.

RATIONALE

For many children in foster care, it is the coercive, threatening, or punitive activities of "others" (i.e., their primary caretakers) that have resulted in their being placed in the foster care system. Once placed in the system, the children continue to feel forced into doing what other people determine is in their best interests (for example, being placed in a foster home or having to go to therapy). In my work with this population, I have found that among the many losses that these children share many of them have expressed anger at losing any sense of control.

The Black-Eye Peas Group Game is a nonthreatening activity that allows children to begin to share and talk with others in a safe, nonthreatening way. It allows the participants to control how little or how much they wish to share. It also promotes bonding among children in a group setting as they begin to identify common experiences through their pictures and storytelling.

DESCRIPTION

Materials

A bag of black-eye peas

1 kitchen timer

Floor space

To play this game, the children and the therapist sit on the floor. Each child is given a handful of black-eye beans and the therapist takes a handful for him- or herself. The children are then instructed that everyone will have ten minutes to make a picture with the peas. A small kitchen timer is set and everyone works as quickly as possible to create his or her own individual picture. When the timer goes off, everyone is asked to stop. Using one child's picture at a time, each person in the group takes a turn guessing what the child's picture might be. After everyone has had a turn guessing, the creator of the picture tells the group what the picture is and narrates a short story about the picture. This format is followed until all the children have had a turn. The therapist goes last. After all the children have guessed what his or her picture might be, he or she tells everyone what it is. Then, drawing on the themes, patterns, images, and feelings that the children have presented in their stories, the therapist makes a therapeutic intervention by narrating a story that incorporates and resolves elements of the children's story in a healthy manner.

APPLICATIONS

Although I originally developed this technique for this particular sibling group therapy, I have found it to be very useful and successful in individual play therapy sessions. A similar format to the one just described can be adapted for individual nondirected play therapy. Its nonthreatening playful format allows children to create pictures through their imagination while allowing the therapist to make significant therapeutic interventions in a safe way. This technique applies well to children who are withdrawn, depressed, or have experienced many losses.

In my experience, although initially children might be a little shy once the game starts they get very excited about the creative aspects of the game. Although making the picture and telling the story are important parts of this technique, it is also useful for the therapist to listen closely to the type of guesses children make about each other's pictures. These guesses can also be incorporated into the therapist's story. In terms of the therapist, this game requires good memory skills, creativity, and imagination.

92

Worry Stones

Judith Anastasia

INTRODUCTION

"Problems" are the common reason children come into therapy. This is often interpreted as the child *has* a problem or the child *is* the problem. I have found that a useful way to talk to a child or other family members is to use the word *worry* as a way to explore the anxiety that is attached to the difficulties that are being experienced in a child's life. In this way, even small children can explore their internal world without feeling something is wrong with them. It helps them analyze the concerns in their life without guilt, blame, or shame. Designating small, medium, or large worries helps the therapist have some understanding of how the child perceives his or her struggles, as well as helping the child distinguish the differences between a big or small apprehension. By expanding the field of worry to other family members, children recognize that others experience difficulties while also normalizing the emotions around the concerns. It is an opportunity to bring family members together around each other's fears.

RATIONALE

Using stones, particularly those that have been washed over time by water, seems to have a healing effect. Their weight, shape, and texture when held in the hand have a comforting sensation. Children relate to stones. They are familiar to all cultural and economic groups. Making a worry *concrete,* that is, having physical properties, allows it to be looked at carefully, held by others, diminish in size, and ultimately be removed. Some props have emotional connotations for children that interfere with neutrality, whereas stones encourage children to express themselves. These solid objects let the child reveal a part of him- or herself without feeling threatened.

DESCRIPTION

This game can be played with an individual child, with groups of children, or with a whole family. It is best suited for children between the ages of 3 and 12, although older children are often comfortable participating.

Materials

Smooth water-washed stones gathered from a beach or stream offer a soothing and beneficial effect. The sea stones should come in three sizes, tiny pebblelike stones, medium-sized stones, and fairly large stones. All the rocks should be of similar color and texture and selected with care. Select a large sturdy piece of neutral colored paper (white, oatmeal, taupe) approximately three feet square or a three-foot square cloth without too much patterning. If using paper, draw a large circle with a black or brown magic marker that covers the whole space.

The therapist and child sit around the large square paper or cloth, which has been placed on the floor in the center of the room. Along the wall the stones are placed in three piles, depending on their size. The therapist explains that these are "worry stones," that everyone has worries, and that worries come in varying sizes. An example of what the therapist might say to the child is, "Worries can change from hour to hour and from day to day. They tend to grow when they are not shared, and they have a way of getting smaller when someone is willing to listen. Take a moment now to think about the worries you have today and notice how big each of them feels. When you are ready, you will have a chance to select as many stones as you would like. If you remember more of your worries as the game goes on, you can go back and get as many stones as you need."

If you are working with a family, start with the youngest member. He or she goes to the piles and selects as many from each group as needed. Each child brings the stones back and places them in front of him- or herself. Continue with the next oldest child, and finish with each parent selecting his or her portion of stones. If you are working with a large family or group, be sure to have enough stones for everyone, with enough stones left in each group for members to go back if necessary.

The therapist must be very aware of timing and the amount of stones each person has in front of him or her. If you clearly see that there won't be time for each worry to be expressed, state that this is a game that doesn't have to be finished and that it can be played anytime, anywhere. With younger children who may have a concern about not using all their stones, have a small cloth bag in which you can place the stones. Before the end of the session, have the child place the remaining stones in the bag and say that the stones will be set aside in a safe place and ready for him or her the next time you meet.

The game begins when the therapist places a stone in the circle and says, "Here is a little worry I have." Once the therapist shares his or her worry, he or she then turns to the youngest member to begin.

Examples of Worries

- Small

    Got my new shoes dirty

    Lost my allowance

    Afraid I will get a bad haircut

    Being late

    Forgetting lunch

    Not getting homework done tonight

- Medium

    Fear I don't look good today

    Being late often

    Afraid of getting a poor mark

    Worry about my parents arguing a lot

Worry that I'm always angry

My brother/sister is always mad at me

- Large

  Not being able to concentrate

  Fear of failing

  Afraid parents will divorce

  Afraid of death

  Not knowing where my sister/brother is

  Fear my father doesn't like me

  Worry that my mom is unhappy

  Have no friends

The "size" of the problem is dependent on the degree of worry a person has about it, not the content of the worry. A problem that would appear small that is being expressed as large is an indication of the degree of anxiety the person is carrying and can also indicate concern about another's reaction to it. If the game is played at different intervals, it is interesting to note the perceived change in size of the problem. Also noteworthy is when other members express the same concern or if that concern diminishes in one person and is heightened in another.

Example Interaction

There are three components that are important in responding to the worries a child brings to the therapist. First, the child needs acknowledgement for the worry from a calm, nonreactive adult. Secondly, the field of concern should be expanded to include those who may also be affected by the problem. And lastly, the distress should be directed back to the significant others who can be of help in dealing with the issue. When working with a child, the therapist is often the supportive link in connecting the worry back to the important people in the child's life.

CASE EXAMPLE

Child: (Places a large stone) I think my parents are breaking up.

Therapist: That is a big worry. Tell me more about it.

Child: My parents fight all the time and my sister never sticks around. She's lucky, at least she can get out of there.

Therapist: You feel stuck at home with no place to go. I imagine you and your sister both feel stuck in this situation.

Child: It is always the same.

Therapist: It's been like this for a while and no one seems to be doing anything.

Child: Yeah.

Therapist: What do you wish could happen?

Child: I wish everyone could get along.

Therapist: I imagine your mom and dad as well as your sister wish it could be better at home.

Child: I guess.

Therapist: If your mom, dad, or sister were here, do you think they would have a big stone in front of them too?

Child: Maybe.

Therapist: My hunch is that if you feel this way, they feel this way too. Do you think you could talk to your mom or dad about how worried you feel?

Child: I don't know.

Therapist: Would it help if you and I did it together?

Child: Okay.

APPLICATIONS

The unique feature about this technique is that it can be useful when working with children with a wide range of problems. This game provides a method of healing with verbally reluctant children as well as those with backgrounds of abuse and neglect where aggression or resistance is a factor. This approach is useful for individual children, families, and groups of children. It is easily transferable from an individual session to a family session without having to change rules or format. It allows children to find a comfortable way to express their feelings. The stones often become an internalized image rather than an actual object. The Worry Stone Game helps access a new form of communication that is not only helpful to children but also to teenagers and adults.

93

Fishing for Feelings

Daniel Yeager

INTRODUCTION

The Fishing for Feelings Game originated years ago in a therapy session with three siblings. It was a spur-of-the-moment elaboration of a much more mundane and boring feelings activity. The 11-year-old sister came up with the idea. With the help of her 6-year-old brother, she drew, colored, cut out, and paper-clipped a dozen brightly colored "feelings fish." The 8-year-old sister and I scrounged for materials to create a fishing pole and came up with a pencil, a telephone cord, and a refrigerator magnet.

This game is now a standard activity in my child and family counseling practice. I have added a few new touches over the years: a boat (my swivel office chair), a pond (blue and green painted cardboard), more fish, and a slightly more upscale fishing rod. But the game still has the look and feel of a spontaneous, homemade game. As such, it is not only useful in its own right, but also serves as an inspiration to other children and families to create their own unique, homemade Feelings Game.

RATIONALE

The typical child who comes into therapy has some difficulties in his or ability to recognize, label, and appropriately express emotions. The Fishing for Feelings Game provides several benefits for the child:

1. Used in the early stages of therapy, the fun nature of the activity helps to establish rapport between the child and the therapist and lowers the child's anxiety about exploring uncomfortable emotions and situations.
2. The activity aids the assessment process by providing the child a means to comfortably convey information about emotions and about behavioral reactions.
3. In playing the game, a child with a limited "feelings vocabulary" learns new terms that will help him or her to more accurately recognize and label emotions.
4. The discussion that ensues can help the child to make the important connection between precipitating events, perceptions, feelings, and behavioral reactions.
5. The problematic emotions, situations, and behaviors that the child identifies during the game can be integrated into the treatment plan, thus modeling a problem-solving procedure for the child.
6. Use of the game with a family (and also the invitation for the family to invent their own Feelings Game) provides insight into family dynamics and also an opportunity to model, teach, and support healthy communication skills.

DESCRIPTION

Materials

"Fishing pole" with magnet on the end of the line

Cutout "fish" with a paper clip placed at the "mouth" of each fish and one feeling-word written on each fish

Optional: fishing pond, boat, bucket, or cooking pot

1. Therapist introduces activity. ("Hey, would you like to go fishing?" The therapist introduces the boat, pond, pole, or fish in ways that will arouse the child's interest and sense of playfulness. Be sure to explain that these fish are "feelings fish.")
2. Child throws the line among the fish and pulls gently until magnet "catches" one of the fish. Child pulls up fish and reads the feeling word.
3. Therapist asks the child to tell about a time that he or she experienced that feeling. Therapist can follow up with additional questions as appropriate to elicit information about child's perception of the precipitating event, child's behavioral response, and so on. Then fish can be placed in a "bucket" or "cooking pot."
4. Continue the process as long as interest holds and time allows. The therapist may want to take a turn as well, taking the child's needs into consideration and carefully steering the discussion along lines that will be helpful for the child.
5. At a later time, the therapist may want to use information that the child introduced during the game for further discussion or for elaboration in other activities.
6. The child can also be invited to make his or her own Feelings Game at home. This can be a good activity for a parent and child to do together.

APPLICATIONS

The Fishing for Feelings Game is helpful with almost all children, ages 4 and older.

The game helps quiet children to open up and provides an opportunity for active children to move around. This activity is especially useful for the ADHD child, as it is an "active" way to teach the child to talk about his or her feelings.

The game can be used with a single child, with groups, and with families.

Section Seven

Other

94

Creating an Ambiance for Play Therapy with African American Children

Alvin Ramsey

INTRODUCTION

Mental health professionals have been challenged to be culturally sensitive as they deliver services to diverse populations. Play therapists who work with children from oppressed racial and cultural groups have the opportunity to create play therapy environments that enhance the therapy process and contribute to positive outcomes for this specific population of clients. O'Connor and Ammen (1997) highlight the point that "It is important for the play therapist to use every opportunity to join the client in celebrating his or her culture" (p. 19). In this article I will briefly describe some of the ways that I celebrate African American culture with African American children and families to facilitate empowerment and resolution of the child's problems. I use the notion of ambiance to convey the idea that my goal in providing culture specific play materials is to create a context that evokes client explorations into ethnic and cultural identity.

RATIONALE

In my work with African American children in play therapy, I am aware that these children bring issues and concerns that derive from the fact that they are black children in America. I do not assume homogeneity among these children, and I clearly recognize individual differences and uniqueness. Furthermore, as I develop a relationship with each child I trust the child to take the lead in sessions to move into the emotional areas that need healing. I respect the choices the child makes about how to use the available play materials and how to involve me in his or her play process.

I am, however, mindful that because of their unique status in American society, African American children need the opportunity to engage in certain processes that special play activities may provide. As pointed out by Boyd-Franklin (1989), empowerment and therapeutic change are especially important treatment goals for African Americans "given the legacy of slavery and the history of racism experienced by Black people in this country" (p. 22). This empowerment work with African American clients in therapy will be facilitated to the degree that the following constituents are strengthened in the child: (a) connection to the African legacy, (b) sense of identity, self-worth, and self-esteem, (c) sense of pride in the African American ethnocultural group, (d) concern for the well-being of the group, (e) sense of mutual trust and dependence on other members of the group.

It is important to emphasize that the person of the play therapist is the most significant element in this cultural ambience. For the cultural process to be effective, the therapist must possess certain qualities. In addition to being trained and competent as a general clinician, the therapist who does empowerment work with black children in play therapy must: (a) be knowledgeable about African American culture and history, (b) internalize the value of ethnic and cultural self-determination as essential for African Americans, and (c) be grounded in a child-centered approach to psychotherapy with children.

DESCRIPTION

The following list contains some of the materials that I have found to be useful in creating a cultural climate as I have entered into relationships with children in play therapy.

Books

A variety of books are accessible for the child to choose from, including books with themes of anger, loss, and other therapeutic issues that arise in therapy. Among this collection are books centered in African American culture. African and African American cultures are rich in stories and folktales, and there are an abundance of good books that capture this oral tradition. Biographies of persons such as Paul Robeson, Rosa Parks, King Sundiata of Mali, and others are obtainable for children. These provide invaluable possibilities for insight, connections to history, and identification. Children show strong interest in coloring books that contain positive images of black people and culture. I have found that aesthetic illustrations add to the quality of the book experience for children. Play therapists are encouraged to browse through the children's section of bookstores to find books that appeal to them. Black bookstores are likely to have a much wider selection of Africentric children's books and sales persons who are knowledgeable about African American children's literature.

Adinkra Symbols

The word *adinkra* means, "a message one gives to another when departing." "Adinkra symbols reflect traditional mores and specific communal values, philosophical concepts, codes of conduct, and the social standards of the Akan people. . . . These Akan symbols are stamped on varied-colored cloths and symbolize parables, aphorisms, proverbs, popular sayings, historical events, hairstyles, traits of animal behavior, or shapes of inanimate or manmade objects" (Willis, 1998, p. 1).

A framed wall chart displaying a set of 80 Adinkra symbols and their meanings is in view in my playroom. Children are often attracted to this chart. They inquire about the symbols and show interest in their meanings. It is important that the therapist have an understanding of the meanings in order to translate the symbols into terms the child is able to understand. Many children draw and paint the symbols and sometimes refer to one of the symbols and weave its meaning into their therapeutic process. For example, T. C., a 10-year-old boy who was struggling to work through feelings and behavioral problems following the murder of his mother wondered in one session, "Do any of these talk about what should happen to those men who killed my mother?" We were able to find two symbols that dealt with justice, the law, and punishment for crimes. The dialogue that ensued seemed to be meaningful to T. C.

Portraits

Two 18 by 24-inch prints by Carl Owens, a Detroit artist, entitled "Strong Men" and "Strong Women," respectively, are a part of the cultural ambiance in my playroom. Each print depicts 35 portrait illustrations of African American men and women who have been inspirational human beings in history. Play therapists may select other portraits of significant African American historical figures.

Lack of school motivation was a significant factor in relation to difficulties an 11-year-old client, K. A., was having at home and at school. In a play therapy session, K. A. was expressing his apathy regarding school and his anger at his mother for not buying him a pair of very expensive gym shoes. In response I pointed to the portrait of Frederick Douglass and asked K. A. if he knew who the person was. He took a close look but could not identify Douglass. I then told him the story of how Frederick Douglass had been a slave and had to take severe risks to learn how to read and to educate himself. He listened attentively as I gently shared with him the highlights of Douglass's life of bondage, escape, and prominence as a black leader. K. A. didn't comment and occupied himself with other play activities for the remainder of the session. When he came to his next session, however, he asked shortly after getting settled in, "Could Frederick Douglass *really* get whipped for learning to read?"

Slave Voices

The strength of African American culture is that it has provided a way for black people to preserve our humanity through the trauma of the slavery experience. The memory of slavery is of profound significance in understanding African American culture and in the change and healing process for contemporary black people. *Remembering Slavery* (Berlin, Favreau, and Miller, 1998) is a remarkable project in which the actual recorded voices of persons who had been slaves can be heard telling stories of their lived experiences of slavery and emancipation. Audiotapes of these slave voices and narrative readings are on hand in my playroom for use as indicated by individual therapeutic circumstances. The play therapist must remain centered in the client's process and use sensitivity, explanation, and timing to incorporate this powerful material in a therapeutically effective way.

Tent with African Blanket

A small 4 by 6-foot, brightly colored, dome-shaped camping tent with a colorful African print blanket inside is included in the playroom. The children in therapy often use the tent and blanket in ways that seem self-comforting. Many of the children who go into the tent frequently wrap themselves in the blanket and appear to be in a safe and nurturing space.

Puppets, Dolls, Sandtray Miniatures

Human figures in the form of dolls, puppets, and sandtray miniatures are an important part of the playroom environment. I have collected a wide assortment of African and African American figures and related symbols and objects. These, along with figures from other ethnic and cultural groups, allow the children to express their thoughts and feelings about themselves, their families, and other issues through their creations in the puppet theater, the dollhouse, and the sandtray. The African and African American figures are essential in facilitating culture specific issues and concerns.

Musical Instruments, Music

Music and dance are vital means of expression in the African American cultural ethos (Richards, 1980). Traditional African musical instruments are included in the collection in the playroom. An African drum and bilaphon (traditional xylophone) were selected for their rich tonal qualities and their symbolic values as cultural artifacts. On many occasions children in therapy sessions have taken these instruments into the tent to play them. Recordings of spirituals, jazz, and other forms of healing music are also available for use in therapy.

Egyptian Writing

Fun with Hieroglyphs (Roehrig, 1990) is a kit published by The Metropolitan Museum of Art in New York City. It contains a hieroglyph alphabet chart, 24 rubber stamps of Egyptian hieroglyphs with an ink pad, and a book with historical information, games, and puzzles. This kit allows children to write their names and other communications in hieroglyphs and facilitates imagination, creativity, curiosity, and pride in learning about an ancient African civilization.

The materials I have described have enriched the play therapy process in my work with African American children with a wide range of presenting problems. Processes of great depth and mystery have often unfolded with the children in therapy and meaningful dialogue with parents has resulted from the use of the materials. It is my hope that the ideas I have shared will be helpful to other play therapists who work with the African American child.

References

Berlin, I., Favreau, M. and Miller, S. F. (1998). *Remembering Slavery: African Americans Talk About Their Personal Experiences of Slavery and Emancipation.* New York: The New Press in association with The Library of Congress, Washington, DC.

Boyd-Franklin, N. (1989). *Black Families in Therapy: A Multisystems Approach.* New York: The Guilford Press.

O'Connor, K. J. and Ammen, S. (1997). *Play Therapy Treatment Planning and Interventions: The Ecosystem Model and Workbook.* New York: Academic Press.

Richards, D. M. (1980). *Let the Circle Be Unbroken: The Implications of African Spirituality in the Diaspora.* Trenton, NJ: The Red Sea Press.

Roehrig, C. (1990). *Fun with Hieroglyphs.* New York: The Metropolitan Museum of Art and Penguin Books.

Willis, W. B. (1998). *The Adinkra Dictionary: A Visual Primer on the Language of Adinkra.* Washington, D.C.: The Pyramid Complex.

95

Matching the Moment: Therapeutic Responding in the Playroom

Wendy M. Miller

INTRODUCTION

As a play therapy supervisor, questions frequently posed to me in supervision involve concerns of pacing and interpretation. "I see the play, I know what I think it means, but if I make the interpretation, I lose the child." Best use of pacing and interpretation has become even larger in the current working climate, where length of treatment has become less flexible. In order to respond to these supervision issues, I began to study my own responses to children in session; to notice how I set my pace with the client, knowing when to lead the process a step forward, and when to wait and maintain the client's pace. I began to notice that I used specific phrases in response to the client's play and behavior, attending to both verbal and nonverbal communications.

RATIONALE

A system that helps negotiate the issues of pacing and interpretation goes a long way in accurately moving the process forward, and in understanding and respecting the client. Some children enter the playroom ready to work, others with similar issues may require many sessions to acclimate. Therapy should be as efficient as possible, however, pushing the child past his or her level of therapeutic readiness is both counterproductive and unethical. Therapeutic Responding allows for a wide breadth of flexibility in responding, matching the client moment by moment and issue by issue, going into deeper process in one area, staying reflective in another.

DESCRIPTION

I. What It Takes

For the play therapist to successfully utilize this technique, certain conditions must be met. The setting must be appropriate for a therapeutic experience. [This environment has been well described by Axline (1947), Moustakas (1992), and Landreth (1991) among others.] In addition, it is imperative that the play therapist utilize critical clinical skills. The following characteristics explain the clinical presence necessary to successfully utilize the appropriate state.

A. *Accurate Conjecture of Internal Experience*

It is the job of the therapist to understand and match the client's presentation. Acceptance of the client and his or her presentation of self in each clinical moment requires the therapist to let go of preconceived ideas and beliefs. Defensiveness or resistance can be experienced by the therapist when his or her own value systems, comfort levels with emotional closeness, or personal space needs don't match the client's. Matching the client's internal state requires an awareness of both countertransference and therapeutic assumptions. To most successfully understand the therapeutic moment, such filters must be minimized.

B. *Distance of Self*

Maintaining a sense of observer or witness helps to keep a part of the therapist neutral and provides time to think carefully before responding. Successful responding to a client is similar to solving a mystery—all clues must be received, none discarded, until it is clear which are really important. Therapist as observer can keep in mind the history and presenting problems without allowing intake data to obscure newly uncovered clinical experience. Both are necessary for accurate understanding.

C. *Accurate Interpretation of Therapy Behavior*

The therapist's awareness of the client's body language, verbal cues, directionality, intensity, and continuity of the activity are paramount in accurate pacing.

D. *Understanding of the Projective Process*

Utilization of symbolism, metaphor, and the client's projection of self into the play are critical in promoting a complete understanding of what is happening for that client in that moment.

II. The Stages of Therapeutic Responding

Utilization of these stages is not a linear process, but involves moment-to-moment awareness of the client's presentation. It is common to move back and forth, and vary greatly within session and across issues. In order to demonstrate this, two examples will follow each explanation, one involving active play with toys, and the other, a more subtle tracking of client nonverbal behavior with sand. Suggestions as to when to move forward and when to pull back are also offered.

Stage 1: **Describe**—Using nonjudgemental language, grounded in the present moment, describe the behavior of the client. The goal here is to let the client know that you are present, observing, accepting, and respecting the activity. The language is that of neutral descriptors. "You picked up that one" (car, yet unnamed) *and* "You are touching the sand" (Stage 1).

Stage 2: **Curiosity**—A stage of open-ended questions, wondering what might be happening to the toy, what is the experience of the toy, demonstrating interest in and curiosity about the interaction of materials and client. The goal here is to maintain the safety level of Stage 1, focusing not on the client, but on the materials and the actions. The language is wondering and questioning. "The car is with the truck. It's moving fast." (Stage 1) "I wonder how it is for that car to move so fast past that truck?" (Stage 2) *and* "What's it like for that sand to be touched?" (Stage 2).

Stage 3: **Generalization**—Although this stage maintains the focus on the toy or action, there begins an attribution of the toy's experience to people. The therapist is utilizing a metaphorical process, attributing feelings, themes, and emotions to the object, moving it from the inanimate to the animate. Care is taken to not label a client's experience directly, instead, the therapist uses the activity and objects to bring out general human experiences. "The truck goes faster and faster, and suddenly, it turned and bumped right into that car" (Stage 1). "What's it like for that car to get bumped?" (Stage 2). "Getting pushed around by bigger trucks might happen a lot to that car. Maybe big ones push the little ones around" (Stage 3) *and* (client starts to smooth the sand very carefully and neatly) "First the sand was smooth, then it had ridges, and now it's smooth again" (Stage 1). "It keeps changing as your hands work with it" (Stage 1). "How is it for the sand to be changed all the time?" (Stage 2). "Wonder what it's like for the sand to not know what's coming, roughness, or smoothness? Sometimes people don't know what's coming either" (Stage 3).

Stage 4: **Personalization**—This stage moves from the general to the personal, assessing the emotional impact of treatment and relating the metaphor of the play to the client's own issues. (truck repeatedly runs over car, car goes up in the air, evading the truck) "Now the car can fly and is chasing the truck" (Stage 1). "What would it be like for the little car to fly over the big truck?" (Stage 2). "Sometimes you might wish you could fly over the big people who both you" (Stage 3). "You've told me you are the littlest one in your family, maybe being run over by the truck is like your big sister running over you. It would be different to be more powerful than your big sister" (Stage 4) *and* "This seems like what happened to you, going from smooth to rough without being able to do anything about it" (Stage 4).

Stage 5: **Frame of Reference**—Once it becomes acceptable to use themes directly, relating the client's actual history and experience, this stage includes specific details of what has really happened. "Your sister picks on you a lot; I wonder what happens if you really do jump on her?" (Stage 5) *and* "When your dad left, that was a really big out of control time" (Stage 5).

Stage 6: **Solution Focus**—At this point the client has faced and acknowledged the problem. This is the time to use the entire process to consider a solution. "So one thing you might need is 'Mom time' without your sister. How can we work on that?" (Stage 6) *and* "Needing your dad around when he doesn't live with you is a big one. Can we figure out how to get more of it?" (Stage 6).

III. Pacing

Movement from stage to stage depends very much on correctly reading the client's response to each interaction. Verbal cues might include confirming or negating your descriptions, indicating the client's willingness to move in that direction. For example, "I wonder how it is for that car to move so fast past that truck?" (Stage 2) could meet with a positive "It's cool, it's the fastest car in the world" or a discouraging "It's just a car." Nonverbally, the same cues can be given. The positive might include speeding up the car, adding engine noises, and moving around in the room, the discouraging could be putting the car down or stopping the play. If the response is positive, it is likely to be acceptable to move to the next stage. If discouraging, the therapist can backtrack and describe, "Seems like you're done with that car for now and have chosen Legos." Of course, the same theme may emerge with the Legos, and another opportunity to move forward will present itself.

Later stage reactions might be more complex. "I don't care if my dad isn't home; he's mean" can require several levels of work from the therapist. Describing what just happened, "I was wrong about your dad, it might be okay if he's not home" both acknowledges the request not to push and keeps the focus on the child's current ability to face his dad's absence. The therapist now also has some immediate experience of the dad issue, which can be utilized at a later time. Perhaps the play moves to building a big walled-in castle with the child as the ruler, and the metaphor has been accepted that no one can leave. It is then personalized to include Dad. A comment might be, "I remember when you talked about it being okay for your dad to be gone but these walls might keep him from leaving your castle." And possibly, "It's been a really long time since you've seen him."

Therapeutic Responding fits most therapeutic contacts. It is especially useful when there is doubt as to when to move therapy forward, or when the child is mainly nonverbal and small clues must be considered. It helps the therapist maintain accuracy and respect in his or her interventions.

References

Axline, V. (1947). *Play Therapy*. New York: Ballantine Books.

Landreth, G. (1991). *Play Therapy: The Art of the Relationship*. Muncie, IN: Accelerated Development, Inc.

Moustakas, C. (1992). *Psychotherapy with Children: The Living Relationship*. Greeley, CO: Carron Publishers.

96

My Body's Nobody's Body but Mine

Claire Milgrom

INTRODUCTION

According to the Canadian Association for Music Therapy (1992), the nonverbal, creative, and affective nature of music facilitates contact, self-expression, communication, and growth. Therapeutically, musical play activities with children can facilitate many different tasks, such as engaging a child, reducing resistance by building a working alliance with the therapist, promoting understanding of self and others, boosting self-esteem and feelings of self-confidence, providing emotional release, and facilitating creative growth.

Working with children who have been victimized by physical or sexual abuse can be especially challenging because their ability to trust is often impaired. It has been my experience that these children may ignore or overtly oppose attempts to engage verbally with the therapist especially around issues directly related to their victimization. Listening to music, singing, composing songs, dancing, and moving in time to music can be an effective and nonthreatening way of initiating and building a relationship with these children when they appear resistant to other ways of engaging. Musical interventions can then be used in numerous ways to facilitate the therapeutic powers of play within the therapeutic relationship.

RATIONALE

A play therapy colleague, Ms. Linda Perry, from the Elizabeth Hill Counselling Centre in Winnipeg, Canada, told me that she sometimes sang the "My Body" song by Peter Alsop with children during sessions. The song teaches children about their right not to have their bodies touched in ways that hurt or make them feel uncomfortable. In instances where children have been abused, the song can be an effective way of empowering them. Empowerment is facilitated by the expression and release of feelings about the touching, alignment with a caring adult who believes and supports the child, placement of responsibility for the abuse on the offender, and the resulting promotion of the child's self-confidence and self-esteem. In my work with children, I have discovered some additional ways to make the learning and singing of this song a particularly compelling intervention with children who have been abused.

DESCRIPTION

The therapist teaches the child the following chorus from the "My Body" song written by Peter Alsop (1985):

> My body's nobody's body but mine
> You run your own body, let me run mine

After children are familiar with the song, the therapist asks them if they know someone who they feel should hear this song or to whom they would like to sing the song. If children name the person who hurt them, the therapist then supplies a puppet, doll, or drawing to represent that person. The child and therapist sing the song together to the representative of that person. If children do not name anyone, the therapist can provide the name of the offender when the offender is known. If the offender is unknown or if there is more than one offender, the therapist can suggest singing the song to "adults or teenagers who trick or hurt kids" or to "people who need to learn not to touch kids' private parts." Children should be encouraged to sing the song to representations of anyone else they feel should heed the words of the song or simply to anyone with whom they would like to share the song. This may be with nonoffending parents or alternate caregivers who they view as supporters or potential supporters. These support people can also sing the song with the child.

When singing the song to the offender, the therapist can encourage children to "really show" how they feel by the tone and volume of their voice, and by adding actions. For example, the therapist can role model "angry" singing, scowling, "standing tall," or pointing at the offender. The therapist can provide children with a large toy plastic microphone (available at most dollar stores) or make a paper microphone to amplify and strengthen metaphorically their voice. The therapist can also encourage children to verbalize what they could do (e.g., run away, tell someone they trust) or what they would feel like doing (e.g., kicking the offender, yelling at the offender to stop, getting their dad to beat up the offender) if the lyrics were not heeded. Finally, children can be encouraged to add their own words and verses to the song, and to talk about feelings and events triggered by this activity about their victimization.

APPLICATIONS

This technique is helpful for children struggling with feelings of powerlessness, anger, and self-blame due to physical or sexual victimization. Children who are not otherwise able to verbalize feelings about their abuse can still experience empowerment, cathartic release, and a decrease in self-blame by learning and providing their own actions to this song, which clearly places responsibility for inappropriate or hurtful touching on the offender. Once the song has been learned, the therapist or child may sing, hum, or whistle the song separately or together while engaged in other activities such as coloring, working with Play-Doh®, or building Legos. This serves as a reminder to children of the therapist's alignment with them in addressing feelings related to their victimization and can provide an empowering soundtrack to play therapy sessions.

References

Alsop, P. (1985). My body. In Blood, P. and Patterson, A. (Eds.). *Rise Up Singing: The Group Singing Songbook*. Bethlehem, PA: The Sing Out Corporation.

Canadian Association for Music Therapy. (1992). *What Is Music Therapy* (Brochure). Waterloo, Ontario: Wilfrid Laurier University.

97

The Stealth Inquiry

H. Mike Kanitz

INTRODUCTION

You have probably not heard the term *Stealth Inquiry* before. That is because it is my creation. In more than 25 years as a supervisor of counselors providing play therapy with children, first through the one-way glass and now with video cameras, I seldom witness children asking a series of questions unless initiated by an adult. I admit to being a slow learner and a power broker in my early years as a play therapist. Any play therapist who has worked with children has heard the admonition, "Stop asking me questions." Possibly resistance was evident instead of those exact words, but the experience did not develop the relationship as intended. Early in my career, I heard Haim Ginott explain how questions were toxic for children. At that time, I thought questioning was part of our genetic heritage, not some source of anxiety in children.

RATIONALE

As a clinical supervisor, I observed that during play therapy sessions children really didn't ask many questions of other children. The interaction with adults was very different than the communication among children. I began to count the questions that therapists asked during a 30-minute play therapy session. Most often the average was more than two a minute. This was interrogation, not counseling or therapy! We are all good police officers! Although counselors didn't always ask these 60 questions in 30 minutes, sections of the session were loaded with questions, which provided that average.

Only when the professional considers questioning a child as a disconnect, and a Stealth Inquiry as a connection, will the dynamics of the relationship eliminate the interrogation factor. Eliminating direct questions in great numbers creates a therapeutic result often missing between child and adult. Adult language is almost always more sophisticated than child talk. The adult stature looming large over the smaller one now adds to the power position, consciously or unconsciously.

DESCRIPTION

The Stealth Inquiry became an attempt to change all questions to a statement. This technique is difficult in the beginning for two reasons: (a) Acculturation creates a habitual questioning mode, and (b) the questioner's ego is seldom in the question. Thus, the interrogating habit is well formed below the level of awareness and the power position is enhanced when adults question children. The following examples will provide an introduction to the process:

Play Therapist Question:	How do you feel about the other children in your family?
Stealth Inquiry:	I would be interested in how you feel about the other children in your family.
Play Therapist Question:	Do you have any close friends?
Stealth Inquiry:	I would like to know if you have any close friends.
Play Therapist Question:	Do you have a best friend?
Stealth Inquiry:	Tell me about your best friend.
Play Therapist Question:	What things do the two of you do together?
Stealth Inquiry:	Share with me the fun things the two of you do when you get together.

As simple as this looks on paper, the habit of interrogation is hard to break. This is very subtle. The Stealth Inquiry engages the child with the therapist's ego involved. This is equity rather than power! You may not know that power and control are even involved, but the child knows, feels, and reacts accordingly. Questions are code for the child that the therapist is the all knowing and the child is the less knowing. Because play between children often includes power and conflict, play therapy with adults already in charge need not be a continuous power play for these little ones. Changing questions to statements allows me to take responsibility for my interventions. This procedure also eliminates the word *why*, which is loaded with negatives for child or adult.

Play Therapist Question: Why did your parents bring you here to meet with me?

Stealth Inquiry: Tell me what you think about being here.

Probing as to why parents made the decision almost always takes a little one into fantasy answers. Gaining information from a Stealth Inquiry provides the play therapist with both different and more details than a direct "why" question.

APPLICATIONS

The Stealth Inquiry technique may be applied to all therapy sessions with children. Whether the child is withdrawn, phobic, or aggressive, the goal is to eliminate the smothering inquisition process. Vernon (1993) comments on ineffective therapist behaviors. "Youthful clients often are reluctant to disclose information, and inexperienced counselors sometimes ask a series of questions to maintain the counselor/client dialogue. Clients can perceive this barrage of questions as an attack" (p. 36). The author is being kind, because experienced therapists in general also ask a series of questions, which interfere with the goal of rapport building.

Many children enter play therapy with a strong need to connect with a human being who is not a parent, teacher, or authority figure. When one observes clinical demographics, by far the normative ages for children taken to clinics are in the 9 to 11 age range. Theoretically, this age group is about to enter the adult cognition stage. Parents call it rebellion and child development specialists call it normal. All the more reason to apply the Stealth Inquiry technique because children have already been asked, "Why are you acting this way?" over and over again. Of course, the

Stealth Inquiry would be, "Help me understand how you feel when people ask you a lot of questions."

Reference

Vernon, A. (1993). *Counseling Children and Adolescents*. Denver, CO: Love Publishing Company.

98

The Use of Filial Techniques in the Elementary School with Latency Age Children

Linda Herschenfeld

INTRODUCTION

While working in the public schools, one commonly encounters many children with feelings of low self-worth. These children express their feelings in many ways, often through acting-out behaviors, social isolation, as well as underachievement in academic areas. Traditional methods utilized in the public school arena involving "talk" therapy fail to help these children to view themselves differently. A more active approach utilizes play and some of the concepts of Filial Therapy to help galvanize these children's self-efficacy.

RATIONALE

Children who endure feelings of low self-worth often have life-long experience of failure. They may receive repeated messages about their inability to succeed. This often translates into a self-fulfilling prophecy. Systematically instructing children in new behaviors and creating the opportunity for them to use these behaviors in a protective environment helps to set the stage for and increase the odds for change. Providing these children with specific communication skills as well as tangible opportunities to cultivate a leadership role through the venue of play helps facilitate a new, more positive view of their own abilities.

Through directed exercises that involve practicing a role of capability, the child begins to take on a role of competence. This fresh purpose engenders novel feelings within the child, which enables him or her to expand his or her repertoire of existent behaviors into other areas of life. These expanded skills often impact the child's social and academic milieu. The general goals of Filial Therapy are congruent with aiding isolated or disengaged children to become more competent and have enhanced participation in their environment. By altering the Filial technique to encompass the older child working with a younger child model, the goals become:

To eliminate the presenting problem at its source

To develop positive interactions between the child and other children and adults

To increase the target child's communication, coping, and problem-solving skills

In this way, the target child may be better able to handle future challenges independently and successfully.

The therapeutic goals for children in Filial Therapy also match the treatment goals for facilitating change in isolated, disengaged, and acting-out latency age children. The goals are as follows:

To enable children to recognize and express their feelings fully and constructively

To give children the opportunity to be heard

To help children develop effective problem-solving and coping skills

To increase children's self-confidence and self-esteem

To reduce or eliminate maladaptive behaviors and presenting problems

To help children develop proactive behaviors (Van Fleet, 1994)

DESCRIPTION

Latency age children are trained in several of the skills taught to parents in Filial Therapy instruction. The children are exposed to child-centered play, and as a corollary to their own therapy, learn the concept of being nondirective and following another's play. The target child learns the structuring skill, mastering how to inform the younger child of the general boundaries of the play session. For example, he or she may tell the younger child, "You can decide to do almost anything that you would like." This apprises the younger child that there are rules and a structure to the play session. These children are also taught the concept of basic reflective listening. By learning this skill, older children learn to show feeling and concern to their younger buddies. Practicing the reflective listening skill helps the older child to learn to convey acceptance of the younger child's feelings and needs. These lessons are accomplished through a series of direct instruction sessions and role play much as they are taught to parents in the course of regular Filial Therapy. Clearly, the level of sophistication of lessons needs to be adjusted for this age group. Nevertheless, it is quite simple to construct lesson plans that address the topic of reflective listening.

These children (fourth and fifth grade) are then paired with a partner in kindergarten, first, or second grade, and the two play in the playroom under the supervision of a child-centered play therapist. The younger child is merely getting the benefit of a mentor, a common buddy system practice in elementary schools. The older child has gotten the opportunity to learn new ways to communicate with others.

This new information about how to more effectively relate to others may translate into additional areas of the child's life. He or she has the chance to play a nurturing role in the life of another person, thereby becoming significant to someone else. After experiencing a measure of success and recognition for the meaningful role he or she has played in the life of a younger child, this exposure often facilitates a transformation in the way a child perceives him or herself. Through child-centered interaction with the younger child, the older child is able to see him or herself in a new role: one of mastery, in which he or she is a competent being, someone who is liked and is looked up to by others.

This new experience of self can gradually translate into other areas of the child's life. He or she may be more willing to take risks in the area of academics or making friends. Although, in the past, these children didn't even bother to try a new math problem, because they were convinced they would fail, there may be a tentative openness to taking small risks. This also applies to the arena of friendship. Since experiencing themselves as someone who is liked by others and who is even consequential in another child's life, the child may be willing to respond to and even initiate social cues such as smiling at a peer or returning a greeting. With continued support, these small steps can lead to larger ones. One often sees increased academic effort as well as heightened involvement in constructive social activities.

APPLICATIONS

This technique works well in the elementary school milieu where there are large numbers of children needing innovative ways to succeed in an academic environment. Children who are able to recognize themselves as capable persons can often make the transition to more acceptable behavior as well as academic success. This technique is useful with students who express their needs by acting out. Children with low self-esteem, conduct problems, school refusal, anxiety, and academic underachievement are among those who respond well to this technique.

99

Native American (Indian) Names: A Play Therapy Technique

Sandra B. Frick-Helms

INTRODUCTION

This technique was developed during a search for methods that would be acceptable for a 12-year-old boy who believed that certain issues were too shameful for someone of his age to express. Treatment issues were addressed in such a way as to help the child feel more grown-up and masculine.

RATIONALE

The technique can be used with young, middle, and older school-age children in individual or group play therapy. If used with preschool-age children it should be used primarily to develop modeling stories. The technique is consistent with cognitive-behavioral and psychoanalytic/psychodynamic approaches. A client-centered approach can be used to determine target issues; play materials, behaviors, skills, attitudes, and feelings, and so on, identified by the client as indicative of the chosen "Indian" name can be used to formulate client-centered empathic responses.

DESCRIPTION

No materials are *necessary*, but the following are useful props: items appropriate to Native American costumes, such as feathers, headbands, headdresses, beaded or fringed items, moccasins, braided wigs, bows, and arrows; art materials; pictures cut from magazines, catalogs, coloring books, and so on; and "sandtray" items symbolic of Native American culture. The way in which Native American tribes gave names to their children is introduced to the child with an introductory statement such as, "Today we're going to figure out your Native American Indian name. The names of Indian tribes mean something in the languages of the tribe. For example: *Apache* is the Zuni word for *"enemy"*; *Cherokee* is the Choctaw word for *"cave people"* and the Creek word for *"people of different speech"*; *Hopi* means *"peaceful ones"* or *"well-mannered* people"; and the Dakota Indians' name for the Iowa tribe meant *"sleepy ones."* In addition to having tribal names with special meanings, boys and young men (often called braves) and girls and young women (maidens) were given names with special meanings. Some names described how the person looked. Others described something the person did that was special. Still others described what the person was expected to become. Alihelisdi is a member of the Cherokee Indian tribe. You can go to her Web site (Stanford, 2000) and find the meaning of "Indian" names. Examples for males are: *Ahanu* (Algonquin for *"he laughs"*); *Degataga* (Cherokee for *"standing together"*); and *Waya* (Cherokee for *"wolf"*). Examples for females are: *Mahwah* (Algonquin for *"beautiful"*); *Ethete* (Arapaho for *"good"*); and *Ahyoka* (Cherokee for *"she brought happiness"*). Today, you and I are going to decide what your name would be according to what you are trying really hard to be."

After the introduction, activities of the therapist and child client or group focus on developing a name that reflects target attributes. Together, the therapist and client focus is on doing and learning things that someone with the chosen name would do and be. Foci of later sessions might include: designing clothes and paraphernalia representative of the name; developing a dance (similar to a rain dance or war dance) that someone with that name would do; having a ritual stressing the qualities of a brave or maiden with the name. A special ritual marking the client's achievement of the name attributes could be used for termination sessions.

APPLICATIONS

Because the interventions can focus on any target attribute, it is appropriate for use with almost any psychological problem/target behavior or with any child for whom a change in an attribute, behavior, thought, feeling, and so on is indicated. For example, if used with an oppositional-defiant child, one target behavior might be the ability to do what the tribal chieftain asks of her or him and the Indian name might be "He Who Walks in Peace with Others." A child with a phobic fear of dogs might focus on facing up to the feared stimulus and have the name, "Walks Fearlessly with Dogs." A sexually abused child might call herself "Peaceful Maiden Who Is Pure and Beautiful," while focusing on issues of aggression, self-perceived blame, stigma, and so forth.

CASE EXAMPLE

Brian was a 12-year-old boy who had been sexually abused at age 4. He displayed depressive symptoms and difficulties in school. Using Strayhorn's (1988) psychological competency inventory, strengths were identified in the psychological skills of "cognitive processing through words, symbols, and images" and "tolerating criticism." Needs for skill practice were identified in the "psychological" skills of "being honest" and "talking about feelings." These became "target skills" toward which interventions were directed. We began by talking about what the Native American name would be for someone who was really good at "cognitive processing" or being able to use words, numbers, and other symbols to figure things out and at "tolerating criticism." Names developed were: "Strong Talker and Writer," "He Makes Pictures with Words," and "Takes as Well as Dishes Out." We talked further about what "He Makes Pictures with Words" or "Takes as Well as Dishes Out" would look like or do. By focusing first on his high skill areas, the idea that he already possessed important psychological strengths was reinforced. From a cognitive-behavioral theoretical stance, the focus on existing strengths facilitated his ability to "make positive self-statements" (Finch, Nelson, and Ott, 1993). From a psychoanalytic/psychodynamic stance, the activities helped "plant" the subconscious or unconscious idea in his mind, that he possessed these positive skills and attributes.

Next, we worked to develop an Indian name for someone who was good at "being honest" and "talking about feelings." Because these were the "target skills" toward which interventions would be directed, I wanted to help him think about and practice ways of "being as good at" these things as he was at "cognitive processing" and "tolerating criticism." (Focusing on ways to "be good at" a psychological skill keeps the focus of therapeutic activities on the positive and what "can be" rather than on the negative and what is weak.) After trying out alternatives, we settled on the name, "Truth Teller Who Knows When He's Happy, Sad, Mad, or Afraid."

We were now ready to work on the characteristics of the warrior brave, "Truth Teller Who Knows When. . . ." We began with a variety of pictures from magazines, calendars, catalogs, clip art, and so on. Some of the pictures were of Native Americans. Others depicted other nationalities and even animals. Brian's job was to find pictures that showed someone or something who was enjoying good outcomes because of being able to be honest or talking about feelings. This variation on Strayhorn's (1988) "Scavenger Hunt," required Brian to actively, cognitively find examples of the target skills. This might be considered, by the cognitive-behavioral play therapist, as a way to "shape" a child's ability to identify examples of the target skill that, once identified, can be practiced in other interventions. It is also a way of developing positive self-statements focused on the target skills. As Brian identified the examples that he found, we discussed what it was about the pictures that made them good examples of the target skills.

Another activity involved developing at least one modeling story for each target skill. We made up a story to specifically meet Brian's situation; but an excellent story focused on attributes of a Native American boy is *Gift Horse* (Nelson, 1999). Brian decided which pictures gave him the basis for making up a story about "Truth Teller Who Knows . . ." and how he was able to get good results because he was good at being honest and talking about his feelings. As the story developed, I wrote it down to be typed in its final form. This activity occurred over several sessions, in which Brian decided what difficulties "Truth Teller Who Knows . . ." had in becoming better at target skills. Research has demonstrated that a mastery model (a model that initially shows some difficulty with the task and then gradually masters it) is more effective than a coping model (a model that demonstrates immediate mastery) in helping children achieve a cognitive-behavioral goal (Strayhorn, 1988). Therefore, I encouraged Brian to include, in his story, some incidents where "Truth Teller Who Knows . . ." tried unsuccessfully to be honest or talk about his feelings. In assisting him to develop the modeling story, I also tried to give instructions that have been demonstrated to result in greater client success in achieving cognitive-behavioral goal, including: asking him to describe the actions of the story model (which seems to elicit greater imitation) and asking him to remember an image of a model from his own memory (Finch, Nelson, and Ott, 1993). Once the story was developed, we took turns reading it with appropriate feelings for the voices of story characters.

After reading the modeling story, we discussed how a story became a movie, including concepts such as writing a screen play, directing a movie, and acting in a movie. We developed a screen play for Brian's *Story of Truth Teller Who Knows. . . .* I role-played a movie director and used exaggerated *directions* in directing Brian to act each of the parts in the movie. Wearing a beret, and using a paper megaphone, I *yelled* things such as "Cut," and "Show me you know what this poor guy is feeling." Then Brian as the director coached me in acting each of the *parts*. By alternating being the director and the actor, clients can use areas of the brain focused on *hearing* and *doing* in the technique of *behavioral rehearsal*. I developed this movie-director version of Strayhorn's (1988) intervention, "performing pre-written modeling plays corresponding to the modeling stories," because I have found that preadolescent and adolescent clients find it a more acceptable way to act out a story than puppet plays, costume dramas, or sandtray scenarios used with younger children. (Note: For children who seem to be more auditory than visual learners, it is useful to use a technique suggested by James (1989) and stage the story as an opera, operetta, or rap song.)

Between sessions, Brian had "homework." I gave him a small notebook to write at least one example (real life, book, movie, TV show, cartoon, etc.) per week of a character who could have been "Truth Teller Who Knows . . ." This homework caused Brian to focus on cognitively searching (a different cognitive operation) for positive models of his target skills. After he and I had practiced directing and acting in *Story of Truth Teller Who Knows . . .*, Brian's homework was to "cast" each member of his family in a different role and direct them in "filming" the movie. Because this involves the entire family in achieving therapeutic goals, it is appropriate for family play therapists. Brian's father was an "emotionally absent" individual who was typically unable to listen to or talk about his feelings. Brian's mother "put her foot down" and told him he *would* participate in Brian's therapy. She reported that Brian took special pleasure in working with his father. For weeks, Brian drilled his father in being able to show feelings appropriate to the "film" characters. This helped Brian to become more skillful at talking about feelings. An unforeseen positive side-effect of the role play was that Brian's father began to show greater ability to talk to Brian. They started setting aside time on a weekly basis to check-in with what was going on with each other. During a follow-up telephone call one year later, Brian's mother reported that father and son were continuing these weekly "feeling" sessions.

If Brian and I had decided to make Indian artifacts or develop rituals, we might have decided that certain colors of feathers for his headdress of shield or bead patterns for his moccasins would signify subskills or composite behaviors. Or we could develop a ceremonial dance or some other ritual that would focus on a brave who receives wampum, a new feather or beads, or a hug every time he gets better at telling the truth saying how he feels. As each composite behavior was described, Brian would role play it while I provided reinforcement, thus providing me with further opportunities to use cognitive-behavioral techniques.

This case example has attempted to show how play therapists can use the concept of developing a name similar to those given by Native Americans to their children, and that is descriptive of a target attribute, skill, behavior, cognition, or feeling. Each child's situation and "Indian" will be different and can give rise to a large variety of ways for the client and therapist to express the target skill(s).

References

Finch, A. J., Nelson, W. M. and Ott, E. S. (1993). *Cognitive-Behavioral Procedures with Children and Adolescents.* Boston: Allyn & Bacon.

James, B. (1989). *Treating Traumatized Children.* Lexington, KY: Lexington Books.

Nelson, S. D. (1999). *Gift Horse: A Lakota Story.* New York: Abrams, Inc.

Stanford, C. (Adawelagisgv, C., 2000). *Native American Baby Names.* http://hometown.aol.com/Alihelisdi/index/AwardsGiven.html.

Strayhorn, Joseph N. (1988). *The Competent Child* (pp. 87–92). New York: The Guilford Press.

100

The Creative Clean-up Technique

Dale-Elizabeth Pehrsson

INTRODUCTION

It's been an active session and now it's almost over. The room is a mess. Should the child clean up at the end of the session or should the therapist clean up after the child leaves? There are advantages and disadvantages to both strategies. I suggest a third method, Creative Clean-up. It is a hybrid approach that allows for choice on the part of the child, respect and efficiency on the part of the counselor.

What should a counselor do when it is time to clean up the playroom? I present a technique that synthesizes both the therapeutic and the practical concerns.

RATIONALE

Therapists and school counselors are caught in a time crunch. They see many young clients. Often they see parents and other family members within the time frame of one session. Usually counselors have no clerical or clinical assistance. They work in cramped space that they often share with others. In schools there is also tremendous time pressure. The counselor's work area must be neat and clean when the counselor leaves the room.

DESCRIPTION

The counseling session is coming to an end and the counselor uses the Creative Clean-up procedure in conjunction with session termination. The steps are:

1. The counselor states, "Johnnie, our time is almost up for today. We have just (five to ten) more minutes." Counselors decide on the time that fits the needs of their youngsters. It is usually five to ten minutes. With little ones it is helpful to state, "We have just a little more time together."
2. The counselor then moves to the next phrase. This phrase implements the procedure. The counselor states, "And now I am for cleaning and you are for finishing."
3. It is an amazingly simple sentence. The children get it. The counselor states in a nonjudgmental manner, nonhurried tone, but firm style that communicates "This is not for negotiation."
4. Next the counselor proceeds to clean up the room. The counselor is deliberate and meaningful in his or her action. For example, make no comments about the mess or number of toys used.
5. The counselor allows time for the child to finish an activity. Some counselors state a limit, "There are no more new toys for using during clean-up." I don't say that. It's your choice, but it can prompt a power struggle.
6. Sometimes, the counselor does not engage in talking during the last five minutes stating, "I'm for cleaning."
7. When the room is clean the counselor states, "Our time is up for the day. Do you want to open the door or do you want me to open it?" This style question can also be applied to shutting off the light. The point is to give the child positive choices and avert the potential power struggle of staying in the room.

APPLICATIONS

What develops over time is that children learn to clean and often volunteer to do so. It also sets the tone that the counselor needs to get the room ready and clients are okay to finish what they are doing. The tone sets the mood. Children are surprisingly unbothered by this process and it becomes part of the routine. Those of us who have tried traditional play therapy in schools and agencies understand what a time crunch is. This is both practical and therapeutic.

The procedure requires a counselor to feel comfortable with cleaning up in front of the client. It requires patience and a nonjudgmental attitude. This process respects the child's need to keep working.

The Creative Clean-up technique is highly effective with all age groups where play therapy is used. It is effective with children doing work regarding locus of control and responsibility. It is useful with assisting the child in developing an awareness of social order. It is used effectively in clinical settings where there are multiple users of the play therapy room. It is useful also to private practitioners who have limited workspace and may not have a separate play therapy room, and it compliments the natural order of school culture.

Theoretical and Ethical Concerns

In life there are consequences to our behaviors. The Creative Clean-up approach allows for a transition back to the real world. It is helpful for efficiency. Used with respect, it does not seem to harm the children in any way. They realize that it is time to finish and get ready for life outside of the clinical setting. Counselors need to note that dismantling the play projects may be too painful for some children to watch. One way to deal with that is having a "saving place." As with all ethical and theoretical concerns, the counselors makes decisions in the best interests of the child.

CONCLUSION

This approach was developed during years of clinical work with children in just about every possible play therapy setting including public schools, university clinics, private practice, and mental health agencies. It combines the concepts of respect, choice, consequences, efficiency, and real-life transition. It works for me and for many of my students and colleagues. I hope it works for you. If not, don't use it. Better yet, come up with some different and better ideas and share them.

101

Future Glasses, Talking to the Future: Visualization of Desired Behavior

Robert W. Freeman

INTRODUCTION

In therapy, working with children at times reaches a plateau. The therapy may be "stuck" and difficult to mobilize. It may be a time to look down the road to the future. Future Glasses or Talking to the Future is a way to consider and speculate about how behavior might be in the future, how behavior may change, and how things could be different. It can provide encouragement to a youngster to consider an image of how things might be. The therapist can use this technique of looking to the future to create movement.

Use of imagery in psychology has been called "receptive visualization." Early work in psychiatry tied images to traumatic events. Breuer, Freud, and especially Jung held that images were a key to understanding the unconscious (Samuels and Samuels, 1975).

Guided Affective Imagery (GAI, Leuner, 1969) is described as the encouragement of fantasies or waking dreams in a psychotherapeutic situation using various verbal prompts to encourage both relaxation and the development of images. As described in Samuels and Samuels (1975), "Leuner uses GAI to help people stimulate their imagination . . . as a basis for free association in therapy, and as a therapy in itself" (p. 201).

Shorr (1972) spoke of his form of psychotherapy called "psycho-imagination therapy" wherein the therapist encourages the client or patient "to imagine certain situations in the time dimensions of past, present and future with the imagination being directed and catalyzed by the therapist" (Shorr cited in Walrond-Skinner, 1986). At a later time, Shorr (1974) discussed "imagery therapy" or the use of mental images as a therapeutic technique. He first induced relaxation and either provided an image or had the client associate to their own created image (Shorr cited in Walrond-Skinner, 1986).

RATIONALE

The therapist can create a possible future and broaden the child's horizon. Unlike foreshadowing, which usually has a foreboding or negative tinge, Talking to the Future as used here has a positive cast—the reach for what might be. Adults tend to plan and think about the future; children are usually less likely to engage in this. Talking to the Future creates an opportunity to describe possible goals or subgoals to a youngster, a way to nudge the youngster to consider some areas where change and development may be needed in the future. A passive child with no friends could initiate contact with another child, be chosen for a team, be noticed. An aggressive/hyperactive child could sit and enjoy an activity, relate comfortably with others, and handle confrontation in a positive manner. A youngster who hits a sister could look forward in time to when "you and your sister get along." Talking to the Future offers the youngster the opportunity to elaborate on what might be, to share in the future fantasy. Talking to the Future takes the focus off the present, and off the anxiety associated with the present, and instead turns the focus to the potential for new patterns. The technique is like touching up a photograph: It involves bringing out existing, perhaps dormant, strengths, expanding on the positive, toning down rough edges, and shaping interactions to produce positive outcomes.

The visualization described in the following is not for relaxation, but rather is more a form of "directed imagery," focusing on a fabricated scene in the future supplied by the therapist rather than the client.

DESCRIPTION

One of my cases best illustrates how Talking to the Future or in this instance Future Glasses can be used as a prop for visualizing the future.

Isabel, a 6-year-old youngster with a diagnosis of elective mutism talked only to her family, and no one outside of that group. As is usual with youngsters in this situation, she was very adept at getting her needs and wants met by pointing, smiling, and manipulating people. After four months she began talking in individual therapy but she still would not speak at school or to her friends. Frustrated at the lack of progress, I tried to think of something concrete to help her begin talking in a broader environment. I took two Styrofoam cups, cut off the tops, and attached some string to the truncated bottoms creating a pair of "glasses." I called them Future Glasses, put them on, and proceeded to talk to the future by imagining how things would look through them in a few months.

> "I see Isabel on the playground at school calling to a friend who is high up on the jungle gym. She calls to the teacher and asks her to help the friend get down."
>
> "I see Isabel talking to Ms. Easton (the teacher) and telling the class about her new kitten."
>
> "Oh there is Isabel telling her friend about her trip to the beach."

Isabel watched and listened intently, "Gimme those glasses," she said.

In this instance, she benefited by my speculating about some desired behavior in the future. She was intrigued enough to want to put the glasses on to see the scene portrayed.

APPLICATIONS

This simple prop gave an opportunity for imagining how she might be in the future. I have achieved this same effect using a ball as a crystal ball, or binoculars or a telescope to look ahead in time. Visualizing the future is a way of desensitizing through imagery. The therapist can redirect anxiety aroused by the thinking that the future will be only an extension of the troublesome present by creating a positive view. Other types of diagnoses lend themselves to this application. For the oppositional child, Talking to the Future might involve a vision or cooperative behavior, for a depressed child, an image of a sunny and positive scene might be used. The possibilities of the technique are limited only by the therapist's imagination.

References

Leuner, H. (1969). Guided Affective Imagery (GAI) *American Journal of Psychotherapy* 23:6.

Samuels, M. and Samuels, N. (1975). *Seeing with the Mind's Eye*. New York: Random House.

Shorr, J. E. (1972). *Psycho-Imagination Therapy*. New York: Intercontinental Medical Book Corporation.

———. (1974). *Psychotherapy Through Imagery*. New York: Intercontinental Medical Book Corporation.

Walrond-Skinner, S. (1986). *A Dictionary of Psychotherapy*. New York: Routledge & Kegan Paul.

INDEX

ABOUT THE EDITORS

Heidi Gerard Kaduson, Ph.D., RPT-S, specializes in evaluation and intervention services for children with a variety of behavioral, emotional, and learning problems. She is past president of the Association for Play Therapy and co-director of the Play Therapy Training Institute. Dr. Kaduson has co-edited many books and maintains a private practice in Monroe Township, New Jersey.

Charles E. Schaefer, Ph.D., RPT-S, a nationally renowned child psychologist, is professor emeritus of psychology at Fairleigh Dickinson University, Hackensack, New Jersey. He is co-founder and director emeritus of the Association for Play Therapy, a national organization that includes international membership. He is a fellow of the American Psychological Association. Among Dr. Schaefer's forty-five books are the outstanding *Handbook of Play Therapy* and *The Therapeutic Use of Child's Play*, both of which have become classics in the field. Dr. Schaefer maintains a private psychotherapy practice for children and their families in Hackensack, New Jersey.